TRAVELS IN THE HISTORY OF ARCHITECTURE

by the same author

Eccentric Spaces

Deliberate Regression

Pharaoh's Dream

The Italian Garden

The Built, the Unbuilt and the Unbuildable

The Shell Guide to English Parish Churches

Thirteen Ways

Reflections on Baroque

TRAVELS IN THE HISTORY OF
ARCHITECTURE

ROBERT HARBISON

REAKTION BOOKS

For Kelly and Livia

Published by Reaktion Books Ltd
33 Great Sutton Street
London EC1V ODX, UK

www.reaktionbooks.co.uk

First published 2009, reprinted with corrections 2009

Printed and bound in Great Britain
by Cromwell Press Group, Trowbridge, Wiltshire

British Library Cataloguing in Publication Data
Harbison, Robert
  Travels in the history of architecture
  1. Architecture – History
  I. Title
  720.9

ISBN: 978 1 86189 435 9

Contents

Preface

At times I have wanted to write a history with none of the expected examples in it, containing in fact nothing recognizable at all, but feared this might lead to something like a garden I remember from childhood, whose maker allowed into it only plants that everyone else regarded as weeds. This would bear the true mark of the autodidact (a title I have little right to, but claim anyway) or the outsider who aspires to overturn every single convention, just for the sake of the commotion it makes.

Like many others I have felt the excitement of Derrida's destabilizing attacks on basic intellectual certainties, but soon realized that I couldn't live day in and day out in the world he conjures up, and was then shocked to find this risky heresy catching on and becoming an orthodoxy. There's an earlier destabilizing mode that won my allegiance the minute I heard of it: New Criticism. I won't try to give its history but just to sketch its consequences for someone trying to write one. Essentially New Criticism denied that history was important. In fact, this movement regarded history or 'background' of any kind as pure obstruction that got between the observer and the thing itself.

'The thing itself' was a poem to begin with, and New Criticism offered a new way of encountering poetry. You had to forget everything you knew or had heard about the work in question. To help you in this exercise the poem's title and the name of the author were often left off so that you had just the words themselves, which you regarded as something like inarticulate pebbles that rattled together in an order that didn't yet have a name.

Of course this deliberate strangening was an artificial procedure, but based on the valid idea that it is the poem (or painting or building) that matters, so that you should make the most direct contact with it that you can, first as a physical object appealing to the senses, and only later as an intellectual construct that depends on cultural conventions and takes its place in a long line of such things. The method was presented as stringent and rigorous, with a hint of the controlled scientific experiment, but as interpreted by me it was highly romantic, based on the notion of the innocent eye and the fresh vision of the child in oneself.

So the believer in this method is particularly unfit to write a history, aspiring, as he does, to see 'a world in a grain of sand and heaven in a wild flower'. In this mode of vision all times are simultaneous, and all works of art have their homes in the mind, not in everyday places or spaces. Yet perhaps one can imagine a kind of history that never loses hold of the sensuous presence of objects, but combines them in a connected sequence that makes sense of historical change. To do this without loss of immediacy maybe you need to believe in the iconic value of some forms and not others, that is, in a kind of canon. Perhaps I simply hope to rewrite the canon, not to topple it, perhaps only (some of the time at least) to give new reasons for the inclusion of the same old monuments.

Of course, a reader will want to know how this retelling of the history of Western architecture differs from all those that have preceded it. First of all it is noticeably compact. I've made no attempt to be comprehensive and have tried to avoid including sets of examples that all show the same thing or nearly the same thing just because they occur in different places. History here is not a flood of names and dates. True to the mystique of the primacy of the object, the book should leave a reader with a vivid sense of particular buildings and places. Hence the idea of 'travels', which start in the experience of being there and keep the sense of distances crossed on the ground, even in their most intense brushes with theory.

A contrary impulse also appears, congruent with the impatience that pares the list of cases down to the absolutely essential – a search for non-architectural artefacts that embody the essence of a period more starkly than any building can. It sometimes seems that the author thinks he can compose the poem of Egypt or the Romanesque, that would consist of images of iconic force that preside like Wagnerian leitmotifs over whole tracts of the subject, so the animal-headed god or the carpet page of a manuscript could express instantaneously the same perspective on reality that would require much digging to excavate from architecture. Some such belief in the revelatory potential of certain specific cultural forms goes part way to explain the intermittently oblique angle of approach in this book. Non-architectural material like Egyptian hieroglyphics and Renaissance allegories are used as shortcuts to get at the core of a style more quickly, and sometimes as a demonstration that architecture is part of something larger, sweeping it up into longer vistas.

Part of what makes architecture special and more physically liberating than other art forms is the fact that one actually visits it and wanders in it, coming round corners to meet surprises that might not have happened in just that order if you had turned another way – or might never have happened at all. So the order of the book tries to incorporate a similar contingency as it wanders purposefully across its ground, hoping that unexpected meetings will strike fire, that leaving out an obvious step will propel you more energetically into a next phase that is upon you before you are aware.

Thus there's a preference for seeing old favourites from slightly eccentric angles and for including a few instances more primitive or more decadent than more sober versions would want to let in. Thus Anglo-Saxon art and Mannerism and Arts and Crafts bulk larger than the coldest calculation could justify. The result will be too wayward for some. My excuse is that in some sense it had to be so, for the writer's sake, but perhaps the erratic path also serves readers too, making them travellers as well, stirring them to find their own new unfamiliar in the already known.

To the writer it has seemed that he worked this story out at a turning point in the history of the world, beginning it in one age and finishing it in another. It's notoriously hard to see one's own moment accurately in a long perspective. The book was originally meant to be a 'History of World Architecture', meaning one that gave all parts of our world their due. A second volume on non-Western cultures is waiting in the wings. At the present moment Western and non-Western can be shown as parallel strands, but not as parts of a single history. While it may frustrate the projector of grand inclusive works, this truth should comfort the student of different cultures.

In the global village, the local seems more precious than ever. Though the specialness of every moment and every culture is what prompts me to include them in the first place, speaking up for the local often seems a hopeless project. In the Aveyron the beautiful stone roofs of farm buildings are losing out to lighter, cheaper, more regular forms of the same thing. Fields are dotted with unusably small shepherd's huts whose roofs are a geology lesson and a meeting of the human hand and natural form on more equal terms than we ever find in cities, where the un-useful precision of modern materials goes unnoticed by those who see only human intention triumphant.

Though this book was written in increasing consciousness of that wonderful and fragile enterprise, the Internet, I can't be sure how much this has influenced its form. At some times the idea hovers on the edge of realization that the Internet could materialize as a single connected order like the one this book is trying to imagine, in which the large is reconciled with the small, the detail with the envelope and pieces of arcane information that you couldn't have imagined just a minute ago provide the capstones of the whole extended edifice. The Internet offers to someone who wants to think discursively the equivalent of a labyrinth with not one but a thousand solutions. For the constructor of orders so far unheard of it is the richest mine, and yet . . . At times it seems to offer a deepening involvement in what is now happening to the earth and culture, at others an incapacitating distraction in mazes of pointless information.

Finding everything in one place paradoxically makes comprehensive history even harder. The Internet reassembles the whole world as a lot of non-communicating moments, each of which, because of the seeming endlessness of every space, has the potential to go on forever, the world of the tiresome autodidact with a vengeance. Yet while the propounder may be trapped in his obsession, the surfer can escape all too easily and develops a protective jitter that isn't necessarily the most productive state of mind.

The Web has been seen as the great rubbish heap of history, like some nightmare of Kafka's where a lifetime could easily be swallowed up in preliminary sorting. But looking into such an abyss of information can be a useful training exercise for a historian. Archaeology has in fact often seemed the presiding deity of this book, not only in the ancient sections, where its presence is literal and constant, but in much of the rest as well, where as one's material emerged from darkness, one tried to recognize the surfaces that could be joined to others to result finally in something recognizable, like a familiar appliance built up through the assembly of fragments, each of which kept asserting its right to stand alone.

Gate in enclosure wall of Khonsu Temple, Karnak, 4th century BC.

I

Egyptian

Ever since Herodotus, Egypt has represented a set of mysteries to be solved. No matter where one starts – the animal-headed gods, the picture writing, the burial customs – immediately one runs up against irreducible strangeness. Now, after thousands of Egyptian texts have been deciphered and read, tombs and temples of all sizes and types uncovered and explored, industrial installations and trade routes analysed, construction methods and building histories pieced together, the civilization still carries a deep residue of strangeness.

These are the people who deify beetles, crocodiles, snakes and baboons. Who embalm and bury in elaborate graves cats, bulls and falcons. Who create whole substitute worlds, whole architectures devoted to the idea of resurrection, including actual vehicles, furniture, clothes, jewellery and cosmetics, and imitation food, servants and buildings – all one needs for a happy and successful earthly life – and then secrete them underground, as if to admit that the entire conception is essentially divorced from reality. Or perhaps just to protect it from the depredations of tomb robbers.

For these are also a people who reliably rifle tombs. Not just the impoverished and alienated or those with nothing to lose: the pharaohs themselves usurp, re-label and reoccupy their predecessors' memorial temples, tombs and sarcophagi. Most openly of all, they turn statues of previous kings into portraits of themselves. Tomb robbery has occasionally been put in context by explaining that it blossoms in times of social disruption and economic collapse. But it is now believed that sarcophagi were often robbed before burial, thus accounting for tombs otherwise undisturbed where the caskets are found empty. So the habit seems more widespread than a desperate response in times of crisis.

Herodotus says they are the most religious people in the world, who invented the calendar to keep track of their unceasing obligations and hundreds of festivals, so frequent they became a kind of spatial structure.

But many things do not fit with the picture of a sclerotically rigid society hemmed in by ritual and obsessed with death. It is true that most of the evidence for revising this view is found in tombs. Walls are painted with lively everyday activity – tending animals, making beer, hunting from boats in the marsh. Delicate stools, chairs and tent-like canopies are piled up. So we get the idea of alert attention to landscape and non-human life, and sensuous appreciation of richly furnished interiors. We only find all this life buried in tombs because anything left more exposed – most of what there was – has disappeared. Yet the suspicion persists that the innocent scenes have an ulterior purpose, if not an occult significance. Such depictions and mementos are not mainly reminiscence but also projection. They are so many allegories of resurrection that focus on activities that suggest renewal, like miraculous growth from Nile mud, archetypally dead-looking yet bursting with life. Even the footstools are coded with emblems of rebirth, winged sun disks and celestial barques.

It is sometimes assumed that the ancient Egyptians expected to ride in boats like those they buried near Khufu's tomb. But there is a powerful symbolism that complicates the question. The celestial journey of the gods, the course of the sun across the sky and the corresponding passage of the moon through darkness are all undertaken in boats. For the most solemn religious rituals the god mounts a ceremonial boat, which is then carried by priests across dry land to another temple that becomes his temporary home. Along the way he stops at crucial moments in barque shrines, stages in the journey marked by buildings. As other narratives are composed of events, this one is made up of stylized locations and prescribed movements.

So, outside the temple of Amun at Karnak there is a Turning Shrine that depicts a change of direction in the journey, turning away from the river – whose course had been followed first along a parallel dry route, a conceptual river – and towards the temple, a progress marked by going in through one door and emerging from another nearby at right angles to it. Once inside the main temple, the procession stops again. The language that uses a building to signify a moment does not fall silent just because it has entered a building. It simply inserts a tiny building into the larger one.

Such processions are features of more than one religion. Apparently the local Muslim saint at Luxor still rides out every year in a barque procession. Favoured images in Catholic Sicily are taken through the town along prescribed courses, and the great moments in the Hindu year take place not in temples but between them, when chariots covered in carved gods like travelling wooden temples are pulled through the streets. But the ancient Egyptian version of such a pilgrimage sounds more literal-minded.

Carrying the god, as if he could possibly need our help to move about, and carrying him in a miniaturized form on a miniaturized boat rather than reminding us of his frailty, simply locates the drama firmly in the realm of representations. Egyptian symbols are taken more directly from daily life than we are used to, but they are fully symbols nonetheless. The barques in shallow pits beside the pyramid are fit for use and have every part one would need for an actual journey, but they were probably never used.

In a long sequence in the *Book of the Dead* the soul of the dead person is asked to name the parts of a boat, giving not their everyday but their spiritual or symbol-world names. This is the final stage in a mental ordeal in which the soul tries to organize its transport in the afterlife by asking countless questions to which he receives evasive answers. Now he is put on the spot and miraculously he knows these far-fetched names that would be utterly hopeless to guess at:

> 'Tell me my name', says the mooring-post.
> 'Lady of the Two Lands in the shrine' is your name.
> 'Tell me my name', says the mallet.
> 'Shank of Apis' is your name.
> 'Tell me my name', says the bow-warp . . .

It is a world of secret knowledge animated through and through, as if the inventor of every human device, even such taken-for-granted ones as the floor and sides of a boat, still inhabits and guards them and watches to see if you are a fit user. This disarticulated analysis is based on a visionary notion of construction as bringing dead wood to life; the boat-building is viewed as a body.

It would be hard to exaggerate the importance that the idea of the boat had come to carry for the ancient Egyptian. To probe it fully we would need to look more closely at the river and its annual cycle of flooding. But even without that we can say that the boats beside the pyramids should not be regarded as simple practical implements whose capacity has been calculated and whose eventual load is stored nearby. Unlike the Egyptian examples, Anglo-Saxon boat burials on headlands looking out to sea or surveying an estuary are actually loaded with the corpse. The boat found at Sutton Hoo, Suffolk, in 1939 had been repaired: it wasn't primarily a ceremonial object or a model but had been subjected to heavy use. It had also been defaced by the removal of essential parts to make space for a special burial compartment. The Egyptian boats aren't often allowed into the tomb chamber. Instead, we find there a selection of prized interior fittings, not a complete set, contra the idea that *everything* required to start up life again is forwarded to the afterworld, but an emblematic series, enough to set the stage once, not to act out the whole play. At least so it seems in Khufu's mother Hetepheres' tomb, the only completely intact royal burial from the Old Kingdom found so far.

Philae, island with its collection of late temples, built from c. 380 BC until Roman times, which were moved to a replica island in the 1970s.

The American discoverers of Hetepheres' tomb at Giza spent almost two years unpacking her small burial chamber. Not because the contents were so numerous, but because they were found piled on top of one another, and because many had fallen to pieces, leaving only ghosts or imprints of themselves. They needed to be detached layer by layer and each newly uncovered configuration separately recorded in order to have any hope of resurrecting the vanished wooden frames (now reduced to powder) to which metal and ivory ornaments had been attached.

The process is a classic example of understanding something by taking it apart. One theory about the buried boats is that their disassembled state embodies the special power of the mind that can take apart and put back together. The full set of pieces reveals the ingenuity of maker or creator more fully than the simpler complete object would.

Disassembly, sometimes brought on by external necessity, has often helped in understanding Egyptian architecture. The late complex on the island of Philae in Upper Egypt, the last place the old Egyptian religion was practised, had to be taken apart and moved in the 1970s before the Aswan High Dam flooded its original site, already periodically submerged by the old dam. This emergency resulted in a clearer idea of earlier stages, revealing superseded buildings and establishing a different sequence of construction.

Another, more dramatic recovery of lost stages through disassembly came from the chance discovery of pieces of the heretic Pharaoh Akhenaten's destroyed temples at Karnak, reused as filler in the Second Pylon and in foundations of the Hypostyle Hall. Further fragments have turned up inside the Ninth Pylon, secreted in such an orderly way that they need only be mounted in reverse order to reveal a whole wall carved with lively scenes of workers putting up the vanished palace of this king.

Akhenaten's are just the most violent instances at Karnak of later stages consuming earlier ones. Continually feeding on themselves, such temples digest earlier stages and the result is a gigantic jigsaw puzzle, a confusion that nonetheless allows experts to reconstruct from partial remnants many vanished kiosks, gateways and courts.

Of course, there were many centuries available for these changes to occur, but the unceasing series of revisions does not fit with our ideas of this civilization as unchanging. In the New Kingdom royal burial practices diverged into bewildering elaborations. Seti I was buried in Thebes, where his mortuary temple is one of the biggest on the entire West Bank. But he also built an elaborate mortuary temple at Abydos, an older and apparently unsuperseded funeral site, later made special by burial there of the reassembled Osiris, pattern of all other resurrections.

Osiris provided the template for multiple burial sites. His dismembered body ended up in thirteen locations, each of which commemorated the burial with a shrine. The dispersed god was also reassembled by Isis who had to fabricate the missing fourteenth part, the penis, which had been eaten by Nile carp. The story of this god, in which he is both found in many places and reunited in one, reflects the Egyptian love of stringing out simple entities into endless series of almost indistinguishable parts and concurrent claims of wholeness.

French kings were sometimes buried in three places, the heart in one, viscera somewhere else, and the rest somewhere further still, each of the locations carrying a different meaning, each deposit provoking special devotions of its own. Egyptian multiple burials – selected body parts removed and stored separately from the main corpse – seem to have been kept together in a single structure, but the second temples somewhere else would still have their own cult observances attached and thus promote a more complex memorial practice.

In fact, monumental architecture in Egypt begins with a royal mortuary precinct that is a kind of city in itself. Djoser's tomb at Saqqara is the oldest monumental stone construction. His step pyramid, the first, consists of six platforms on top of each other, decreasing regularly in stages. The form derives from a traditional memorial in the form of a low mound of mud brick that looks like a windowless room or a smaller version of a single one of the Djoser steps. These were called mastabas by workers on nineteenth-century excavations, from the Arab word for bench. Probing of Djoser's pyramid has shown that it began as a mastaba and arrived at its present dimensions by several increments. Intermediate stages, intended as final to begin with, were ambitiously extended to arrive at the heroic mass we have now. The result seemed so remarkable that the architect's name was preserved and he acquired legendary status. Imhotep, also remembered as a mathematician and physician, was later deified, and through the link with medicine became confused with Aesculapius.

Djoser's complex is stone-built throughout, but some of the forms reproduce other kinds of construction. Outer walls, made of fine ashlar, resemble brick fortifications. A grandiose entrance gallery, whose columns imitate bundled reeds, was roofed in stone slabs carved to look like huge logs. Perhaps the most interesting feature of all is the Sed court, into which you emerge from the gallery. This is framed by delicate pavilions representing provinces of Egypt. Forms are flimsy, recalling slender wooden posts supporting tent roofs or thatch. Some are fluted and, in view of their refinement, were dated to the Greco-Roman period by early twentieth-century investigators. These are dummy chapels of solid stone with no real enterable space. Crucial for the Sed festival ritual were boundary markers towards the end of the course. Holding appliances whose function is not well understood, the king ran between the markers, proving his vitality and reasserting the union of the two halves of Egypt under his rule.

Egypt, as a whole made of parts, was conceived as Upper – the southern part of the country towards Nubia, represented by the colour white and the lotus flower – and Lower – the northern part towards the Delta, represented by red and the papyrus bloom. The king united these differences, symbolic shorthand for cultural variety, most vividly in his regalia, which included a composite double crown, the Upper Egyptian cone inserted in the Lower Egyptian ring. The most complete representation of

Stepped pyramid of Djoser at Saqqara, c. 2650 BC. The earliest monumental building in stone and the first by a named architect, Imhotep.

Dummy pavilions in Djoser complex at Saqqara, imitating canvas tents in stone.

the Sed festival that cemented the union occurs many centuries later on re-discovered blocks from Akhenaten's destroyed temples at Karnak, where a long passageway connecting a temple to the palace depicted the festival in great detail.

Djoser set the pattern for royal burials of a walled mortuary complex centred on a pyramid. A few more stepped pyramids were built, and then came the idea of filling in the steps to make a single sheer slope. The earliest attempt to survive, the Bent Pyramid at Dashur, is one that went wrong. Too steep, it began to collapse, and attempts to shore it up resulted in a crooked profile. Soon after this time pyramids began to be accorded elaborate names. The first was called 'Sneferu appears in glory', and the famous triad at Giza was named 'Horizon of Khufu', 'Khafre is great' and 'Menkaure is divine'.

Names convert the buildings into beings and make a confusion between the person and the tomb; the large looming shape becomes articulate. The names are like charms to be repeated over by the elect, and it is most unlikely that they were in common use. It is a contrary process from the kind of naming we know best, which aims at brevity above all.

At around the time that they pick up names, the pyramids pick up meanings. For now the primitive mound – associated with the lump of matter from which the world is born – has become a more diagrammatic figure, a picture of the sun's rays spreading out and fertilizing the earth. This accompanies the growth of the solar cult and is clinched by the finishing touch on the masonry cone, a gilded granite capstone like a miniature pyramid. The rays made solid in this way also provide a stair or

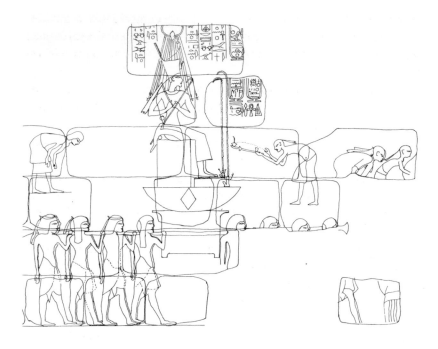

Reconstructed relief of Akhenaten's Sed festival, *c.* 1350 BC, from stone fragments found buried in foundations of later buildings at Karnak.

route for the king to ascend back towards the sun, from the aspiring steps of Djoser's pyramid towards a more conceptual image of ascent.

Khufu's, the first of the Giza group, is the largest and has the most complicated inner structure, enclosing three burial chambers, instead of the conventional *one*, two of which are hollowed out of the superstructure instead of the bedrock beneath, which was the norm. These are connected to the outside by sloping shafts that exit higher up the cone and have sometimes been associated with ventilation, but are more likely to have an astronomical function, being carefully aligned with stars in Orion crucial in the king's heavenly journey.

The pyramids have provoked some of the most far-fetched of all human speculation. They are visible from space, and the notion has sprung up that visitors from outside the solar system built them. Elaborate calculations have been produced to show that the three largest at Giza form a pattern matching stars in Orion's belt as they appeared in 2600 BC, though how such a simple figure, delayed through the reigns of at least four pharaohs, could have given any satisfaction to anyone along the way or justified the expenditure by those who would see only the first or second dot of three is hard to see. Undeniably, these three are aligned on the cardinal points with surprising accuracy, and the levelling of the sloping ground and regularity of the construction show remarkable control. So we jump from such evidence of technical skill to the idea that the overall configuration must mean something. But the three were not always three, and even now the idea that they form a group is our perception anyway.

Speculation about how the pyramids got built, socially and physically, has also travelled in strange as well as rational paths. Engineers have argued plausibly that ramps for raising stones to the upper levels would have had to be more than a mile long and more time-consuming and difficult to construct than the pyramids themselves, and are thus unlikely to have been built. But contemporary illustrations of ramps survive. A system of shorter ramps, perhaps wrapping around the central core, is now favoured. The construction of the core has recently received greater attention. The largest pyramids have precisely laid ashlar cores; in later ones, rubble and brick are covered with a single layer of limestone to achieve a cheaper, quicker result, which looks like solid stone construction until the facing is robbed for later buildings.

The labour force needed for construction has also spawned myths. Tens of thousands of slaves appear struggling under the eye of overseers with whips in the biblical epics of Hollywood. More plausibly, it is suggested that the inundation that made moving the stone easier also laid off farm workers who were free to spend the idle months of the agricultural year working on the pyramid. And the workmen's villages found at a number of sites suggest a settled workforce of skilled craftsmen who were too valuable to drive in the heartless way that Herodotus and Cecil B. DeMille have suggested. But an enormous gap still subsists between prosaic technical accounts of stonecutting procedures and the transcendental goal of the labour. Very few times in the history of human effort have the energies of so many gone to produce such an overpowering One.

The attempt to discover or attribute personalities to the kings who built the three great pyramids at Giza has been going on a long time. It seems likely that the character traits in fanciful tales told seven hundred years later about Khufu are deduced from the overpowering scale of his pyramid. He appears as the archetypal tyrant with a strong superstitious streak. His grandson Menkaure – whose pyramid is clad in red granite lower down, which runs out part way up – is turned into another fairy-tale king and portrayed coping with a prediction that his life will be cut short by staying up all night.

When Old Kingdom figures (like Khufu's son Djedefhor) are given vivid features in the ancient historical record, it only seems to interfere with our attempt to reach the truth about them. Like Imhotep, Djedefhor is another mythically wise man, who discovered four lost chapters of the *Book of the Dead* and became the subject of a cult, though he missed becoming king. The kings of the next dynasty are some of the most interesting of all, because of their descent from the great pyramid builders, their theological innovations and the tantalizing survivals associated with them. The names of their tomb complexes survive: 'The *ba* of Sahure gleams', 'Neferirkara has become a *ba*', 'The *bas* of Raneferef are divine' and 'The places of Nyuserra are enduring'. These kings are the first to build temples unconnected with their own funeral cults, a series of sun temples at or near Abusir. Nyuserra's complex is focused on a giant open-air altar of cross shape formed by the hieroglyph 'offering' repeated four times around a central disk, a notable instance of the Egyptian urge to give physical substance to words.

Egyptian writing has understandably fascinated and mystified outsiders. Pictures and writing form part of a single continuum in later temple reliefs, which seem to cover every available surface inside and out with messages. Walls, ceilings, beams, columns are all subjected to this habit of inscription. It is impossible to find a seam in the overlay that would help one tell which came first and whether the building ever existed without this omnipresent decoration.

At the end of the Fifth Dynasty royal tomb chambers begin to be comprehensively inscribed with texts that translate hopes and fears in the face of death into procedures: charms, curses, pleas and formulas, mostly couched as if they could be uttered by the dead person. More than eight hundred texts have been collected from a few tombs around Abusir, all of which show extensive sharing of texts, which must represent a traditional corpus that has existed a fair while before finally appearing on the tomb walls themselves. Putting the words exactly there is a kind of literalism that seems very Egyptian. As well as these 'Pyramid Texts', the tombs and temples of Abusir have yielded large caches of papyrus that tell a great deal about temple practices and hence how these spaces functioned.

Decipherment has gone further in Egypt than in many ancient cultures, yet reading the best translations of the Pyramid Texts one realizes that decipherment can never be complete, of texts as old and strange as those the Egyptian hieroglyphs carry. Perhaps all the signs are read, and perhaps we know how most of them would sound, but there are still many that withhold their meaning. Nouns in the Pyramid Texts are often simply blanks. The suppliant asks to be granted or promises to donate a certain kind of container or staff of office, a certain sweet liquid – either a drink or an ointment – a kind of food or a piece of clothing. Perhaps these are just the clearest gaps in our knowledge – things. About nuances of the relation between the speaker and his partner in speech, uncertainty is probably deeper than we have any idea.

The mystery that so long baffled Europeans, of the lines of small images that must be writing, even though they are not made of letters, partly evident because the little creatures all face the same way and repeat themselves in recognizable sequences – this mystery must have ceased to exist or at least become less compelling for those who lived around it every day. For most of us, though, to enter an Egyptian temple is to become an illiterate peasant, surrounded by symbols we cannot understand, knowing that much meaning is being transacted from which we are shut out.

A person temporarily in a place whose language he does not understand, and therefore cannot read, duplicates only a few features of this plight. He will go back to being at home in a swarm of familiar symbols before long; this is only an interlude. And then only occasionally will he come on an inscription with some of the power of picture, more primitive and accessible in wordless pub and shop signs, more withdrawn from view in long rows of hieroglyphs.

The high-water mark of writing as the main decoration on urban surfaces has already been passed – in photographs from Victorian England an unheard-of number of gigantic painted and printed inscriptions appear on every flat surface in the middle of cities, mostly the names of sellers or their products. Victorian writers barely mention this barrage (which has now moved to airwaves and wires), as if they had become blind to it through familiarity.

In ancient Egypt public inscription must have been more special. Shops would not have advertised themselves with written notices; street and road signs were unknown, so that temples might have almost a monopoly on public inscription. But it would probably take less of an ordinary Egyptian's attention than we imagine when we try to calculate what all that picture-writing must have seemed like. Most of it he would never see, shut up in temple compounds where he could seldom go. Far from being flooded with signals he couldn't understand, the average person very rarely saw them at all.

Features of royal tombs in the hills opposite Luxor are sometimes attributed to rivalry with earlier rulers. But these complex underground edifices were sealed as soon as they came fully into use and had been seen by very few before that moment. The idea of architecture as public display, even as public at all, is highly restricted in most of the ancient Egyptian structures we know.

Tombs on the West Bank are full of wonderful imagery, like the motif of kings regenerated through divine suckling, becoming the baby son of a mothering goddess. This takes an extreme form in Tuthmose iii's tomb where he is suckled by a tree (Hathor as the Lady of the Sycamores). Further down the scale a royal gardener turns the main room in his tomb into a grape arbour, its ceiling covered in a net of painted vines. But until recently few had seen either of these spaces, which had a specific and we would say non-architectural function, if architecture must be enterable to exist at all.

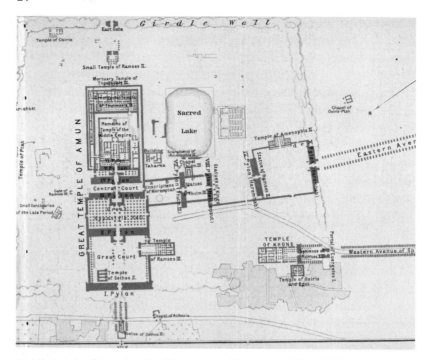

Karnak, temple of Amun-Re, plan of central part of the most ramifying of all ancient Egyptian temples, extended over a long period from 1600 BC until Roman times.

Even the great temple complexes on the other bank of the Nile give a misleading impression in their present state, lacking the high walls of mud brick that would have kept all but priests and royal parties from entering or even seeing into the exciting series of spaces. The temple of Amun at Karnak is the most complex and ramifying of all Egyptian buildings and now makes an open and democratic impression. It seems a loose series of open courts and closed, darker halls, alternating irregularly, with unexpected eruptions on cross axes like the temple of Ramesses III breaching the wall of the first court. This is actually a barque shrine, a temporary stopping place in the ceremonial progress, not a full-fledged temple. Because its grandiosity is out of scale with its circumscribed function, it has sometimes been mistaken for another kind of object.

The constantly shifting spatial narrative of the main temple is the result of countless individual decisions, which occur over the 3,000 years of the building's life, a span that includes sackings by foreign armies, which prompt further improvements and repairs. Like other structures continually embellished over long periods, Karnak temple must have perplexed some donors over how to make their mark. One solution was to preface all that already existed with a new court or a new gate, creating a grander introduction to the whole. Or one could start at the other end,

Karnak, temple of Amun, Hypostyle Hall, begun *c.* 1294 BC, view from the forest of closed bud papyrus columns looking toward the central spine of open papyrus columns with window grilles above.

as Tuthmose III did with his Festival Temple, adding a new culmination to the triumphal series. Or intrude on an existing open space with a 'kiosk' – seeming temporary by its location, but overpowering by its scale like Taharqa's, or colonize an existing court by inserting large images of oneself between every pair of columns, as Ramesses II did at Luxor.

The present looseness and freedom arise in part from what is missing. In their *Topographical Bibliography* Porter and Moss catalogue some of the hundreds of statues that are known to have clustered round the feet of columns in the Hypostyle Hall, already a space with little room for manoeuvre. It is one of the most powerful of architectural conceptions, a large squarish interior occupied by a forest of campaniform columns whose trunks are 10 to 15 feet across and whose giant blooms hit the roof 72 feet overhead in the central aisle. There is no roof now, so one struggles to imagine the space lit only by the window grilles that line the taller central aisle. Gloomy now, it must have been far more sepulchral then, a cave rather than a forest.

Karnak, temple of Amun, relief showing a barque procession on north internal wall of Hypostyle Hall.

The sizes of these columns are not demanded by the weight of the superstructure resting on them. Similarly, the narrow spaces between them are only in a trivial sense determined by the spanning capacities of stone lintels. This space obeys an intention, not just a necessity, and presents a solemn and inward-looking world.

Only at certain times of day would the reliefs of the barque procession on the north wall be readable without help. More often they would loom there not exactly visible. Even harder the further you got from the windows to read the hieroglyphs high up on columns in this totally inscribed, intermittently visible space, a heightened rendering of the primal swamp from which all life is supposed to have sprung, where deliberate flooding at certain times of year made the illusion stronger.

The name of the main god worshiped at Karnak means the 'Hidden One'. As one goes further in, the floor rises and the ceiling drops until

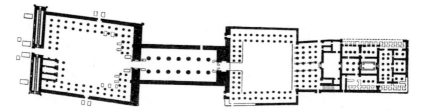

Luxor, plan of temple, *c.* 1400 to 1250 BC, showing skewing of first court to meet axis of sphinx avenue leading from Karnak, omitting both the mosque inserted in the wall of the court at upper left and remains of Christian churches scattered around the left-hand edges of the plan.

the inner sanctum is the smallest, darkest space in the whole sequence, an effect that can be experienced now more powerfully at nearby Luxor than at Karnak. At Luxor, one can look back along the route one has come, down the graded series of progressively more secret spaces and feel like a small kernel hidden somewhere deep in the earth.

The main axis at Karnak grew longer and sprouted an extra cross axis linking the temple with the precinct of Mut to the south. This was not the only branching movement: a temple of Monthu (last member of the Theban Triad) to the north was linked by formal gateways to the main temple and also to another Monthu temple further away at Melamoud. Further complexes to related gods hive off in different directions and form a catalogue of fashions in Egyptian religion. Their different proximities to the main thread would make a rich spatial study, but the most important ramification is the connection with Amun's temple in Luxor two miles away, along an avenue lined with hundreds of sphinxes brought in at a late stage from other locations. The plan of Luxor shows clearly how the attractive force of nearby Karnak has pulled its first large court out of straight alignment. This space becomes a sloping parallelogram to meet the route from Karnak and join it to the axis of the sanctum at Luxor.

Later interference with its form is also more obvious at Luxor. When the Romans took over the temple and incorporated it in an army barracks, the inner sanctum was apsed and re-dedicated to the Roman imperial cult, while the Hypostyle Hall was thinned out, an architectural form that suited neither the Roman worldview nor Roman practical requirements. The Hypostyle Hall at Karnak is often compared to a fertile reed swamp from which life was generated in the first place. Momentarily this seems apt at Luxor too, with its thickets of bundled papyrus columns forming the high colonnade between courts.

Another intrusion at Luxor appears in the first court. A mosque, built mostly of reused ancient material, occupies half of the north side, from which it looks down on its predecessor. In fact, this mosque has taken over the place and some of the fabric of an earlier Christian church, one of a group that colonized the ancient precinct.

Most plans in guidebooks leave out both the mosque and the churches. Many Egyptian temples went through a stage of Christian infiltration, a phase that has been largely erased in an attempt to get back to the earlier monument in as purely Egyptian a state as possible. The mosque survives at Luxor only because it is impossible to detach the ancient ruins from the modern town. To see a plan of the ruin that acknowledges the outlines of the various churches strewn through the site comes with the force of revelation. It is messier, of course, but lights up the long intervening history. Instead of fleeing from the sites of blasphemous old cults, new creeds replacing them invariably reoccupy their sites, perching as near

Luxor, view towards the northwest corner of the first court, showing the 13th-century mosque intruding into the space.

to the abomination as they can, if not on top of or inside it. The archaeology of early Christianity in Egypt is presently kept separate from that of ancient Egypt, but this seems an impoverishment. At some point in the future it will be recognized as arbitrary to exclude the history of these sites after the demise of the old pagan cult.

The island of Philae is famous as the place where the last surviving open observance of Egyptian religion was finally stamped out in AD 535 by the Eastern emperor Justinian, the builder of Hagia Sophia in Constantinople. Far from the centres of power, Philae was by then a kind of holdover. Soon after, a Christian monastery occupied the temple of Isis, traces of which have recently disappeared in archaeologists' reconstruction of the ancient pilgrimage site, left behind on the old island at the time more ancient remains were removed to preserve them from flooding by the dammed-up Nile.

The siting of Philae was crucially important; it was the nearest point one could occupy to one of Osiris's thirteen burial sites on the island of Biga, which laymen were strictly forbidden to enter. Biga was also regarded as the source of the Nile, an island in the middle of it from which the river sprang, as if from its opposite, forming another myth of death and rebirth like that of the god, violently dismembered, patiently collected and sown in the ground from which he rises again. The god's story could be an allegory of Egyptian archaeology, or, more particularly, of the chequered history of Philae, threatened with flooding by the Aswan

High Dam and moved piece by piece to another island not far away, no longer next to Osiris's grave or the river source, which, being myths at home in the imagination, cannot so easily move.

The oldest trace of building on Philae (dating from the Late period) has been obliterated by the Ptolemaic and Roman constructions that dominate the site. But as it stands Philae contains all the main distinguishing features of the latest phases of Egyptian religion and architecture, the cults of mother goddesses like Isis and her husband Osiris, the ritual forms of birth house and cult terrace, and architectural innovations sometimes traced to Hellenistic precedent. These include irregular planning that yields oblique views instead of the rigid axial symmetry of older temple complexes.

At Philae the configuration was not planned all at once and has to fit into a cramped island site. But the designers respond to the constraints with new forms including an open-ended courtyard of funnel-shaped perspectival form, a freer kind of outdoor room than any met in Egypt before, which has been traced by at least one historian to Hellenistic colonnaded squares.

The capitals of the colonnade include the liveliest variety, with occasional acanthus leaves and composites formed of the blooms of more than one plant that seem conscious of Corinthian prototypes. It is above all an illusionistic perspective, bounded on one side by shrines and enterable rooms, matched on the other by an arcade whose 'windows' open onto the landscape beyond, essentially a piece of architectural scenery.

The magnificent pylon covered in sunk relief to which this colonnade leads is encroached on by a little temple to the architect-god Imhotep.

Philae, west colonnade, a variety of vegetal forms in capitals, early 1st century AD.

Philae, Roman kiosk that once had an elaborate wooden roof, formerly attributed to Trajan (in whose reign its decoration was carved), now Augustus.

These lopsided proportions and crooked entrances are carried even further by the courtyard within, where a large birth house fills up the left side, leaving an exciting diagonal passage between itself and the temple, a scenographic effect that exploits rather than conceals the collisions brought on by the crowded site. Birth houses were employed for staging pieces of religious theatre, which turned the birth of Horus – and by implication the king's rebirth – into a play, at a time when Egyptian religion enters a lurid populist phase near its end.

Another foreign infiltration, the large roofless kiosk on the eastern edge of the island, whose details are Egyptian and its proportions classical, is now attributed to Augustus, not Trajan, and hence comes near the beginning of the Roman occupation of Egypt. At last, towards the end of the Roman period, the island was reoriented by the addition of a large new entry gate, which gave special prominence to another smaller shrine to Augustus that had turned its back on the temple of Isis.

In ways we can't fully appreciate, we have always received our Egypt through the filter of Greece and Rome. Many of our key terms for naming ancient Egypt are Greek, like 'pyramid' and 'nome', or Greekified, like 'pharaoh'. Obelisks are few and far between in Egypt now. Most of the survivors were transported to Rome, some to enhance imperial might, others to decorate constructions devoted to Egyptian cults in Rome, which

Sarcophagus of
Seti I, c. 1279 BC,
in its current location
in the basement
of Sir John Soane's
Museum in London.

Abu Simbel, rock-cut temple, two of the four gigantic statues of Ramesses II forming the facade, one of which was shattered by an earthquake in ancient times.

were certainly not Egyptian buildings, but aped selected Egyptian features more or less conscientiously. Like the sculpted figures of Antinous, Hadrian's favourite who died in Egypt, which present him dressed as a pharaoh, they perplex us. When cultures as apparently diverse as these two begin to copy each other's most intimate inventions it induces something like vertigo. Egypt can't be moved to Rome or London. Seti I's sarcophagus, buried now in Soane's house in London, has lost all the blue mastic that spelled out its important inscription. In the damp northern climate the words fell out of those delicate crevices.

The Greeks stood in awe of Egyptian learning, and early phases of Greek sculpture probably show a more profound absorption of Egyptian ways than careful but superficial Roman imitations. But in neither case is our real debt to Egypt adequately revealed. For hundreds of years they provided the model for forms of civility the Greeks could only aspire to. At least as far back as Mycenae, where Egyptian artefacts of various kinds have turned up, Egypt had exhibited an unattainable standard of refinement.

To represent the learned, thoughtful side of Egyptian civilization we might choose Khaemwaset, son and heir of Ramesses II, an early antiquarian who went around the country digging up lost statues and repairing decayed temples. And to represent the gigantesque Egypt of popular imagination, we could choose his father, deified in his own lifetime. In the halls of the rock-cut temple at Abu Simbel Ramesses is shown making offerings to himself, and on its outer face, a pylon-front extracted from a cliff face, he is repeated four times in seated figures 60 feet high, trampling on enemies, towering over knee-high wives and inspiring generations of megalomaniac rulers to come. The only real variety in this mind-numbing façade was provided by an earthquake, which removed the top half of the second figure from the left. So it was left to time and natural disaster to supply a humanizing touch of variety to these inflated boasts.

2
Greek

Mycenae isn't exactly Greek, but was always thought so, and thus from an early stage efforts were under way to tie it culturally to later Greek institutions, artistic forms and stories. Nineteenth-century excavators never deciphered Linear B, the Mycenaean script, a non-Greek alphabet for a proto-Greek language. But so strong was their wish to link their discoveries to the weightiest written remains of Greek civilization that they named the most magnificent burials that they found after Agamemnon and Clytemnestra, whom they knew from tragedy and epic.

This habit of linking the legendary past with specific places and objects was nothing new. The ancient Greeks themselves were always doing it, and Pausanias, travelling round in the second century AD, was shown Helen's bath, Patroklos' breastplate and Hippodameia's bed. Temples by his time resembled museums in collecting together works of high art and objects of historical or superstitious significance. Experienced observers like Pausanias were already discriminating among these categories and rejecting certain relics after sceptical inspection. In fact, Herodotus had shown the way six hundred years earlier.

Pausanias pays a kind of lip service to Mycenae, but it does not detain him long. Nowadays the landscape dominates the view, and the stone city is dwarfed by the stony place it sits in. Today different grey-green tones and yellow flowers impress the visitor, but this place was originally devised for a more violent existence. Even now the most entertaining elements are defences, like the secret passage through the walls to a hidden cistern, the maw that made Henry Miller think of snakes and which he balked at entering. There are, of course, more refined examples of masonry at Mycenae, like the beautifully tailored clefts running between sheer walls to the entrances of tholos tombs.

But the most powerful and meaningful Mycenaean constructions are the ruder Cyclopean walls, originally finished in their upper reaches with sun-dried bricks. Here we gauge best the distance between Greece and

Mycenae, entrance in the citadel wall to a secret passage leading to a cistern outside the walls and 18 metres below the surface. 13th century BC.

Egypt: Greece from the start a conflict-ridden world, Egypt saved by geography and a unified state from large outlay on the fortification of every settlement. There is one other built form besides walls and gates to note at Mycenae because it portends so much for the future – the megaron, a large room sitting behind its columned court, framed by a porch and vestibule like its sacred descendants. From this unlikely source springs the greatest Greek contribution to the history of architecture, the Doric temple.

The earliest temples do not survive except as post holes in the ground and clay models dedicated in sanctuaries. In fact, the presence of such models is the clearest sign that we have come upon a sanctuary. No other use for these tiny buildings is known than dedications in a sacred place. One of the most famous models, found in the Argive Heraion, portrays a modest structure of wood and mud brick or even flimsier materials. For someone coming from inspection of Doric temples, though, the little replica is a revelation of electrifying force. Its porch has only two columns

Votive model found
in Argive Heraion,
near Argos, of an
early temple form
in wood and
mud brick,
8th century BC.

as yet, and is still focused on its primitive function of keeping weather off
the walls and protecting the entrance. But the idea is already there, of a
formal introduction to the building consisting of vertical elements as high
as the walls. In the unusual equality between the porch and the building
lies the germ of an encircling colonnade. Already we find an odd lack of
interest in lighting the interior: there are tiny breaks in the side walls,
and the only sizeable opening in the gable, which will soon become the
main site of sculptural decoration, reclaimed from everyday function for
elevated meaning.

Elevation is not the only purpose of the earliest architectural sculpture in Greece. Fitly, the earliest of all is a kind of gable built into a wall
that intimidates both as technical feat and figured expression. The Lion
Gate at Mycenae consists of a huge monolith – the lintel – capped by a
triangular carved stone carrying the famous lionesses, now lacking their
heads. They worship or guard a column of top-heavy Minoan form. An
object of reverence so abstract and unfigurative must be a symbol, it is
commonly thought, either a metonym for the palace and hence the ruler,
or for the goddess, whom we are shy of representing directly in such an
exposed place. Structurally, the decoration is a clever disguise, deflecting
the wall's weight from bearing straight on the lintel, which doesn't stop
it from enshrining a boast at the same time. It asserts that this citadel is
doubly guarded – by walls and by co-opted beings.

Mycenae, Lion Gate, *c*, 1250 BC, the earliest architectural sculpture in Greece, representing either the mother goddess or the ruler.

At Mycenae the carved animals are doing architectural work, and supplying animation to a diagram of structural forces. Such symbiosis between the figure and the structure, between living bodies and the geometry of the building, is an abiding theme in Greek architecture, binding decoration firmly into deeper levels of the site. One of the seventh-century BC temples at Prinias in Crete has no provable connection with the mainland, but its frieze of carved riders marks a crucial stage in this dialogue between living beings and geometrical perfection and offers a primitive version of the most persistent concerns of Greek architectural sculpture.

Far more than Rome, ancient Greece comes to us in wrecked and partial form. So our idea about the special importance of sculpture as the pre-eminent Greek expressive form may derive partly from the more complete destruction of Greek painting. And yet . . . the physicality of stone and the bodily emphasis of Greek art mean that in sculpture above all their sense of how ideas are embodied is revealed.

At Prinias a row of nearly identical bareback riders fills identical rectangles of stone. They all face left, raising their puny spears, dwarfed by their huge mounts. Later, on the Parthenon frieze, horses will be scaled down to give proper prominence to those walking beside them. At Prinias an idea of geometrical consistency takes precedence over detailed interest

Prinias, Crete, surviving remnants of a temple frieze showing mounted riders, *c.* 630–580 BC.

in anatomy. But it is a stage in the same struggle to capture and subdue life and movement to the rhythms of architecture without snuffing it out entirely.

The earliest stone temple in Greece widens the field of play considerably, reaching further back into primitive darkness and introducing a population of monsters and monstrous hybrids, beings that fill necessary spaces in the terrain of the psyche and exercise abiding fascination for the Greeks. The temple of Artemis on Corfu was purposely destroyed at an early date, but is generally regarded as the first stone temple. Only fragments survive, most notably a reconstructed pediment in the Corfu museum. Here primitive disproportions outdo even Prinias. Of course, a pediment's triangular shape always pushes one strongly towards different scales in the taller centre and the squashed ends, solved throughout Greek sculpture with standing, kneeling and lying figures, and at least once with semi-serpentine species.

At Corfu the problems are aggravated by the tumultuous subject chosen. The whole space is dominated by a contorted representation of a Gorgon whose head overlaps the frame. She is the formulaic guardian, threatening all who approach. She, who has burst out of ritual stasis into narrative, is flanked by her disturbingly small offspring and, in the corners, by even smaller renderings of the great gods shown battling giants who are more like dwarfs. Large heraldic lions fill long intervals between Gorgon and gods, further signs of unresolved struggle between hieratic pattern and flexible narrative.

A further stage in the humanizing of architectural sculpture was reached a few decades later in metopes from a Hera temple at Foce de Sele near Paestum, south of Naples, even though these little reliefs are cruder and wilder than the Corfu pediments. This series of scenes contains a high proportion of deadly combat: Herakles stabs his opponents, or carries two of them upside down, or shoves one rudely before finishing him off. Physical energy is portrayed as a good in itself, but violence is also redeemed by an opposing force of composition – the struggles are constrained by the frames, and a giant and a man, by matching each other's agonized contortion, satisfy the geometric fiat of the rectangular panel. So, for all the boisterousness of the carving, these panels are really about obeying the rules.

The earliest temple at Paestum, contemporary with these reliefs, carries no figure sculpture, only some vegetable ornament on the lower surfaces of capitals on its backside (but facing the former settlement), a location that makes them easy to overlook nowadays. Though there is no localized carving to speak of at Paestum, in some sense it is everywhere. The porous local limestone of which the temples are made, grey in the earlier Hera temple, ochre in the later one, together with the raggedness of surfaces eaten by time, makes the columns into a lot of articulate individuals.

Even without such accidents one can see in the major destination we have now arrived at, the fabric of the Doric order itself, that the Greeks have succeeded at infusing their feeling for the single human figure into the more impersonal elements of the building. Further accidents increase the effect of columns distinguished almost to the point of personification. Neither temple has its roof or its walls, and the Basilica is missing most of its frieze. The resulting openness lets light play freely on stone

Foce de Sele, near Paestum, Campania, a metope showing Herakles in combat with a giant, possibly Polyphemus, *c.* 550 BC.

'Basilica', c. 550 BC.
Doric columns as
almost personified.
Paestum.

surfaces and allows views through one temple to the other, until their strange proximity seems almost an allegory of the Greek penchant for setting up contests or rivalries. Imagining the juxtaposition as an athletic event ranging two heroes against each other, one slow and steady, the other quicker and coarser, we come up against the twentieth-century discovery that the buildings may have been dedicated to the same goddess, Hera, not Neptune as the eighteenth century thought.

In the eighteenth century the temples were given names that have stuck, though long ago overturned. Paestum in Greek was Poseidonia, and so it stood to reason that its grandest temples would be dedicated to the patron of the settlement. The proportions of both buildings are easily read as masculine, with columns much heavier and more assertively present than their contemporaries in mainland Greece. So they were regarded as temples of Neptune, one called Basilica (a Roman format) because it had aisles, and the other Neptune. The names influenced how people saw the buildings. Piranesi's ink and wash drawings in the Soane, for instance, convey the almost oppressive force of these walls made of columns. Hera was the deity at Foce de Sele too, where the carved scenes were all male battles, mainly conducted, it is true, by Herakles, whose name has been translated as 'glory of Hera'.

Yet we return to our sense that Doric temples are assertions of self-confident maleness, turning away from the interior toward the wider world beyond, advertising themselves at a distance but on a human scale. This scale is not a matter of size but of proportion. Columns are a series of individual human bodies that carry the consonance deriving from that parallel when viewed from a distance, even if they intimidate by sheer size close to.

Something in the builders' attitude to the materials gives the stone a peculiar presence. Southern Italy has no sources of marble, but even the relatively coarse local limestone at Paestum glows in the light. Modern observers pore reverently over the pitted surface, soaking up the idea of stone that is colonized here and there by plants and at dusk by swallows. The Greeks certainly understood stone but may not have cared about these superficial sensuous effects, for they plastered columns to smooth them out and painted the backgrounds of metopes and friezes with strong reds and blues. In the museum at Paestum are gaudy reconstructions of the roof of the Basilica by German archaeologists, showing howling faces, flapping wings and large floral flourishes on the skyline.

If we must have the temples coloured and their stoniness obscured, at least we would like muted earth colours like we find on Greek pots, but apparently potters had found blue and red pigments for architectural details that did not bleach in the sun but remained bright. French Beaux-Arts architects of around 1900 pitched themselves wholeheartedly into imagining the best temples weighed down by rich and sombre ornamental schemes like Victorian interiors.

If Greek architecture was originally less pure and single-minded than we prefer to think, it was still full of subtle refinements, like carefully calculated fluting on the columns. In the later temple of Hera at Paestum, external columns have twenty-four flutes, larger internal ones twenty, smaller sixteen. Egyptian architects had already experimented with entasis in the shafts of columns, a swelling in the middle, which combats sensations of precarious thinness. But with the Greeks such corrections became an obsession.

In an ideal world the deviations should be invisible and contribute to a deep sense of rightness overall. But sometimes, taking so much trouble to incorporate meaningful irregularities, Greek designers must have wanted to let it show. Columns of the Basilica at Paestum have the most exaggerated swelling of any surviving Greek building, pronounced enough to be detectable by the eye, confirming a general sense that the building is almost alive, its little variations affecting us as gentle movement, like breathing.

The key to this architecture is subtle difference that can almost be mistaken for sameness. The spacing of columns is different on ends and sides, different also at corners and in middles. Columns faintly congregate or cluster at the important places, and by this means convert uniformity into nuance and emphasis, carefully judged but not insistent. Paestum offers a relatively crude and friendly version of this Greek obsession, which was taken to unheard of heights in the Parthenon.

At Paestum the rivals lie a couple of hundred yards from each other. The temple of Zeus at Olympia and Athena's temple in Athens were much further apart, but acutely conscious of one another. So much so that the Parthenon is widely assumed a specific response to the previously largest temple in Greece, trumping it in a multitude of specific ways. The citizens of Olympia's manner of redressing the balance was to order another huge gold and ivory cult statue from the same Phidias who had made an *Athena* of those materials for Athens. His *Zeus* would be bigger, only feasible if he sat down, inspiring the joke that if he ever stood up, this statue would carry off the roof.

For Pausanias Olympia was a site of the most intense religious significance. The modern revival of the games is not much help in understanding the powerful meanings attached to athletic contests by the Greeks. Pausanias begins the account of his visit to Olympia – the longest treatment of a site in his entire travels – with reports of the mythic and legendary foreshadowings of the games. Here Zeus and Chronos wrestled, the first individualized struggle of all, and here Apollo and Hermes raced. Later, Herakles laid out the courses for runners and chariots. Later still or earlier, Pelops, a local hero who gave his name to the lower half of Greece, won a bride in a chariot race previously lost by thirteen suitors who paid with their lives.

An archaeology of layers lies behind the highly ritualized contests of the present. Ordeals have become 'games', but apparently when new events are introduced into the games they are more lurid than the older ones and more likely to end in death for one of the contestants. Perhaps this unsettling fact simply reveals the Greek genius for reinventing the primitive and allowing old origins to re-erupt in the present.

Looking at a site like Olympia, Pausanias never thinks of separating aesthetic concerns from the train of associations they pull along behind them. He combines the cataloguer's interest in physical remains with a voracious appetite for the stories that go with them. Describing the pediments of the temple of Zeus, the greatest monument of the severe style,

Pausanias is carried away by the import of the scenes, which he connects to Homer, to the local landscape and to philosophical ideas of the well- or ill-spent life.

None of his interests is subordinated to any of the others. The story of Pelops is not told just to clarify what the stone figures are up to, but taken more seriously than that. Pelops is one of the legendary founders of the games and this race of his – for which the pediment shows the prepa- rations – is therefore in some way the first Olympic contest of all, and so the qualities the hero exhibits in it cast their shadow on all later happen- ings at the site.

Pausanias' engagement with the stories behind the pediment prob- ably makes the sculpture mean more to most modern observers. It survives in the site museum in mutilated form, displayed as free-standing groups on the ground, a few feet from the wall behind. Older photographs show that the sculptures have been de-restored recently. Missing bits needed to complete the course of an arm or leg, formerly supplied in plaster, were removed in the 1960s, leaving a truer impression of the shattered incom- pleteness of the pediment.

Apparently, pieces continue to be identified in the marble store that fit somewhere in this puzzle, and perhaps the de-restoration was mainly meant to make further piecing together easier. Just as likely, the removal of all the smoothing out in plaster is ideological. The archaic pediments from Aegina now in Munich have been similarly de-restored by the removal of a more prestigious restoration carried out by Thorvaldsen.

Presumably the theory is that each of us must piece the fragments together for ourselves, not taking someone else's word for it, never en- shrining one idea to the exclusion of others. Then again, not everyone will want to imagine the pediment and then the temple whole again – this is the thinking – such is the modern fascination with the fragment, not an entirely voluntary prompting, but the result of a historically conditioned compulsion.

Pausanias talking about what still exists – even if semi-ruined – is one thing. The bulk of his narrative, however, treats of what is no longer there. He populates a site now grown up in olive trees and asphodel with a clamouring crowd of presences, mainly memorials in bronze on marble pedestals. The subjects and donors come from all over the Greek world – Sicily, Asia Minor and Egypt, as well as the mainland. Which means that Pausanias is always wandering off, though briefly, to these other spots. Like the modern games, the ancient ones were occasions for unusual meetings, and nowhere can one get a quicker sense of the interconnected- ness of the Greek world than in Pausanias writing about Olympia.

He does not need the stimulus of foreign place names to set off on journeys. In the midst of a long analysis of the chryselephantine *Zeus* we suddenly find him talking about whether elephants' tusks are really teeth or horns. Only later does he connect the subject to the ivory elements of the *Zeus* statue. This statue was made in a studio that Phidias was permitted to build close behind the temple, a studio that reproduced the dimensions and conditions of the temple interior and thus allowed the sculptor to work out perspective effects, compensating for the viewer's nearness to the towering figure. The great *Zeus* vanished long ago, of course. The modern historian is reduced to attaching long footnotes to the denuded site, filling in the missing historical stages of the most important disappearances: though Caligula had a scheme for taking the *Zeus* to Rome, it was never carried out, and the colossal figure probably ended its days in Constantinople.

Many of the dozens of bronze statues described by Pausanias survive only in their inscribed marble bases, which allow a ghostly tour of these obscure hints of what is missing and where. One of his most enticing descriptions evokes a group of eight Greek heroes drawing lots to see which of them will go against Hector. Apparently the visitor walked between the two halves of this group, becoming temporarily part of it. One of the two Riace bronzes, figures pulled out of the sea off Calabria in 1972, has been put forward as the *Agamemnon* from this group, another trophy on its way to Rome.

Amazing traces survive at Olympia, formerly jumbled in dark temple interiors, now neatly laid out in the museum. In Pausanias' time the old temple of Hera held more numerous and venerable relics than grander Zeus' that superseded it. These included Pelops' wife's bed and a richly carved cedar chest in which a Corinthian dictator had once been concealed, so the story went. Pausanias catalogues every episode on the

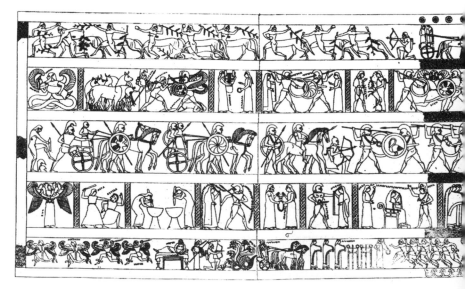

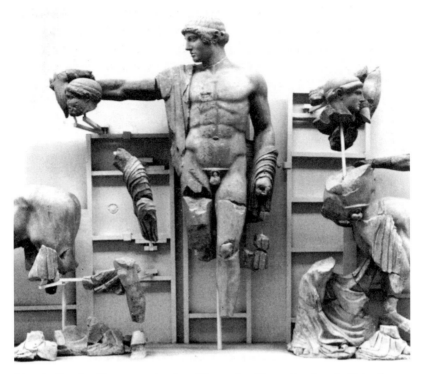

Olympia, Temple of Zeus, reconstruction of the centre of the west pediment with Apollo flanked by Theseus and Peirithoos, a prime example of the modern taste for presenting fragments as aspects of an irreparably shattered whole.

Frazer's reconstruction of the so-called Chest of Cypselus as described by Pausanias, who saw it exhibited in the Temple of Hera at Olympia. No trace of the chest remains, so Frazer based his reconstruction on a large Greek ceramic vase now in Florence.

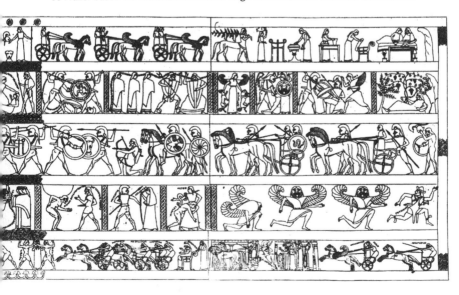

Columns of the great Temple of Zeus at Olympia, toppled long ago by an earthquake.

chest's crowded surface, making a confusing flood of story. This passage prompted J. G. Frazer (of *The Golden Bough*) to produce elaborate visualizations of the chest, derived mainly from a large ceramic pot, the François Vase in Florence. Now this reconstruction seems misguided, and we relish the gaps Pausanias reminds us of for their own sake. Instead of trying to fill them we savour the ironic contrast between a prosaic present and a myth-laden past, between our scientific recovery of the merest shreds and the wealth of the scene described by Pausanias.

The great temple of Zeus was tumbled by an earthquake and no one has ever tried to put it back up. It remains perhaps the most beautiful instance of nearly total collapse. On the south side, columns lie in concertinaed dissection with varying gaps between drums roughly aligned with one another. Much of this effect, as of the exploded diagram of a building, is the result of tidying by the German archaeologists who since 1875 have done exemplary work at Olympia.

The stone is limestone of powerful grey colour, so shelly that it sometimes looks like nothing but hundreds of shells glued together. An elaborate set of ramps at the entrance prompts thoughts of the ritual processions catalogued by Pausanias, who describes the great altar, which lay somewhere to the north-east and was composed entirely of the ashes of sacrificial victims held together by Alpheios river water, nothing else would do. Similarly, no wood could be used to burn the offerings but white poplar supplied by a man who had a special concession. Earlier, Pausanias had described the two personified rivers (the Alpheios one of them) at either end of the east pediment, not stuck in as idle filler but active participants in the race.

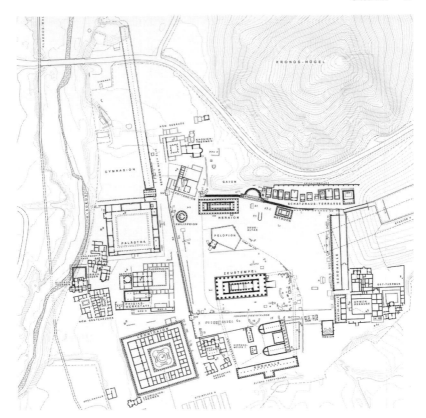

Comparative plans of Altis at Olympia and the Acropolis at Athens, the one set on a level plain, the other on a steep promontory, a meeting-place for the whole Greek world as against the focal centre of one city.

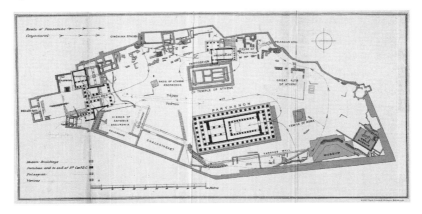

The bulk of his commentary concerns statues and dedications of athletes connected with the games, including disasters at sea travelling to and from Olympia. These proportions put architecture in its place. Olympia is above all a locus of memory where much has happened and continues to happen, commemorated in forms that obscure the lines of the temple, gathering round it, fanning out from it, blurring the clear outline of the Doric structure. Too much had occurred at Olympia to let architecture stand alone.

The Acropolis in Athens, eventually the site of a famous attempt to outdo the temple of Zeus at Olympia, had lived through a more chequered past than Altis, the old core at Olympia. The Acropolis, a distinct natural feature to begin with, has seen a clarifying reduction of its functions over a long period. Its later history has been erased by the purification that began in 1834, immediately after the establishment of Athens as capital of newly independent Greece, and its earlier history has only recently been recovered by scientific study.

With understandable if regrettable fervour the first Greek archaeologists dedicated themselves to removing every Ottoman trace from the site, scraping away all evidence later than the classical heyday of the fifth century BC. This included the mosques erected in the interiors of the Parthenon and Erechtheion, the remains of Christian churches that had preceded them in both places, Byzantine gates and governor's house and Ottoman defences of the promontory, in dismantling which the elements of the temple of Athena Nike were discovered almost entire, hastily incorporated in beefed-up seventeenth-century battlements.

The result of this cleansing was to give the whole outcropping the stark appearance it has had ever since. It consists now of three striking constructions widely spaced on a stony platform. They form a powerful irregular composition, memorably sketched in 1911 by Le Corbusier as if the buildings were the sparse furnishings of a large outdoor room. All three are grand replacements for simpler predecessors, and the latest to be built, the Propylaia, never completed, while creating a delusive impression of its own regularity, binds the others in a sophisticated single composition.

Perspective of the Acropolis in Athens taken as the visitor crosses the threshold of the Propylaia, from Le Corbusier's *Vers une architecture* of 1924. The size of the outdoor statue of Athena, known from texts but now missing, is greatly exaggerated.

Erechtheion, 421–405 BC, whose hybrid form is explained by the assortment of functions it performed.

Recent excavation has filled in earlier stages in the history of the hill. In Mycenaean times it functioned as a citadel and held the ruler's palace, of which little survives. After political upheaval in which the last Peisistratid tyrant was driven out of Athens, the hill ceased to be the ruler's stronghold and was turned over completely to sacred purposes. By the time of the prestigious buildings that remain, the Acropolis had become a ceremonial core incorporating various relics of legendary events essential to the city's identity.

Legends and relics determined the peculiar form of the Erechtheion, which is three buildings in one, ingeniously joined to each other to make diverting variety rather than confusion. Like the older Hera temple at Olympia, this less imposing, secondary structure contained the most venerable image on the Acropolis, a wooden *Athena* that fell from heaven in primordial times. The building also enshrined graves and traces of events tied to precise locations that could not be altered, so the building was tailored to fit them, not they, it. Graves included that of Kekrops, the legendary first ruler of the city, whose daughters are commemorated in the famous caryatid maidens. They remind us of a grisly but uplifting story of early civic virtue, and they also hark back to the origins of architectural form in the human body.

The Ionian order was traditionally derived from the form of a young maiden. Doric and Ionic orders have deep psychological and cultural roots. They are named after the two main Greek language groups, which coincide with a geographic distinction – Doric settlers arrived in mainland Greece, Ionian in Asia Minor. At the beginning that is how the architectural forms were distributed. The appearance of the Ionian order on the Erechtheion is one of the earliest on the mainland, which is sometimes explained functionally as a way of setting the later structure off against the Parthenon.

Naturally the earlier temple exercised a powerful influence on its neighbour. The new Parthenon of 447–432 BC was and remained the largest temple in mainland Greece. No other building has been found to incorporate so many refinements in the form of deviations from simple rectangularity. Every line is bowed away from straightness; every interval is individually adjusted. Most of the variance is too slight to be visible to an unaided eye – only in certain spots can we see the stylobate – highest step of the temple's stone plinth – declining slightly away from the centre.

All these adjustments would have made the temple much more difficult to build. Its contemporaries may have been better than we are at detecting them, but it is not agreed that they all tend in a consistent direction. After all the theories that the adjustments correct the building into optical regularity, it seems possible that their intention is quite different – to lessen the monotonous sameness of the Doric format rigidly adhered to.

Having finally achieved this miracle of inconspicuous individuality in every element of a temple, it seems the Greeks never bothered with it again. Interest in such optical distortions declined, and they are not found together in later temples, not even Apollo Epikouros at Bassae, often attributed to Iktinos, architect of the Parthenon.

Perhaps the Parthenon is one of those achievements like Shakespeare's plays that so exceeds the previous norm that it dampens further effort in the same direction. Never was a classical Greek temple so prodigal in its squandering of sculptural ornament. The famous frieze now mainly in the British Museum was originally placed in a poorly lit location behind the colonnade, so that the continuity of the action was continually broken by the columns standing in front of it.

Later observers have speculated that this obscurity would spur viewers to repeated visits in which they slowly pieced together the obstructed narrative. What the narrative shows remains undecided. Perhaps it portrays the yearly Panathenaic procession that passed along the flank of the building on its way to the east front where the newly woven peplos was presented to the goddess. Elements of the procession known from descriptions are missing from the frieze, like the large wheeled boat across whose rigging the peplos was draped like a sail. The bundle that, according to this reading, represents the peplos in the frieze is visually insignificant and the gestures surrounding it seem un-momentous.

Or is it an un-literal, abstract version of the procession? Or another celebration of the victory at Marathon, equally apposite to the temple's civic role? According to any of these interpretations the progress ends in an assembly of the gods, which falls at the east end under a pediment depicting the birth of Athena at dawn.

The gods in the frieze are larger than other figures around them, but are shown sitting casually on chairs, Ares especially in a remarkably relaxed pose, curling a foot around his spear. It is thrilling to see them behaving so naturally, but in bringing them down to earth Phidias (responsible for overall planning) has given up the old hieratic power of the divine image which keeps its distance.

Writers like Jeffrey Hurwit have recently stripped the Parthenon of its aura by demoting it from a temple to a locked storehouse, 'the central bank of Greece'. In some sense Perikles invited this interpretation. He justified the misuse of funds forcibly collected for the joint defence from members of the Delian League on pragmatic grounds and argued at the same time that the expense of Phidias' great statue could be recovered – its gold could be stripped off and sold. So the modern critic argues that the Athenians had a thoroughly pragmatic view of the monument.

One might cast a similarly cold beam of scepticism onto the venerable inclusions in the Erechtheion, the sort of literal enactments of myth that appeal only to the most naive. There one could see the hole in its roof made by Poseidon's trident as he fought over Athens with Athena. Likewise the god's little salt sea, a mysterious spring now given an architectural

Gods in the Parthenon frieze, shown as larger than the human beings next to them but in relaxed and human, not ritualized, postures. Ares props his foot on the chair-leg. c. 443–438 BC.

shape by framing it in stone. In a courtyard off this chamber grew the olive, Athena's gift that had helped her win the contest. The whole story is remarkable because it shows gods competing for human favour. We might imagine that all the literal traces left behind by the myth inspired sophisticated architects with secret derision. But Pausanias, who does not mention the Parthenon frieze, pays meticulous attention to the placement of a series of altars on the Acropolis. He betrays no sign of rational disbelief in his account of the Erechtheion as the guardian of the city's founding myths. But he also finds time to marvel at the amazing gilded flue shaped like a palm tree that Callimachus devised to take away the smoke from his miraculous lamp with an asbestos wick.

Nietzsche blamed a new scientific spirit for the destruction of myth and tragedy and the old gods of Greece. He follows the process not in sculpture or architecture, but in literature, and the main culprits are Socrates and Euripides, great innovators of a self-consciousness that undermines belief. There is no doubt that some Greeks outgrew their myths. Plato advised keeping stories of gods' misbehaviour away from the young, and allegoric interpretations appeared as a way of reclaiming archaic narrative of which one could no longer swallow the literal sense. So the gods became weather effects or moral entities or aspects of the human psyche. Nietzsche was roused to furious irony by such dilution of the primitive power of stories. He, whose thought was helplessly agonistic, was in some ways the ideal interpreter of ancient Greece, which is a constant presence in all his books from The Birth of Tragedy to Twilight of the Idols. He pits the myth of Prometheus (Aryan, masculine) against the Garden of Eden (Semitic, feminine), but the battle is already lost before the sides are announced. The true primitive is irrecoverable, and Nietzsche himself is implausible as the advocate of reverence, for his Dionysian rhapsodies are wishful, nostalgic, tormented.

We too inhabit the other side of this divide. The anecdote in Philochorus of a dog that wandered into the hallowed spaces of the Erechtheion in 306 BC and lay down on an altar is one of our main helps in trying to figure out what its spaces were for. We always learn most when taking ancient buildings apart, usually because previous efforts to stick them together are now causing them to rot at an accelerated rate. So the construction history of the Parthenon is disentangled while removing rusting clamps inserted early in the century. Now conservation is far more sensitive, its interventions all reversible. But just beyond the boundary of the site, car engines make a mockery of such refined calculations.

The naiveties of Pausanias lead to exciting revisions of accepted views. Now a reflecting pool is posited in the cella of the Parthenon, an idea first mooted in his discussion of how colossal ivory images are cared for under various conditions. Also from Pausanias come the liveliest suggestions about how spaces at the Propylaia were filled. A picture gallery and a dining room for important visitors may have occupied the largest rooms in a building many tourists probably regard as a kind of guardhouse.

The most shocking instance of our modern scientistic view of reality intruding on ancient structures appears at the temple of Apollo at Bassae, built soon after the Parthenon in a much more remote location. Photographs taken before 1987 show the temple standing alone in an inspiringly desolate landscape. Its colonnade, made of blue-grey limestone, looks almost complete. Old photographs show this colour and this powerful relation to setting, but no one can see these features any longer at Bassae, for the building sits under a plastic tent that hides it from the landscape and turns it yellow. The building is now held together by a system of wooden and metal splints, and visitors are kept out of its interior.

The temple of Apollo at Bassae has been subjected to scientific overkill by a formidable team of every imaginable kind of expert, who have begun a lengthy study that will duplicate much of the work of an earlier archaeologist. Frederick Cooper laboured at Bassae for twenty years, approximately the length of time it took to build it in the first place. His work left the temple undisturbed and resulted in a series of printed volumes that have become the best place to study it, now that the site has been thoroughly desecrated by modern science.

Bassae is anomalous in many ways. Known to be later than the Parthenon and reputedly designed by the same architect, it represents a step backwards, abandoning many of the refinements perfected at the Parthenon, including entasis and inward inclination of columns, outward inclination of entablature and bunching at corners. It also faces north, perhaps in deference to Apollo's winter sojourn among those mythical northerners, the Hyperboreans.

Bassae appears in histories of architecture on account of two startling innovations, neither of them any longer perceptible on the spot. Here the architectural conventions were turned inside out, and the sculpted frieze was run around the inside of the cella instead of under the external colonnade, perhaps a comment on the unsatisfactory visibility of the larger and longer Parthenon frieze.

This richly decorated space also included the earliest known example of a Corinthian capital, set off like a cult statue as the centrepiece of a screen wall towards the back of the cella. Both these extraordinary features are now missing: the frieze is in the British Museum and the capital exists only in early nineteenth-century drawings and pitifully incomplete fragments. It was inexplicably smashed by local inhabitants soon after its discovery by British dilettante travellers.

Frederick Cooper's studies have enriched the space further. In his inventory of every stone lying around on the site he found seven different

Battle friezes from the Temple of Apollo at Bassae, 420–400 BC, now in the British Museum. Unusually they ran around the inside of the cella, not the outside.

types of ceiling coffer in limestone and marble, in grids of different scale, some of which run diagonally in diamond shapes. Cooper has reconstituted this ceiling as something resembling a work by Vasarely, the Hungarian Op artist. Contrasts of blue limestone and white marble – also present in interior columns and capitals – and of growing and shrinking patterns, create a hallucinatory effect. For Pausanias the marble roof, which collapsed long ago, was the outstanding feature at Bassae. The colour contrast of blue colonnade and glittering white roof was then visible externally from distant mountains, and echoed near at hand in marble triglyphs highlighted against dark limestone metopes.

Not everyone will follow Cooper into his rhapsodies over the meander pattern on the Corinthian capital 'deeply rooted in contemporary philosophy'. This discussion draws on early forms of map-making and ends in one of the strongest statements of the view that Greek architectural refinements are not primarily aesthetic in character but 'inherently philosophical or religious'.

Cooper's results are often thrilling and his exploded or floating drawings of all the fallen and scattered fragments in the disposition in which he found them are unexpectedly beautiful. Among the peripheral benefits is his discovery of ancient marble quarries in the Mani, mistaken for a sacred site in the 1970s, which seems to solve the problem of where the non-local materials came from. He has carefully detailed the large aseismic stone platform on which the temple stands and argued for Iktinos' authorship of three diverse buildings in Athens, Bassae and Eleusis by finding similarity in the very uniqueness of each.

This is not the only irresolvable conundrum thrown up by this nonstandard building. The ordering of the sculptural frieze remains extremely

Bassae, Temple of Apollo, late 5th century BC, restoration of the interior showing the lone Corinthian capital, the earliest known, set out from the end wall.

problematic. Three different, related stories seem to be incorporated, two Amazonomachies and a centauromachy. They appear to start in the north-west corner and run clockwise until they arrive there again. The panels were not carved *in situ* – the Parthenon frieze is unusual in this respect – but in a studio on site. Dimensions were miscalculated and at least two sides had to be cut down, an operation clumsily carried out. In fact, the disposition of scenes seems thoroughly haphazard. The carving is crude but lively, the conception almost Baroque. Figures lunge from the frame in contorted movements that look forward to much later stages in the Greek vision of conflict. The classical moment of balanced forces has been left behind.

Perspectival shifts built into Greek architecture further east were far more radical. At three sites near each other in Asia Minor, emulation pushed Ionic temples to gargantuan size. At least we incline to view size as an overriding determinant, in whose train follow multiplication of members like peripetal columns and such strange features as roofless-ness of the main space, concealed from the visitor to Didyma until fairly late in his first encounter with the temple. Some of the wildest innova-tions at Didyma, like all the mysteries of the central space, may have been

Didyma, Temple of Apollo, 3rd century BC and later, interior, which was always unroofed, looking back toward the platform of the oracle and two symmetrical entrance passages.

accessible only to a select few. But every visitor would have seen the relatively small, dark entrances to narrow sloping tunnels, and some petitioners at least would have experienced the shock of coming from them into the vast high-walled emptiness that feels like a basement. At the other end, in place of the expected cult image of Apollo, stood a small building within the building, a diminutive temple ringed by laurel trees sacred to the god.

The striking rooflessness of the huge cella is sometimes disputed. Ironically, the presence of the sacred grove inside the building, which preceded even the dedication to Apollo, sometimes tips the argument in favour of rooflessness. Each of Didyma's architectural oddities can be explained in part by its function as an oracle. Under the portico, where the entrance should be, appears a huge doorframe – its jambs the largest monoliths in any Greek building, its threshold 5 feet higher than floor level – and thus unusable by ordinary mortals. It is sometimes thought that oracles were spoken from this portal as from a stage, to those who had just threaded the forest of colossal columns, embossed with oversized carving on their lowest drums.

Thus were suppliants intimidated by architecture and subsequently excited by the scenic novelty of traversing the enormous 'yard' of the cella, from which one turns back to find another gigantic entrance staring at one. This consists of a wide flight of monumental steps filling the space between the tunnel entrances next to the outer walls. At the top of the steps, a colonnade screens the oracle chamber, from which two labyrinth-stairs lead up to the roof, the final destination of this curious backward-turning route and scene of who knows what rites, because these stairs with powerful meander patterns on their ceilings surely have more-than-practical purpose.

At Didyma the standard components of a Greek temple are taken apart and recombined in unnerving new orders. Not only in its present ruined state did it produce the eerie sensation that the inside is another outside, where the façade viewed from behind forms another front. By means of such reversal, space is powerfully subjectivized. The truth about reality no longer seems fixed, but shifts as one changes one's position. Even architecture is reduced to scenery in a private psychodrama.

The temple at Didyma was such a grandiose project it dragged on for centuries without approaching completion. Back and sides never received the full complement of columns and the site continued in a state of dynamic becoming.

The plan, which strikes us as so eminently Baroque, belongs to a much earlier moment than the bold Hellenistic detail. Among later improbable plans, the great altar at Pergamon stands out. Strictly speaking, the architecture is more like a plinth or container for an altar than the altar itself. Maybe we could think of the mass of sculpted stone topped by a colonnade, forming three of the walls of an enclosure that isn't there, as a crystallized form of the pile of bones or ash that marks the place of sacrifice and then becomes formalized as the platform for further sacrifice, the base for further acts like its own producing cause.

The altar at Pergamon certainly looks like something that has got itself into the wrong order. The frieze has swelled to such size that it changes places with the arcade, sinks or tumbles because of its great weight to the ground and writhes there with energy that will never come to rest.

Confronted by the floridity of the Pergamon frieze, more like an entire building formed of bodies loosely cemented together, we may even experience a sneaking sympathy with St John who called the weird construction Satan's Seat. At some point in the Middle Ages it was taken apart to construct hasty defences against Muslim armies, in which it remained entombed until a German archaeologist began to pry it loose in the 1870s, which explains the odd fact that the entire frieze has ended up in Berlin where it has remained, except for the years 1948–58 that it spent in Leningrad, where it inspired a phantasmagoric novel by Vasily Aksyonov.

We would like to assimilate all this violent conflict that threatens to pull everything, every lunging stone torso and limb, down about its own ears, to the old pattern of civilization subduing barbarism. But in this welter we can find no suggestion of harmony, only a brutishness that exhilarates us in spite of ourselves.

Many sculptures of Pergamene provenance ended up in Rome, and they provide us with a coda on Hellenistic subjectivity. Recently the Italian

Pergamon, altar, section of frieze now in Berlin showing Athena contending with giants, labelled on the sculpture as Alkyoneus and Ge (or Gaia), 180–150 BC.

archaeologist Filippo Coarelli and his colleagues have noticed a cryptic little diagram on the base of the most famous of all, The Dying Gaul in the Capitoline Museum. Now on its own, this figure was originally part of a group, and the star-figure scratched on its plinth shows the elaborate diagonal matrix formed by four bodies. Even in isolation this Gaul exerts an unexpectedly strong pull, only partly arising from its fame since its rediscovery in the Renaissance. The disconsolate pose combines melodrama and geometric ingenuity of a high order. Blood is flowing; limbs converge and overlap. Head and heart are no more and no less than counters in a perilous game based on ambiguous portrayals of one's enemies expiring.

Here Roman reuse of Greek culture makes a cameo of something originally operating like an expanding nebula. It had begun as the furthest reach of Greek incorporation of sculpture into public space to create centrifugal drama. Transporting such fragments to Rome performed another kind of Baroque wrench or dislocation, which left the trophy with the power to destabilize the mental world of the looter.

3
Roman

The site is probably the most impacted in the world. Its earliest levels sometimes lie 20 metres below modern streets. In the Piazza Navona, which keeps the shape of the stadium of Domitian, there stands a Baroque church that bears a complex relation to late, deviant antique forms. Once inside, you can descend into a series of first-century domestic spaces long reputed to include the brothel where Agnes, the virgin martyr this church commemorates, was exposed naked to punish her Christian stubbornness. Not that the ancients lived in cellars, but that we now walk about on top of the accumulated debris of the intervening centuries.

Rome is both deeply layered and heavily loaded. The history of the city has meant, contentiously and intensely, many things for many centuries. Gibbon took another tack from devotees of Agnes as he contemplated the ruins and set off on a strongly pro-pagan enterprise lasting twenty years. Freud found in the complicated picture of the city constructed by modern archaeology a figure for the structure of the psyche with its buried layers and haunted passages.

We cannot dig ourselves out from under all that Rome has meant, and who would want to? But we can start by dispelling a crucial illusion, that Roman civilization derives from and resembles Greek. The Greek element in Roman architecture is mainly superficial and can impose itself only on those who do not realize how Roman imperial buildings are made and what they are made of.

By 200 BC concrete of various types was the preferred material for large Roman structures, commonly faced in composite forms of masonry and later in brick with travertine or marble trimming at openings. A few honorific structures like temples continue to look much like their Greek models, but even those are often not true trabeated structures. Even the porch of the Pantheon is an arched composition that now lacks the false ceiling that would have made it look like post and beam construction.

Pantheon, Rome, c. AD 118–28, curve of dome overhead, on which the path of the sun is traced by a circle of light admitted by the oculus, the only aperture in the great hemispherically domed cylinder.

Behind that and dwarfing it is the innovative part of this building, the rotunda consisting of a large brick-clad concrete cylinder closed by a hemispherical concrete dome of daring thinness (its thickness decreasing from almost 20 feet at its base to less than 5 feet at the oculus), originally clad externally in gilt-bronze tiles, concrete whose composition varies as you ascend through the structure, incorporating large chunks of stone in the lowest layers, pierced by many voids and threaded by brick relieving arches whose most important work was done while the concrete was still curing. The scale, the geometry and the conception of unbroken interior space are entirely un-Greek. Here the individual no longer measures himself comfortably against the proportions of the building, which are regular, harmonious and completely out of reach.

The interior cladding and decoration of the Pantheon have since been altered and only partially reinstated. In each coffer of the dome a metal rosette would have glittered like a star. So at least it is read by those who see in the curve overhead a model of the expansive Roman idea of a unified imperium like a well-ordered cosmos. Lower down, the walls were revetted in thin plates of costly marbles, an un-Greek technique and the standard treatment for grand public buildings, such as baths and law courts.

A number of prominent Roman building types like the huge public bath complexes were unknown in Greece and unimaginable without arched and vaulted construction in concrete. The largest Greek constructions, still post and lintel, are often impeded or enhanced by forests of interior columns, like the temples at Paestum, or were probably unroofed, like that at Didyma.

It seems likely that the search for cheap methods of construction to meet housing or perhaps storage needs in a rapidly expanding city prompted arched construction in brick (not an especially cheap material), but that once forms of concrete were developed the possibilities of large spans led to the familiar oversized Roman interior, which of course one finds domestically only in imperial palaces and villas. Apparently it was inconceivable for an ordinary person to build a vaulted dining room on a modest scale.

So wealthy but not imperial dwellings in Pompeii, for instance, look more Greek than large public buildings in the capital. And it is true that the classical orders of Greek derivation are never displaced as the highest form of architectural ornament, though Roman elaborations on the Corinthian order take it into new aesthetic territory. But they have become decoration, applied as semi-columns to the outside of the Colosseum and the Arch of Titus. Or just as fictitious, as almost freestanding elements, for which the entablature makes an invigorating detour, as on the arches of Septimius Severus and Constantine. In fact, some of the most beautiful Roman sculpture occurs in friezes and Corinthian capitals on temple elevations, more convincing than pure figural sculpture in Rome.

So in Pompeian interiors the columns and entablatures are a kind of theatre, like the even more diverting architecture painted on walls further inside. It is tempting to say that the Roman sense of architectural form found some of its fullest expression in these fictional buildings glimpsed at the edges of the room and beyond in perspective vistas. A surprising wealth of such decoration survives, above all from Pompeii, where the sequence of styles was first worked out by historians; Second, Third and Fourth styles they are lamely called, and the boundaries blur. The First style, seldom mentioned, consists of marking stucco walls in horizontal bands to look like masonry. In the Second, architectural vistas appear, apparently constructed of a mixture of solid and flimsy elements, with pavilions glimpsed over walls or peeking round corners.

The Third style retreats to simpler overall organization, slender arcades making space for large empty rectangles in which a picture appears to be hung or from which a far-away landscape emerges. In a room rescued

Pompeii, fictional architecture in a wall painting from a living-room in the House of the Vettii, mid-1st century AD.

from the grounds of a Renaissance pleasure pavilion near the Tiber, an astonishing spatial narrative spins itself out on a black ground, a world where rickety towers and equestrian statues emerge and disappear in sidelong diagonal movement.

The Fourth style becomes more explicit about its riddles, presenting figures that are sometimes meant as statues, sometimes as breathing beings in imaginary alcoves. Next to them are landscapes hung like pictures or viewed through openings. These can be among the most diverting instances of architecture (eked out by art) conceived as a fictional world. It is often said that theatre scenery is the inspiration for such

Sabratha, Libya, theatre backdrop, early 3rd century AD, a genre that spawned some of the most adventurous productions of Roman Imperial architecture.

imaginary spaces and you can see why. Like mirrors these painted illusions make us more self-conscious about ourselves as actors and cause the rooms they decorate to become slightly unreal.

In Rome no stage scenery survives except in lurid contemporary description. But in distant parts of the empire we find the extravagant baroque backdrops common on Roman stages from an early period. At Sabratha in Libya the scenery is three storeys high, as in the large Roman theatres, and maybe 10 feet deep, which leaves room for steeply curving arcades and abruptly jutting porticos. It is an architecture unnaturally rich in openings, many of which would have been filled by statues.

Paradoxically, this flat and functionless construction conveys a powerful sense of architecture as movement. Instead of columns all in a line we find them zigzagging in and out like a restless crowd coming forward, then dropping back to safety, linked in pairs but inconsistently.

All we know about theatre scenes in Rome itself is that they incorporated precious materials – four onyx columns in one, colossal marble ones in another. The most extravagant description sounds unlikely: in the Theatrum Scauri scene, 360 columns made room for 3,000 bronze statues in three storeys of marble, glass mosaic and gilt wood. The love of fiction meets the love of rich substances, so instead of pure fakery, expensive stuffs are squandered in creating imaginary effects, doubtless combined with fake ones. One result must have been a devaluing of the classical orders as profound visual material to be handled reverently.

It comes as a shock when something close to stage design appears as a solid building in the street outside. Not as a brothel or gaming club, but a library containing the tomb of the benefactor who gave it to his city – Celsus' library in Ephesus was built in an extremely prominent location. Like a stage set it is divided into plentiful bays and storeys, which rather than matching the internal arrangements simply create a crowd of niches and porticoes holding windows and statues, as if it were a city of small pedimented structures that through zigzag movement have broken free from each other.

This format has the maximum amount of each element of a classical order – at least twice as much entablature and frieze as it would if the columns were set in straight lines – bases and pedestals in excess, almost two complete layers of columns with their lavish capitals, deep carved coffering for 'roofs' on bays thrown out a few feet in front of their fellows, until the observer is confused about where the building ends and the sky begins.

The library at Ephesus shows us the other side to Roman practicality, a fanciful architecture that springs from rational deconstruction of classical formulae, followed by irresponsible recombination as weird as anything by Piranesi.

In fact, the Romans were prolific inventors of architectural fictions, which abstract the most recognizable elements of buildings and give them almost exclusively symbolic functions. The triumphal arch is a piece of wall that has worked itself free, to appear at leisure somewhere else in the city, or an entrance with nothing inside it, so a pure idea of entering upon a new phase. The form begins closely tied to a festive occasion, the

Library of Celsus, Ephesus, built by his son as a memorial to a provincial governor; it included his tomb. First quarter of the 2nd century AD.

procession of a victor, like a play for which it provides a dignified scene. In one proposed story of its origin the arch develops from the decorated city gate, appearing first astride an existing route, then becoming more independent, like a piece of urban sculpture that attracts more admiring notice because it sits apart, impeding nothing when the festive occasion has passed.

The awkward terrain on which Septimius Severus' arch is planted makes it unlikely a public thoroughfare ever passed through it. By the time it appeared, the Forum it decorates was well on the way to becoming the field of monuments we know, a calcification of Roman history that replaced the lively commercial crowds described in Plautus' comedies with a stone population. The triumphal arch was itself a calcification of activity, covered, in the most elaborate later instances (Septimius Severus, Constantine), with reliefs recording military campaigns in stone. Rome's most important contribution to architecture is the inventive development of the arch's spanning capacity, so there is both a justice and an irony in their also contributing to Renaissance courts this apotheosis of the arch as a pictorial form, holding up not a roof but a large inscription.

Septimius Severus' arch is innovative both in its profusion of carved narrative and the scale of its inscription, which fills the entire upper storey. The rumour or theory has sometimes got about that the dedicatee is buried in his arch. Relatively recently this belief has been held regarding the Arch of Titus, which may simply reveal a wish to find a functional excuse for all the masonry, to give the mass some useful work to perform. Titus' arch, like Septimius', contains chambers at the top and a relief of the dead emperor taken to heaven like Ganymede by an eagle.

By Septimius' time Roman sculptural narrative had degenerated from the vigorous clarity of Titus hauling off booty from the Temple in Jerusalem to a comic book with pictures in rows like crowded print on a page. These are full of interesting data for military historians, but battle itself makes very little appearance. In its stead, the commander is shown addressing his troops on three different occasions and problems of supply are enthusiastically confronted. All very Roman in its concentration on the politics and logistics of war.

The true legacy of these monuments and of Roman architecture as a whole lies in their deifying of the secular. Modern tyrants are the eagerest learners, but governments not mainly dictatorial have also seen this particular writing on the wall. Pliny takes the jaded view that triumphal arches are just a means of raising statues above the level of ordinary mortals. He asserts that this is all you need to create secular gods. The crowning elements he refers to are missing from all surviving arches, a gilt-bronze hero driving a quadriga, flanked by members of his family and minor goddesses.

Busts of Roman emperors decorate the fence posts around the Sheldonian Theatre at Oxford and many entrance halls and libraries in country houses. It is more likely to be an idle learned reference than a real genuflection or survival into our day of the old pagan religion that tried to assure continuance by deifying the last ruler, and by worship of the recent past to make an end to the present order unthinkable. The Romans themselves were capable of dealing unceremoniously with the past when it suited them. When Constantine built his arch he cannibalized the monuments of his most eminent predecessors to adorn it. The result is a hodge podge of styles and stories, which incorporates large rectangular panels of Marcus Aurelius, circular carvings of Hadrian and horizontal narratives of Trajan. It has been said that the theft is homage and shows whom he revered. But he replaced their heads with his own in a clumsy rewriting of history. Squashed in between the ample roundels and the cornice below is a crowded little band carrying Constantine's only original contribution to the sculptural programme. It shows crucial moments from his own life, and its dwarf qualities might be thought to tell against it, but evidently not in the eyes of its creator. Luckily for the current dignity of this monument we can no longer distinguish the yellow (*giallo antico*) marble of the columns, or the purple (porphyry) of the backgrounds, an indoor style of richness moved awkwardly outdoors.

Later arches like this one seem verbose, packing in sculptural narrative as if an arch could be a book. Perhaps they were influenced in this by an earlier invention in the field of monumental narrative that has been attributed to one of the greatest Roman architects, Apollodorus of Damascus, who had earlier proved himself a spatial genius in the planning of Trajan's Market.

His invention (if it was his) is the figured column. A single column erected apart from any building, to call attention to something or someone is an old form of commemoration. At a certain point the idea of mounting a figure on these isolated columns appeared. Apollodorus' contribution was to treat the 'unused' surface of the shaft as a site for messages, for in fact a long continuous scroll of images, like a book. Apparently Trajan's Column, first in the genre, existed in the beginning without its long inscription, consisting of 114 distinct scenes containing more than 2,000 figures, which reads from bottom to top and makes no concession to the observer on the ground. The figures do not get larger or the compositions simpler as they get further away. The nearby libraries, of which the column finally formed one volume in the collection, were not part of the original scheme, so viewing the reliefs from an upper storey was not intended from the start. With Trajan's Column the great masters of scale have lost the thread. Scenes that can be absorbing when taken one at a time are cancelled by sloping neighbours jostling them above and below. The frieze constitutes a picture album best studied in books or plaster casts.

The column also makes obscure reference to another feat of Apollodorus' constructive skill in an over-literal way. The Dacian campaign it commemorates was finally won using a pontoon bridge across the Danube, devised by Apollodorus. This bridge was 127 Roman feet long, and Trajan's column is exactly 127 Roman feet high, a far-fetched parallel that would never be duplicated in a successor, of which the column boasts one near at hand, which survives. It is generally thought that Marcus Aurelius' column is inferior; but while carrying on the impractical plan, it has at least learned that Trajan's scenes are too small. So its narrative is less finely detailed, hence more readable.

Columns crowned with statues were still being set up in the Forum as late as AD 608. This followed in the wake and spirit of Diocletian's set of five memorial columns near the Rostra. Diocletian's seem an indiscriminate proliferation, from a late stage of the notorious Roman monument craze, but Smaragdus' later commemoration of the Byzantine usurper Phocas, though composed of recycled elements, worked, if simply getting the subject's name remembered is what you go by. It is too easy to regard all recycling as a sign of failing powers, a cultural moment in which the spark grows dim. It can indicate vastly different states of mind or circumstance, not only failed conviction or scarce resources, physical dearth or forgotten skill, but receptiveness, inventiveness and the memorializing habit. The history of Rome is littered with many miracles of remembering and of forgetting. The former include the outlines of

Temple of Concordia Augusta, Rome, on a coin of AD 36 showing the busy sculptural crown of the building, parts that never survive.

Marble plan of ancient Rome, a few of the 1,000-plus fragments known. These have been pieced together, but their location in the city remains unknown. Early 3rd century AD.

the Theatre of Pompey in current street forms and buildings, and the latter the migration of names until the Forum of Nerva gets called Trajan's, and Trajan's Column is known as Hadrian's in the Middle Ages.

The whole business of matching topographical references in ancient literature or artefacts to surviving remains is a minefield. Apparent aids are often treacherous: Roman coins are always showing buildings, but it is hard to tell wishful projection from careful recording. The famous marble plan made in AD 203–11 is a frustratingly slapdash stone copy of a parchment map showing the monumental centre at a scale of 1:240. It used to be mounted on a temple wall until metal clamps gave way and it ended up on the floor in thousands of pieces. These began to re-emerge in 1562, until there are now more than 1,000 fragments known, of which about fifty have been identified.

This serves as a painful allegory of our attempts to know the past. Astonishing amounts survive but more is lost completely, like the colossal statue of Nero that gave its name to the Colosseum. Rays of the sun

23 Roman feet long issued from the head of this gilded bronze figure, which was moved standing up by 24 elephants.

Already in ancient times the earliest stages of the city's history were shrouded in mystery. In the centre of the Forum lay the Lapis Niger, a pavement of black stone with a cone of black marble like an aniconic deity, accompanied by an unreadable inscription in proto-Italic letters. The inscription is still largely unread and all our learning has achieved only a sceptical mistrust of the ancient interpretation of this spot as the grave of Romulus. Like many other peoples, the ancient Romans carried on old rituals of which they had forgotten the origins. No explanations survive for the weird annual rite of throwing 27 rush dolls into the Tiber from the Sublician Bridge. Such outmoded rituals became the choicest relics of their past, as random Roman fragments become in their turn the oldest remnants of ours.

Some of the most lavish complexes of the ancient city remain half uncovered, like the linked series of grandiose public spaces known as the Imperial Forums. In the 1930s they got mixed up in a piece of Fascist urban planning that exploited and also obscured them. The ceremonial Via Impero ('Street of the Empire') was driven diagonally across them in 1932–3, putting a premature end to excavation of their grandest component, the Forum of Trajan. The name of the modern road was ambiguous,

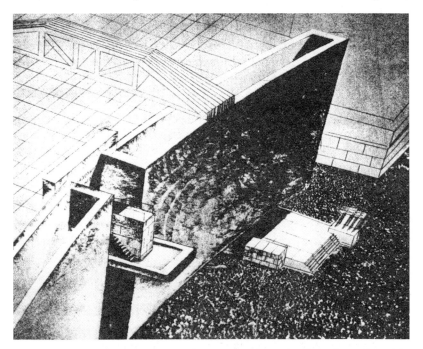

Proposed ornament of Via Impero, Mussolini's Street of the Empire, design for a Palazzo del Littorio by a team led by Giuseppe Terragni, incorporating a huge cape coated in porphyry robbed from ancient buildings to frame a speaker's platform, 1934.

referring to the ancient and the revived imperiums at once. In 1934 an architectural competition was held to add an imperial-scale Party building, the Palazzo del Littorio, opposite the Basilica of Maxentius and in sight of the Colosseum. Among the entries was Terragni's staggering proposal for a vast curved shape coated in porphyry, a traditionally imperial material, which would have been robbed from who knows what ancient sources.

Neither this nor any other proposal was ever built, but the ceremonial conception influences and impedes understanding of the remains. The current excavation must still skirt the wide diagonal of Mussolini's boulevard across the site. Partly in reaction against Fascist grandiosity, current interests favour such non-imperial remains as cobbled ninth-century thoroughfares showing continuous occupation in disregarded times. The taste for fringes, undersides and forgotten episodes is also gratified by discoveries like the four training schools for gladiators east of the Colosseum, which first came to light in 1937. These are not major works of architecture but can be coaxed to yield up ingenuities of plan and mixtures of use. In the project of filling in empty spaces in the map of the ancient city they play a crucial part, turning the largest monument of all, the Colosseum – until Victorian times the world's most extensive structure – into a ramified institution rather than just an isolated geometrical figure.

In similar vein one can find space for the vast banks of warehouses that lined the Tiber. Not only Roman monuments but Roman commerce too assumed a far larger scale than any hitherto known. And then there is Roman housing, which remains in a few sets of island blocks, stretching to five or six storeys and threaded by cavernous lanes whose cramped dimensions had been fixed at times of lower building heights. Perhaps the most curious evidence of the enormous scale of ancient urban existence is an artificial hill, Monte Testaccio, which consists entirely of discarded clay containers, oil and wine jars finished with and collected in one place. Even Roman rubbish assumes heroic dimensions.

The two sides of Roman architecture, the honorific and the practical, sit side by side at Trajan's Forum. One of Fascism's best services to archaeology was the freeing of the large complex to the north of Trajan's Forum known as Trajan's Market, which had long been partly visible, built onto and surrounded by later structures. The ancient development was carried out in a densely settled part of the city where it dug into a steep hillside to create a whole connected mini-district in brick-faced concrete with its own internal streets lined by what are usually taken to be shops. Many of these small units are incorporated in larger groupings, most interestingly on two levels branching out from a vaulted hall. This element has been called the first shopping mall, but other spaces may have served

Trajan's Market, Rome, brick-faced concrete trimmed in travertine, c. AD 110–12. This ceremonial front facing Trajan's Forum conceals the varied scales and everyday functions of the complex.

non-commercial functions, like the large apsed spaces, perhaps lecture halls served by the libraries in Trajan's Forum, according to one historian (Coarelli). Another (Richardson) does not accept the whole idea of public–private mixed-use development. For him the 'Market' is offices not shops, a bureaucratic warren from which the empire was governed.

Whatever combination of functions one imagines, Apollodorus' complex is un-monumental, non-axial in plan and efficient in its use of space. This is architecture in an entirely different key from the adjoining Forum of Trajan, designed at the same time by the same architect. The restorations of the 1930s doubtless influence one's view to some extent. The market buildings have been completed in a style suspiciously like the post offices of the Fascist era, a stripped-down classicism inspired by Roman ruins, De Chirico's paintings of empty squares, and undecorated Modernism in equal measure. So a featureless monumentality of sheer brick surfaces creeps in where it probably does not belong.

Monumentality is indisputably present in the building type that fascinated Palladio above all others. The first large public bath in Rome was built by Agrippa in 25–12 BC. This was followed by a series of imperial bath complexes in the centre of the city, beginning with Nero's near the Pantheon and ending with Constantine's on the Quirinal.

Diocletian's comes near the end of the series and survives most nearly intact. More than any other ruin it puts one in awe of Roman planning, as much when bits of it turn up in far-flung parts of the city like the domed space of San Bernardo, a reused corner pavilion at the outer limit of the whole compound, as when one stands in Michelangelo's reworking of the baths' central hall which saved it by turning it into a church.

Turning a bath into a church, extracting transcendent meanings from the most explicit piece of Roman prose – Michelangelo was by no means the last to find sublimity in these secular institutions. Palladio

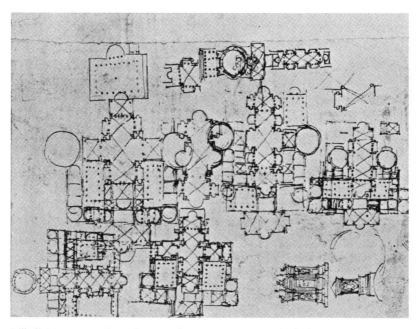

Palladio's reconstructions of c. 1550 of the Baths of Agrippa, extrapolated from slender remains.

became an expert on this class of building, and his drawings are still used as the most telling illustrations of their original state.

It has sometimes been assumed that Palladio's symmetrical layouts are fantasies taking their cue from insignificant remaining fragments and extending them far beyond what any concrete evidence could justify. But in fact more of the fabric survived when he measured the remains, and recent work often confirms the accuracy of his extrapolations. His greatest liberty is to supply complex vaults where what is left provides no clue to the roof, but perhaps crumbling bits of concrete that have since disappeared were his starting points.

For the combination of functions since identified – baths of several different temperatures, with swimming pools, sports fields, gardens and libraries attached, and showy works of art dotted everywhere – seems to have turned the everyday function of cleaning oneself into a riot of the senses. In the Baths of Diocletian the backdrop for the main pool was a great theatrical *scaena* in coloured marble. Thus the clean outlines of today, which inspired Piranesi's tomb-like solemnity, create a misleading picture.

The baths constituted whole worlds in microcosm. Eventually they had their own subterranean supply networks. The tunnels for wheeled vehicles beneath Caracalla's baths allowed resupply of linen and fuel to heat the water without the bathers ever knowing it was happening. A network of service stairs would also have permitted repairs to the fabric, including the roofs, without interruption in the service. And then there were the drains, another system of routes that carried another kind of traffic. Roman waterworks have understandably preoccupied many later students. Piranesi produced whole sets of images that turn obscure chambers in the sewer system into sublime poetry.

Large imperial baths consumed immense resources. Emperors donated forests to supply them with fuel and levied special taxes to maintain them. They staggered on into the sixth century, long after the political collapse of empire, finally falling out of use when the aqueducts were cut in barbarian invasions. Turning Diocletian's Tepidarium and Frigidarium into a church saved them from further pilfering and eventual ruin. 'Pilfering' could, of course, include Michelangelo recutting a shapeless piece of the temple of the Deified Trajan to make a base for the mounted bronze figure of Marcus Aurelius, which survived through the Middle Ages because of an imaginary Christian connection. Trajan's Column served for a time as the *campanile* of a little church built against its base, hiding and thus protecting its inscription, and a long list could be collected of all the pagan temples saved by turning them into Christian churches.

Rome is so special among cities by virtue of the greater involvement of its oldest monuments in what has happened since. Scholars now trace the marbles of the Baths of Caracalla in their flight across the city to

Piranesi's rendering of the dramatic space of a ruined Roman cistern, from *Antichità d' Albano e di Castelgandolfo* (1764).

S. Maria in Trastevere, a reused ancient column on a reused ancient base, probably from the Baths of Caracalla.

become, say, the extremely beautiful arcades of Santa Maria in Trastevere, more beautiful because they do not match their surroundings and are eked out with extra base sections, too richly carved for the purpose and cemented in upside down.

One could tell a clearer history of Roman architecture by editing out all that has happened since, as the archaeologists did when they got their hands on the Colosseum after the unification of Italy and the loosening of the Church's hold. Before this, it had a meaning now lost to us unless we read the accounts of early nineteenth-century travellers, who fall on their knees before the cross and revere the sand underfoot as much as the stones rising on every side.

To these visitors the Colosseum is primarily the scene of martyrdoms in the arena and provokes shudders along with exhilaration at ts size and completeness. This sombre tonality has largely departed, and so has a botanical wonder of the world that coexisted with it. Before being cleansed of them in the interest of scientific study of building form and technique, the Colosseum was the home of 420 different species of plant, some so rare and unexpected in Europe that their seeds have been supposed carried by exotic animals brought to the arena from as far away as Persia. The plants were catalogued by an English botanist in 1855 and swept away a few years later in pursuit of a more monocular vision of history.

The bibliography for individual Roman monuments is wonderfully vast and continually growing. And the conventional bibliography does not include Bruegel on the Colosseum, Hawthorne on antique sculpture,

Pieter Bruegel the elder, *The Tower of Babel* (1563; Vienna, Kunsthistorisches Museum), based in part on the painter's memories of the Colosseum.

A rare survival of a late 19th-century collection of classical casts; Slater Memorial Museum, Norwich, Connecticut.

or the whole subject of plaster casts. Bruegel, one of the most interesting intersections of cosmopolitan and deeply local perspectives there has ever been, turned his memories of the great elliptical mass in Rome (approximately elliptical, more correctly a polycentric ovoid form whose geometrical construction is currently debated) into a compelling vision of the Tower of Babel. His painting is an ambiguous spectacle of beguiling ingenuity riddled by an underlying futility. Much enthusiastic observation is overseen by a pessimism inescapable like the weather.

Perhaps Bruegel's picture is already part of the history of the Protestant response to Rome, most interesting when most ambivalent in texts like *The Marble Faun* and *Middlemarch*. A crucial part of the story is the history of casts after the antique, which cleansed and purified classical civilization for Protestant sensibilities. They made possible the transport of Rome to such far-flung outposts of the empire of Greco-Roman culture as the Slater Memorial Museum in Norwich, Connecticut, where by a miracle of forgetfulness the dense population of dusty presences has survived into a present when almost everyone needs to be told who they are. The decline of casts, attributable just as much to cooling ardour for the antique as to a more stringent notion of authenticity, ranks among the saddest signs of a lost Victorian seriousness.

Now we stand to Rome as they did to Egypt, baffled by the language and fooled by poor imitations in places like Las Vegas. The Roman tolerance of Egyptian religion is different from any fad of ours, though. At least we do not want to think that an emperor dressing as a pharaoh means no more than a Western leader donning token native garb during a state visit. Still, the obelisks that the Romans went to such lengths to import and display had undoubtedly lost their profoundest depths of significance in the course of the journey.

A mathematician turned the first one brought to Rome into the pointer of a giant sundial for Augustus. Bronze labels and markers stretching over a couple of hundred metres were sunk in the pavement, thus giving a practical twist to this embodiment of sacred geometry. Perhaps Roman curiosity about other cultures led no further than a great department store of religions that could find room for whatever foreign cult, however weird, Syrian, Egyptian or Zoroastrian, as London can accommodate Turkish, Albanian and any other ethnic enclave that might be required by the global drift of populations.

Roman religion remains a mystery. On the one hand, the Pantheon, temple to all the gods or none, most rational of constructions, whose internal height equals its diameter and inspired some of the most crazily consistent projects of the Enlightenment, like Boullée's spherical monument to Newton. And on the other, augur-infested superstition that flourished best at the edges of empire, in exciting, irrational and unclassical monuments like the temples at Baalbek, true locii of Eastern darkness that feed their uncertainties back into the capital.

Occasionally, the strongest sense of the Roman effect on the world is gained at the edge, from the astounding regularity of a training fort on the North York Moors or the undeviating straightness of a Roman road in the wilds of Northumberland. But the provinces are in certain ways even more remote today, less securely bound to the centre than when the

Etienne-Louis Boullée, *Monument to Newton* (1784), which literalizes the sphere inscribed in the Roman Pantheon on an even vaster scale.

Temple of Bacchus, Baalbek, Lebanon, 2nd century AD, where Eastern exuberance overpowers the classical system it sets out from.

carver in Bewcastle, Cumbria, sat down to combine, though not as a conscious programme, the late antique decorative forms transmitted by the empire with Celtic monstrosities grown locally.

Of course, the idea of a classic time when everyone could count on secure grasp of a consistent culture is a dream that cannot survive prolonged contact with the reality of an antique world in which various states of unease are normal. Like the ancient Romans we are still tantalized by those myths of completeness that the Pantheon and the baths in their different ways try to fulfil. And we are still puzzled and propelled by dreams of Roman grandeur, like those rumours of buried pieces of a lost obelisk bigger than the others, said to be lurking deep among the foundations somewhere in the centre of Rome, like the great damaged body of the ancient city itself, subsisting more or less intact beneath the present one.

4
Byzantine

It comes as a surprise to find Handel treating Justinian as just another Roman emperor in his opera *Giustino*, because for most of us Byzantium is not simply more of the Rome we already know, moved to another place but culturally continuous with the western branch. No, for us Byzantium is a weird and distant world, of lives hieratic like its art, full of such obscure artifice and ghostly stand-offish figures as we find in Yeats's *Sailing to Byzantium*. Byzantine literature isn't especially familiar; it consists mainly of rumours: something called the *Book of Ceremonies*, turning gorgeous court ritual into verbal prescriptions; or dynastic chronicles by jaded functionaries, denizens of palace corridors full of spleen and thwarted ambition. Comedy and tragedy seem equally remote from this setting, their places taken by different styles of pomp.

But pomp in these hands can be very alluring: Paulus Silentiarius loses himself in the marble meadows of Hagia Sophia and shows us how to convert sensuous texture into spiritual perception. It is done with such prosaic-sounding means as a flood of place-names. In imperial Roman buildings coloured marbles of far-flung provenance (recognized immediately by knowledgeable observers) were advertisements of Roman power. In Silentiarius' description, by contrast, the names bring the whole world into the interior, further signs of the divine plenitude that the building exists to express.

According to Procopius in the *Secret History*, Justinian was a vindictive monster. But in Hagia Sophia, his biggest building project, the emperor successfully spiritualizes materials and themes that further west had always been engines of dynastic boasts. Justinian's dubious claim to spiritual authenticity may in fact be confirmed most powerfully by two culturally destructive acts. He closed the Academy at Athens and put an end to the practice of the old Egyptian religion, which survived deep in the country at Philae.

Hagia Sophia, Istanbul, 532–7, view of roofs from a minaret.

Hagia Sophia, interior: side galleries and quarter dome.

Hagia Sophia's close relation to imperial Roman precedent isn't very evident any more, encrusted as it is with later structures including sultans' tombs and enormous buttresses anticipating earthquakes. Transitional buildings that would clarify the development, like the cathedral at Bosra

Hagia Sophia, innermost of the two narthexes.

in Syria, are all ruined or have vanished completely. Hagia Sophia follows after in a series of efforts to adapt Roman arched, vaulted, domed forms to Christian purposes. Liturgical needs called for a longitudinal format, hence the common conversion of the basilican form of Roman law courts to religious use. But it was hard to give up the exhilarating space and heavenly symbolism of a central dome as realized most grandly in the Pantheon.

Hagia Sophia is a compromise between these two forms whose dome shades off into semi-domes that blur the transition from the central space supported on four thick masonry arches to outer walls of brick, more amply pierced with openings than central plans generally allow. The dome itself is different from Roman domes in its shallow profile and in the dense circle of windows at its base, which make it appear to float. Procopius expressed this apparent detachment by saying that it seemed suspended from heaven by a golden chain.

The intricate side galleries that might detract from the inclusive unity of the space actually reinforce it, by making one aware of the gigantic scale of the whole. The effect is also enhanced by a carefully planned preface of high narrow narthexes placed sideways against the main space so that the contrast of these narrow tubes with the billowing larger vessel makes the sensation on entering overpowering.

The lower reaches of the interior are sheathed in rich and sombre marble sheets, purple, green and maroon, all dusky with time, while upper parts including undulating ceilings are coated in gold mosaic, mostly plain except for large Greek crosses, four huge cherubim in the pendentives and a *Virgin* in the apse. There's presently a debate about whether the lost *Pantocrator* – Christ as Ruler of All – at the apex of the dome survives under the Muslim inscription that presently occupies this spot.

The question of imagery in Hagia Sophia may be something of a distraction, because this interior makes its effect in sweeping gestures, not in elaborate narrative, so the field of gold overhead seems a sufficient rendering of heaven all by itself. Detail appears at the fringes in marble chewed like coral into the capitals of the gallery, in all the coloured marble and in a few figural mosaics that remain on lower walls.

It is true that many rich appliances lovingly described by Silentiarius have disappeared, like the silver altar screen, ambos and pulpits. Their place is taken by lavish Muslim furniture filling much the same functions. These and the four huge metal discs with Koranic texts, forged on the

Sinan, Shahsultan and Zal Mahmud Pasha mosque in Eyüp, Istanbul, 1578–90, an interior derived from Hagia Sophia.

spot and too big to get out through the doors in one piece, are visible signs of the building's vicissitudes. A thousand years as a church, four hundred as a mosque, seventy as a museum. Like the mosque at Córdoba, Hagia Sophia is perhaps the richer for this overlay of incompatible cultures. The Muslim conquest was not a gentle affair, but at this distance the Muslim imprint seems relatively mild, and both creeds though present are equally superseded.

The scale of Hagia Sophia was not equalled or even approached in the nine Byzantine centuries that followed. Architecturally, the inheritors of the big church are the big mosques of the Ottoman capital, many of which adopt the format of a large clear space under a shallow dome. The form of the great Ottoman mosques thus differs from those in any other Muslim country. A tantalizing question remains of whether Hagia Sophia exercised more than formal influence on its successors.

For someone visiting Istanbul / Constantinople in the present, Byzantine remnants, aside from Hagia Sophia, are hidden like needles in a haystack. The large mosque complexes founded by and named after sultans are visible from far off and make themselves felt in the streets around, but the smaller Byzantine churches lurk in poor neighbourhoods far removed from main thoroughfares.

This obscurity has doubtless played a part in saving them, not a thought likely to occur to a first-time visitor, who accepts immurement in shabby surroundings as these buildings' essential mode of being. A few of the more important survivors have been freed from their nearest neighbours, demolished to leave an empty space around the relic.

St Theodore / Vefa Kilise Camii, the archetypal small Byzantine church in Istanbul, bears signs of its conversion to new uses in blocked-up narthex arcades, half filled in with something like sash windows in green frames. Surprisingly fresh bits of carving – grapes on capitals, vines on pilasters – are mixed together with crude replacements for missing parts. Over the central door, a sheet of corrugated plastic on brackets forms a little entrance porch.

This is the building's disguise or veil, concealing wonders within, which include a set of three melon domes immediately behind this façade like a botched ruin in Piranesi. The little domes are, or were, all lined with mosaic, which makes the most varied glitter out of the separate curves in each segment of the melon. A standing figure in every segment looks diminutive yet finely detailed from the ground. As far as you can see them, that is, for they've been crudely painted over with dirty white since the photos in the art history books were taken. One can read the archaeologist's report on early twentieth-century excavations for which permission was abruptly withdrawn. Contentions evidently continue that we haven't completely understood.

Vefa Kilise Camii, one of the small Byzantine churches of Istanbul, sometimes identified as St Theodore. 11th century, narthex c. 1300.

There's a second narthex where time-softened marble trimmings stick out from the fresh plaster that surrounds them. The plan is the venerable Greek cross-in-square type with a dome over the crossing, surprisingly high above, as if at the end of a tube.

The apse of the church is still the focus of the mosque, but with a twist. Mecca isn't due east of here, so the mihrab has to angle itself at 15 degrees to the axis of the church. Everything at the east end except the windows is skewed like that, including, of course, the pattern in the carpet, which suggests the alignment for prayer, because in this creed people continue to pray towards a particular place, not a general direction like east, which in Christian practice stands for sunrise as a type of Christ's resurrection.

These adjustments, to be met over and over again in the Byzantine churches of Istanbul, form one of the most moving instances of cultural overlay. It can be carried out with clumsy directness as here, the Islamic markers all off-centre in a strongly axial space, or with great refinement, as in the marble and gilt fittings in Hagia Sophia, which form part of a harmonious overall effect in which one banished creed is inscribed on another.

The mellow walls I remember in Kilise Camii ('church mosque') from some years ago are stark with new white paint that relents only around the painted decoration in the dome and apse, which may be true

Kalendarhane Camii, Istanbul, example of a 12th-century Byzantine church reoriented as a mosque.

eighteenth-century Rococo or early twentieth-century folkish. These are the moments that make you aware there's something older underneath that the present is blanking out, while allowing highlights to peek through the coating of modernity.

What hands in which to leave such precious relics! you might say, but the scale of the Byzantine survivors is so un-monumental and local that they easily seem features of a neighbourhood, not objects of international concern. And you connect more directly with buildings inhabited and used than with those that have had to become museums.

A few fascinating rooms in the Archaeological Museum proceed church by church across the city to reconstruct as much as possible of the missing richness of appliance and decoration. Most of the churches realized semi-virtually in the museum can still be visited, as empty shells. Now they have two bodies, one of them where they always were, the other here in ideal space, where the most precious scraps – an arbitrary sample left behind because it was buried or overlooked when other bits headed for Venice – are displayed with analytical clarity. Better not to set the two forms of knowing in opposition to each other, however, but to relish the hope of fusing them in the mind and thus coming nearer to the lost original.

Certainly there is no possibility of summoning back a vanished Greek population to fill all these churches with Orthodox practice. The fifteenth-century Greek population fled the Ottoman invader – in what numbers we can only guess – and returned hesitantly thereafter. So taking over churches for mosques in part simply recognized this shift of population. One of the latest chapters in the story is one of the saddest. Unrealistic Greek dreams of retaking Constantinople and the old Greek territory in Asia Minor ended with the military defeat of 1922 and the expulsion of the Greeks from Turkey and the Turks from Greece.

Piecing together the lost churches of Constantinople is trickier and more interesting because, like the remains of ancient Rome, they are found in a living city, not a deserted archaeological site. This distinction isn't perfectly clear-cut when you look closely: functioning bits of the city are liable to turn into archaeological sites on occasion. So in the 1960s the attempted construction of a highway overpass led to the discovery of one of the most interesting Byzantine structures, Anicia Juliana's church of St Polyeuktos, originally planned as a rival to Justinian's projects by a self-willed and learned woman with more distinguished family connections than the emperor. She appears in one of the gorgeous manuscripts she commissioned, surrounded by gold leaf, at the centre of an intricate geometric figure.

Her church is a remarkable example of physical dispersion. Like a jigsaw puzzle scattered around the house, pieces of it turn up treasured but unrecognized outside San Marco in Venice, in Barcelona, or closer to home in the garden of a museum in Istanbul. From verbal descriptions, photos of the other pieces and a glimpse of one fragment at a time, depending on where you are, you can try to conjure up this extraordinary interior, probably richer in low-relief carving than any other Byzantine building.

The other fascination of Anicia's church, besides its curious dispersion and reassembly in the work of scholars, is its way of treating a text

St Polyeuktos, Constantinople, 524–7, fragment (a pier) mounted outside San Marco, Venice, formerly misidentified as deriving from a church in Acre, Syria.

as its main ornament. A lengthy poem is threaded through the building, travelling across cornices and around the curve of arches in spidery, deep-cut letters. Only a small portion of the poem survives in this sensuous and befuddling form, but you can check on the rest because it was included in the *Palatine Anthology* put together by Cephalas in the tenth century. One would like to chart the fit between places in the building and twists in the movement of the verses, but this is beyond anyone today, even if we could plot the poem more or less precisely through the space. As with monumental Koranic inscriptions in medieval mosques, the idea of the building wedded to particular words, even built of them, until it almost *becomes* text itself, that idea is probably more powerful than exactly what is said at most points along the way. In such inscriptions – too mild a word for this interfusion between literature and architecture – the meaning of architecture has finally become explicit and is told to us like a story.

We can read the church's poem in the Loeb translation, hoping to find a key to what the Byzantines wanted from their sacred buildings, but its message is now dim because – in that version at least – the poem does not even attempt the transformation of stones into symbols. It even complains of practical difficulties met and overcome by the patroness during construction, a site diary elevated into admonitory permanence to go on distracting visitors for the entire life of the building.

One of Justinian's churches also boasts a single lengthy inscription that circles the space. The lettering at SS Sergius and Bacchus is dignified but not gorgeous and like all the rich capitals in the church looks (or looked until recent cleaning) as if it has been loaded with coats of white-wash.

This church is probably so lavish because it was a chapel attached to the vanished Hormisdas Palace. An old controversy still continues over whether it or Hagia Sophia is older. It treats the themes of dome and gallery in exquisite miniature form, the dome like a forecast of Islamic melon domes, divided into segments now concave, now convex, the galleries shifting in and out as if in anticipation of the Baroque.

The printed translation of this message that isn't poetry points out that saint-dedicatees of other churches are often inactive hermits. By contrast, the emperor has chosen a hero-saint of deeds – one who lost all his blood serving the faith. It even mentions a container in which this blood was collected or displayed to do its good work. I imagine this an inverted version of the dome overhead, a bowl with frequent creases as it alternates between flat and curved segments.

There is something lovably clumsy about Sergius and Bacchus, not in the plan, which is intricate and recondite, but in the execution, which doesn't get things straight or smooth, an irregularity more noticeable in the plan than the experience.

The greatest irregularity in Byzantine art creates a rupture so violent it amounts to a blank space or pure discontinuity. The destructions of war wield powerful influence on the history of art but take place in some sense

SS Sergius and Bacchus, Istanbul, c. 527–36, view up into melon dome.

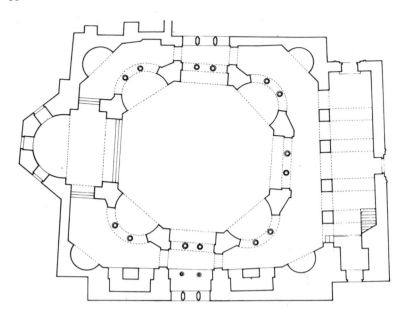

SS Sergius and Bacchus, Istanbul, plan showing an elaborate system of galleries inside a simpler outer shell.

outside it. The destructions of iconoclasm are different, because they are ideological, and therefore exercise a powerful fascination. The iconoclasts elude one, in part, of course, because they leave behind no artefacts through which you could study them. And there is something inherently improbable, almost paradoxical, in an outbreak of Protestantism in the East, source over centuries of the richest, most exotic imagery, which had stunned and diverted the Roman world from its prosaic course.

The richness of early Byzantine art entails, admittedly, a stilling of pagan movement and high spirits in the interest of hieratic solemnity, and maybe it makes a logical progression to move from sleepwalking figures as expressive of spiritual states to the disappearance of bodies altogether.

Not that it happened in this gradual, peaceful way by a kind of inner, uncoerced conversion. The so-called Iconoclastic Controversy became violent, and not only images but also lovers of images were physically defaced. Perhaps these convulsions focused on art tell us something crucial about that art, whose hypnotic and domineering statements put viewers on their mettle and could provoke a violent resistance.

Undoubtedly, though, the iconoclastic surges were not entirely internal to the art they appeared directed at. It seems more than coincidence that they occurred in a place bordered by the strongly aniconic culture of Islam. From Syrian provinces came emperors and soldiers with austere views, who supported the clearing out of images. In a single year, 765, the churches of Constantinople were stripped of their decoration, and all icons that could be found were destroyed along with their owners. At this distance, such horrors simply invest the frozen images with fresh mystery and interest.

Several times in these centuries art provoked a kind of revolution that resulted in almost complete erasure of the record. So early icons survive only on the peripheries of the empire and especially in one of the most inaccessible places of all, the monastery of St Catherine in the Sinai desert. At other moments as well collapse at the centre encourages flowering at the edge, as in the Despotate of Epiros in eastern Greece during the Frankish occupation of Constantinople in the thirteenth century. Thus we account for the surprising concentration of Byzantine architecture in the provincial capital of Arta.

Byzantine art appears from the start as a late and debased style, a backsliding from or sclerotic hardening of Roman realism. So in place of fluent reliefs of Marcus Aurelius in highly regulated ritual appearances, we get the Emperor Theodosius sitting stiffly on the marble base of a granite obelisk in the Hippodrome of the capital. These reliefs don't look at all like someone in particular, and, most improbably, the four sides of the base show four views of the emperor in the royal box. The cast is slightly varied each time, as reliefs concentrate successively on the extended family, the court, lower tiers of the crowd, marshals, dancers. Costumes differ just enough from scene to scene to provide mild diversion to those looking really hard. But everyone faces forward, and expressions

Relief of c. AD 390 on the base of an Egyptian obelisk (late 15th century BC) in the Hippodrome, Istanbul, showing Imperial family and court in hieratic poses.

and gestures are generic, not specific. The individual and the momentary have been devalued, until even in the arena Byzantine faces stare rigidly into eternity.

It is definitely a turning away, and if one thinks of art as a progress, a regression. But a regression from the soulless expertise and crassness of the portraits of emperors with careworn faces on young nude bodies, or what looks like reverently rendered sacrifice and is actually the burning of the tax rolls. The Byzantines have given up fluency in pursuit of an otherworldliness that turns up even in unlikely secular locations. Records of court intrigues and grisly penalties for falling out of favour like blinding, maiming and disfigurement do not persuade one that this culture was spiritual through and through. Still, it undoubtedly aspired in that direction, in its cool and obscure manner and in strange and effete forms like ivory diptychs and micro-mosaic icons. The diptychs are even more baffling than the stadium reliefs in their stolid repetitions, and micromosaics perverse in fineness beyond the powers of human eyes to appreciate without some intervening aid. There's a contradiction in a devotional image that needs a magnifying glass to plumb its depths. But like many other Byzantine images, these pictures make us feel the inadequacy of rational comprehension: they require submission.

There is no reason to expect that complex works have a single purpose, however, or that Byzantine art remained uniformly true to some original aim over ten centuries. It seems far more consistent than most

Pseudo-Kufic inscription under the eaves of Fethiye Camii / Pammakaristos (Joyous Mother of God), Istanbul, after 1315.

12th-century rock-cut church in Cappadocia, from which roof, floor and a whole side wall have fallen away, revealing the fictitious nature of the structure more clearly.

styles, but it throws up its rogues and aberrations, among which may be ranked a form of architectural decoration sometimes called pseudo-Kufic.

This occurs on late Byzantine churches and consists of patterns made of tile inlaid in brick walls that look vaguely like Arabic inscriptions, or a cross between Arabic and Greek that no one can read. These are placed near cornices like real inscriptions, as if for ease of decipherment. Might they represent a collaboration between Arab workmen and Greek designers, or an attempt to produce the tantalizing effect of Koranic inscription on viewers for whom Arabic is a complete mystery? Is it a premonitory inkling of the later absorption of all these territories by the Ottomans? Or just a feckless pulverizing that reduces the exotic to nonsensical trimmings? Pseudo-Kufic may be a hoax, or a powerful form of mystification: even the greatest Byzantine works provoke disturbing ambivalence – will we be transported into another realm, or left cold by lifeless stiffness?

This ambivalence lies at the heart of Byzantine culture. Contradictory voices tell us that the only valid image of Christ is the consecrated bread and wine of the Eucharist, or that by denying images we risk not recognizing Him on the Day of Judgement. The Empty Throne has come to stand for the fate of Byzantine art. There is a close connection, even a symbiotic relation, between over-rich Byzantine poetry that loads the altar with the congested symbolism of throne, tomb and table all at once, and the attack on all attempts to represent the sacred. By horribly apt ironies one must now look for early Byzantine mosaics in Damascus and

Jerusalem. Work of this period survived iconoclasm only in mosques decorated by Byzantine workers. Fresco cycles almost entirely missing from Constantinople survive in the humble cave churches of Cappadocia, where pious hermits hid, to be visited by pilgrims who left behind rumours of the capital in visual narratives filling the walls of these hollowed-out spaces, caves made to look like architecture, with 'columns' and 'vaults' discovered in the soft rock, not constructed in the usual way.

Byzantine civilization gives disturbing glimpses of a culture devouring itself by doing away with its own most elaborate products. In the years after the second bout of iconoclasm, introduced like the first by another usurper-emperor, all the writings of the iconoclasts were destroyed, until they exist now only in fragments quoted by their opponents in order to refute them. The self-swallowing tendencies in iconoclasm are matched in a curious way by the crippling restrictions that even the richest Byzantine art imposes on itself. Such strong repressions come close to a way of internalizing iconoclasm within the image.

5
Romanesque

The word 'Romanesque' stresses continuity with classical antiquity, but the most compelling feature of early medieval art is the intrusion of barbaric energies surging in from the north and east. In Irish, Anglo-Saxon and Viking objects the beast-life met in much earlier human products like Sumerian cylinder seals comes rushing back along with tangles of vegetation that form themselves up into interlaced pattern that has forgotten specific natural origins.

The hunt for the ultimate sources of these motifs has taken interesting paths. By the time we meet them as architects, the Northern tribes are Christianized, and most art on larger scales than objects of personal adornment comes from monastic contexts. Monasticism was a cultural form that began in Egypt and arrived in Ireland and then in northern England carrying much mental baggage determined by the peculiar geography and history of a certain bit of the Mediterranean. Coptic sources have even been adduced for that most Northern motif, writhing serpent-life converted to tightly laced pattern.

The carpet page of the Lichfield Gospels (so called because this eighth-century Northern manuscript ended up in the cathedral founded at Lichfield by a Northumbrian missionary) hides a cross in a nightmarish sea of growth, a company of animals who fill up the entire rectangle except for the barely perceptible zigzags of the cross threading its way through the crowd. The animals' tails and legs turn or degenerate into something close to pure line. The entire maze is living tissue and the overall effect like a riddle challenging you to pick out the overriding truth, and to overlook the distraction of serpentine limbs, instead of tracing them till they run out like persistent errors.

In the moralized interpretation, the animals represent evil forces, over which the cross triumphs. But the cross is swallowed up and the twisting animals nip at the heels of the letters on the page opposite, threatening the composure of the text. Animistic pagan motifs seem far from subdued.

The Franks Casket, whalebone carved with phantasmagoric combination of biblical narrative, Roman history and Teutonic myth, first half of the 8th century.

A small casket from roughly the same time and place illustrates a turmoil of cultural forces in a more explicitly disjointed form. The Franks Casket is carved all over with lively scenes in flat relief that stand out like writing against a dark ground. In fact, the scenes are surrounded by writing, mostly tall runes with a little Latin mixed in. The scenes show the Magi adoring the Christ Child next to grisly sacrifices from Northern myth, the Emperor Titus storming Jerusalem, armed warriors attacking Egil in a fort, Romulus and Remus suckled by a wolf in the forest (where the runes form a lush extension of the trees like the fringe on a carpet) and another bit of Germanic myth (this piece now in Florence) with seers and a talking beast.

The casket was not a sacred object to start with, though it may have ended up at the shrine of St Julien at Brioude in the Auvergne, the region where it was discovered in the nineteenth century being used as a workbasket. The inscription on the front says nothing uplifting about Christ's ability to subsume all these pagan stories. Instead, it's a weird kind of poetry, a riddle asking us to guess the material of the box we're looking at. The verse tells of the beaching of a whale (called 'the king of terror'), informing us obliquely that the box is made of whalebone, a substance instinct with life.

All the stories filling the sides of the container constitute a continuous phantasmagoria of personages in movement, undergoing tests, arriving at destinations, finding out secrets, repelling threats, losing everything. The apparent disorder of the material is actually a molten, unsettled state before meanings become fixed, when history, legend and divine revelation can still inhabit the same space.

Most of the surviving signs of monumental ambitions in Anglo-Saxon culture aren't strictly architectural but consist of incomplete stone crosses that stood in place of a building or marked an important grave. Fragments of hundreds of these, some as much as 17 feet tall, are scattered across northern England. Inscribed monoliths are not unique to Britain and Ireland, but this Christianized transformation into the free-standing cross is a peculiar insular development.

Although the crosses could function as memorials – the inscription on the cross at Bewcastle in Cumberland points that way – they belong to a different genre from those Roman commemorative columns in urban locations, seen always in the wider architectural context, a singled-out element of the enveloping built fabric. Pre-Conquest crosses in Britain often inhabited lonely spots, not centres of civilization. That must have been in some sense the point – they were beacons in dark places, not crowning ornamental touches in the capital. Early medieval imitations of the antique, like the bishop of Hildesheim's bronze reduction of Trajan's Column, were as likely to be set up indoors.

Still, the evolution of the crosses is not a straightforward progress. The earliest examples are among the least wild, with figural scenes of disconcertingly classical composure. But these too represent untamed survivors in remote spots, standing out against hard weather. Much detail on the early eighth-century cross at Ruthwell in Dumfriesshire has been washed away, but much remains. The scenes are vague and shadowy, but the inscriptions, though incomplete, are not fuzzy. On front and back, borders are filled with beautifully calm Roman letters forming texts that jump unexpectedly from one row to another. This inconsistency is nothing to what you meet on the narrower sides, where birds and small animals perch in vine scrolls.

Here the edges are inscribed with runes squeezed into a long upright string of space, but written across it, so there isn't often room for a whole word on a line. Besides, the text circles the shaft in four sections, against the direction of the lines. So much for the riddling layout; the text turns out to be a poem in the Northumbrian dialect known to modern readers as The Dream of the Rood, a fantastic work spoken by the cross that was forced to bear the crucified Christ. When the Ruthwell cross speaks, it says something a cross might say and utters the stone's long-harboured lament.

Like the box calling attention to the whale that provided its substance, the cross asserting that stones have feelings too might be taken as an over-wrought conceit, but once again the idea has been buried so thoroughly in its riddle-form that it seems to operate in secret. From the beginning art is to be unravelled or deciphered, its earliest form already knotted.

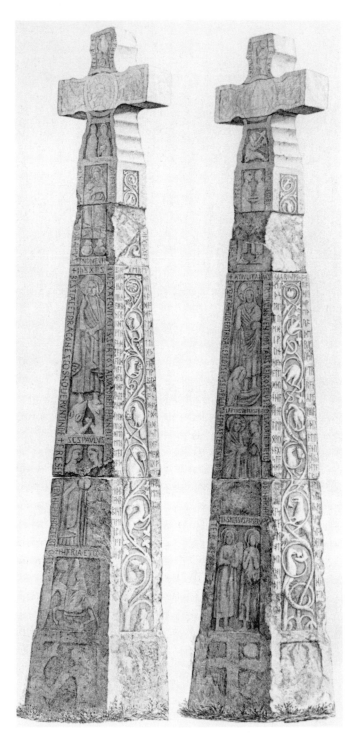

Ruthwell Cross, early 8th century, an engraving of 1866–7 that shows the combination of scenes, vegetal scrolls and inscriptions in Roman and runic more clearly than modern photographs.

St John, Escomb, Co. Durham, *c.* 670, one of a small number of completely preserved Anglo-Saxon churches of typically high and narrow proportions.

Saxon cathedrals, where we might expect to find the most elaborate meanings, have all disappeared, replaced by ambitious Norman successors. The modest Saxon churches that survive intact usually achieve the feat by getting themselves completely forgotten, like St John in Escomb, or St Laurence in Bradford-on-Avon. Escomb, which may pre-date the crosses and the casket by a decade or two, is a simple additive structure whose boxlike elements are made of reused Roman stones.

Anglo-Saxon proportions are easily recognizable: the vessels are like tall, narrow coffers with steep gable roofs. Small round-headed windows look down from high in the walls. Openings between the parts are even more tall and narrow than the spaces, so that you feel squeezed as you pass or look through. Thus the chancel at Escomb isn't fully visible from the nave, and the nave would have been occluded from the porch.

External decoration of Saxon stone buildings consists of illogical patterns in the masonry, stones laid in herringbone courses as if the building is woven out of reeds or imitates a wall-hanging. Elements that were originally structural are now treated decoratively, so post and lintel forms, or arcades with stilted peaks instead of arches, are stuck onto the fabric as surface ornament rather than systems of support. Wall arcades were used decoratively in late Roman architecture, of course, but in Saxon building we lack the straight form in wood that preceded the fiction in stone.

In Norway early wooden churches survive in small numbers from the twelfth century, the century after conversion to Christianity by English missionaries. The first generation of buildings, whose posts were planted directly in the ground, hasn't survived, but the simple device of standing the timbers on stone plates solved the problem of rotting posts in churches built after about 1130. Although there's an uncanny resemblance between the tall narrow interiors of these stave churches and the standard Anglo-Saxon spaces, the narrow height is arrived at differently. In these wooden buildings a ring of posts, tied together by braces and detached from the walls, creates something like a nave and aisles.

These 'aisles' are extremely narrow and contain the only seating along their outer edge. According to one theory, this rough approximation to basilican form is a conscious reference to Old St Peter's in Rome – though if an echo, a muffled one. The posts are far more slender than classical columns, but turn up with cushion capitals copied from contemporary stone buildings, as well as more archaic grimacing heads. The combination in a single structure of classical intimations and strong survivals of old vernacular forms reminds us of the mixed identities of heroes in the Norse sagas, who divide their year between farming or trade and Viking raids. Surviving remnants from the oldest Norse churches consist of richly carved decorative elements – doorframes and window grilles teeming with beast life, saved and reused on structurally more sophisticated successors. The most savage and exciting elements, far from daylight consciousness, are brought along from an earlier phase and lie stranded in another historical time, like the pre-Christian heroes that people still want to hear about but wouldn't be at home with in the present.

The true Romanesque is marked by more coherent and hence imposing plans, and by greater clarity of structure combined with intense physicality of stonework and integrated sculptural ornament that maintains the vigorous beast-life found in early manuscript illumination. Somewhat unhistorically, we read Romanesque backwards from Gothic and see the masonry, perhaps appearing as a great feat of intellectual clarification to its contemporaries, as above all massive and unpenetrated, creating dark if numinous interiors where one feels one's way by other senses than the eyes. Always the light-filled vessels of Gothic lurk nearby as the standard of comparison.

Very large Romanesque buildings like St Philibert in Tournus and Durham Cathedral may feel high enough when you're inside them, but their silhouettes are long and low, by contrast with the more spindly outline preferred by Gothic. At Durham the main vertical accent, the central tower, has been heightened in successive stages with a finally un-Romanesque result, awkward under close inspection – the highest storey sits on an earlier set of battlements, now superfluous.

At Tournus strong sub-units are combined but not exactly integrated, if judged by the demanding later standards of Gothic. The result is two-ended, on the German, imperial model. The westwork looks like a fortified introduction to the whole. A Hungarian invasion had set fire to the previous church and the rebuilding reflected the determination to withstand such threats just as they became less likely. St Philibert's remains had arrived in 875, rescued from Viking raiders by monks who had travelled many circuitous miles seeking a safer home. These relics pushed out the earlier martyr-dedicatee Valerian, though the presence of two foci at east and west ends could have accommodated both saints' shrines – the ambulatory leading pilgrims past Philibert's axial chapel in the east, the second space for Valerian above the west narthex accessible by double stairs from the aisles.

A narthex under the west chapel harks back to an early Christian or Eastern form, also met at Durham, where the explanation may be more mundane: ground at the east was less suitable for building on. The function of this so-called Galilee at Durham is uncertain, though eventually it held the relics of Bede, matching those of his mentor Cuthbert at the other end of the church. Durham also wears an aspect of fortification and formed part of a citadel, along with the Norman castle that came to serve as the bishop's palace.

So Durham like Tournus looks fortified and for a similar reason. Like the monks of Noirmoutier who settled at Tournus, those of Lindisfarne had fled Danish raiders with Cuthbert's relics and spent a hundred years wandering round northern England before they reached safe haven at Durham, where these relics prompted the Norman rebuilding of an Anglo-Saxon cathedral, the last in a series of Norman churches of cathedral scale that included Winchester, Westminster and Ely.

At Tournus the most interesting stages are the latest ones, the eleventh-century narthex and the twelfth-century rebuilding of the nave. At Durham the narthex is lighter and of lighter construction than the rest of the church, an almost non-directional field of columns without axial emphasis, like a liberation from the earlier preference for strongly axial naves, while at Tournus the narthex provides a low, crypt-like introduction to the high nave, with heavy groin vaults springing from squat columns. There are four of these, making a quincunx, like the cross-in-square familiar in mid- and late Byzantine churches. After the enveloping stonework of the narthex, coming into the nave at Tournus is like being set free. A single simple series stretches ahead, of massive circular columns in small masonry, pink like brick. They are extremely tall, without capitals, and connected to each other by tall round arches springing abruptly from the flat disks of the column-tops. Demi-columns attached to the walls support further larger arches at right angles to the arcade, which cross the nave and make a series of membranes that sketch a continuous but hypothetical barrel vault.

For the mysterious truth is that instead of the single tunnel that this nave seems to call for, the space is closed by a set of five barrel vaults running at right angles to the nave between these membranes,

St Philibert, Tournus, early 11th century, nave with its distortions of classical arcades and system of five cross-vaults.

or diaphragm arches. This complex system makes it possible to have larger clerestory windows, but creates the impression that the space is composed of five separate containers. This novel solution to the problem of vaulting high spaces was picked up by only one later Romanesque building, St Vincent in Mont-Saint-Vincent nearby. So Tournus is neither typical nor a pointer to the future, but remains a distinctive fulfilment of certain Romanesque ideals – to express the solidity and consistency of a clear structural idea without distracting adornment.

St Philibert is not as consistent as it first seems, however, and may once have been less bare than it is now, when it looks as if it has been restored by a Corbusian Modernist. Recently, rich painted decoration of Romanesque date has been uncovered on the undersides of arches, and an elaborate mosaic of the Seasons and the Zodiac has been revealed in the ambulatory. So it appears that unadorned stone was not left to speak for itself.

But Durham Cathedral, one of the most complete and consistent large Romanesque churches, does fulfil the Romanesque ideal of the interior as a practically monochrome and unadorned world of stone. Part of the explanation is that Durham was stripped of many furnishings in 1539 at the Dissolution. But more importantly, kinds of richness that amount to adornment are thoroughly integrated in the fabric. First of all comes the system of alternating columns and composite piers in the nave arcade, almost equally massive but different in their visual effect. The columns are single and self-contained, the piers multiple and tied into the whole three-storey elevation. So the rhythm of the forward progression of the eye down the nave is varied and lingering. The difference is reflected in the vaults where bays are joined in pairs and emphasized by some of the earliest rib vaults in Western architecture.

Rib vaults were nothing new in Islamic architecture and are seen, for example, in the lavish cubicle in front of the mihrab at Córdoba, which is accorded the status of a separate room. But Islamic designers focus on the geometric rather than the structural possibilities of rib vaults, so ribs constitute teasing patterns in spaces of no special technical ambition.

At Durham some of the advantages of rib as against groin vaults begin to be explored. At first these seem mainly aesthetic gains – the knitting of the ceiling overhead into the wall fabric, so that the whole structure embodies a single process of thought, the ribs continuous with the overall system of support, as indicated by strings of stone traced from floor to ceiling. Ribs depart from and return to attached columns, demonstrating the interconnectedness of the embracing web of structural members.

At Durham this structure like a web of lines is not being used to lighten the fabric, far from it. Ribs here are a form of emphasis or insistence enhanced by toothed mouldings on either side of the central member, to create what is essentially a kind of decoration. The designer has found that pointing the transverse arches gives him more flexibility in vault sizes and shapes, but so far these possibilities lie mainly dormant.

When viewed in section, the roofing of the nave galleries looks like a first heavy intimation of flying buttresses, as if the master mason at Durham stands on the verge of discovering the whole skeletal format of later Gothic. But it has lately been established that these lateral arches weren't intended to take off any of the weight of the vault from the walls, for they are not bonded to them and sometimes stand clear of them.

So Durham turns out to be accidental proto-Gothic. Still, even within the bounds of Romanesque solidity it reaches towards greater unity of parts and finds novel ways to lighten its aggressively massive effects; the heroic plinths on which the composite piers sit are boldly undercut as if to assure us of the designer's competence and also of the uncompelled expressiveness of the masses of stone. Even more startling is the scoring of the huge columns in patterns matching across the nave but varied along it, and readable from great distances. The scorings are themselves huge and not delicate, but achieve a remarkable lightening of the single-ness of the columns. Nonetheless, even in the most decorative moments at Durham we aren't far from austerity: patterns had been painted on columns before, but this more sculptural method that plays with chang-ing depths of shadow keeps to the sober colours of stone.

The choir vault at Durham, perhaps the first of all high rib vaults, was thought to be unsound in the thirteenth century and replaced, leav-ing traces of the original profile. Otherwise, leaving aside early Gothic embellishment of the east end, the complete set of Romanesque rib vaults survives. As any visitor knows, it is more usual to find such buildings improved and altered over the centuries with additions in different styles, re-roofed because towers fell into naves, or reclothed to bring them up to date and fit to hold prestigious tombs.

So at Tewkesbury, an important abbey in south-west England, an incongruous late Gothic vault is plonked on top of the Romanesque nave, whose giant order may derive from descriptions in Vitruvius, an author found in many monastic libraries. The evolution of complex ribbed vaults was extremely rapid in fourteenth-century England, and innovations in three-dimensional geometry at Tewkesbury upstage the poor old Roman-esque interior, though the Romanesque central tower and a western arched façade that recalls German imperial sources hold their own.

At Gloucester, not far away, the Romanesque fabric was subjected to even more ingenious disfigurement. As at Tewkesbury the Romanesque nave received a new vault, while in the eastern parts instead of an expen-sive rebuilding from scratch, the monks and the mason decided on a kind of camouflage. An internal skin or membrane of stone was inserted in front of the solid Romanesque walls, sometimes panelled like blind trac-ery, sometimes an open stone filigree through which the old masonry could be glimpsed, the width of a narrow passage away. The Romanesque shell remains, and a complete Perpendicular interior sits inside, barely touching it.

At roughly the same time that a rational approach to structure and integrated decoration was developed at Durham, in French towns along the pilgrimage roads to Spain a great flowering of visionary sculpture occurred, giving expression to primitive conceptions of Christian belief. The grandest depictions in these programmes get focused onto the space above the principal entrance, a vestigally architectural entity, the

Durham Cathedral, nave with early rib vaults. Built 1093–1133, the vaults at the end of this period.

half-circle between an arch overhead and rectangular wooden doors beneath.

Through exigencies of situation one of the most powerful of these tympana gets shunted to a side door and sheltered under a projecting porch on the monastery church at Moissac in Quercy. The subject of the tympanum is the apparition of Christ sitting in judgement at the end of the world, as reported by St John in the Book of Revelation, but harking back to Ezekiel's vision of the four beasts covered in eyes and turning every which way, as well. Christ at the centre is large and still, framed by beasts in violent turning movement, who are further framed by stiff and preternaturally slender angels.

Next in the radiating hierarchy comes a set of 24 tiny kings or elders seated in neat rows but all craning eagerly to get a sight of the core of the vision. They are comically various in the shapes of their crowns and the styles of their beards, and they all brandish cups and viols that give 48 more opportunities for depicting movement.

Moissac, detail of tympanum showing the Last Judgment with Christ surrounded by the Four Beasts of the Evangelists, two angels and 24 elders, c. 1115–30.

The unutterable strangeness of the vision has plausibly been explicated by comparing it to the court of an oriental potentate, filtered via Moorish provinces in Spain. Huge rosettes decorating the lintel are borrowed from Spanish textiles, and the trumeau or pillar between the doors has sprung into Assyrian life as a tower of lions and lionesses standing on each other's heads. Thus do we explain to ourselves the un-Christian weirdness of the most powerful of all Romanesque sculpture.

Moissac, central
doorpost, interlaced
lion and lioness
standing on each
other's back.

The portal at Moissac, an inward-turning, not an expansive feature, is a more concentrated version of the sprawling façades one finds at the same time further north, that much further from Spain, in Poitou. Some students of early medieval sculpture have detected a progression away from disorderly effusion towards realism and greater technical mastery in Gothic. From this perspective the brocaded façade of Notre-Dame-la-Grande in Poitiers stands at a lower stage of development than its more focused contemporaries like Moissac.

Notre-Dame-la-Grande, Poitiers, facade whose arcades are framed by overscaled derivatives of classical orders and whose surface is carved with a rich jumble of scenes in relief, second quarter of the 12th century.

At Poitiers the entire façade is covered in carving of different depths and scales. At first it seems to be controlled by an architectural system, but when you look more closely it turns out to be just a picture of architecture, based on an 'arcade' partly closed, partly open, of arches partly round and partly pointed. The arch over the central door recedes in diminished echoes of itself, a weakening of the architectural idea in the interest of richness, which is pursued less wholeheartedly by the side arches. A giant order springs up at the sides and frames the whole composition without engaging the roof. Two heavily pierced turrets grow into the main body at the ends.

Narrative reliefs are dotted across the space over the arches like stone patchwork or collage. Even parts of the same scene are allowed to lead separate existences and seem to bump accidentally against the stones that complete them. Logical oddities abound in how the material is laid out, rising from small to large as it mounts the façade. Even the illogicalities play their part, though, in the overall impression of something natural like coral, a living coruscation that suggests now vegetable exuberance, now a bodily orifice, all scarred or flawed by the gaps produced by an enthusiasm that never dreams of keeping everything in focus at once.

This façade at Poitiers has many neighbours attempting something similar, which shouldn't be judged by the standards of later, more sober Gothic. If one sympathizes with the goal of imparting life to a fabric of stone, animating dead matter with an exuberance like the generative force of Nature itself, then nothing in later, grander Gothic surpasses this.

There is a descendant of Moissac, perhaps not a literal descendant, the chronology remaining uncertain, but a sculptural programme that goes further into violence and worship of the grotesque, so far that it might justify some of the strictures that St Bernard aimed at Romanesque excesses. At Souillac the trumeau becomes a writing mass of beaked and clawed creatures that attack pitifully small human figures. It's like a manuscript border brought horribly to life.

Souillac, doorframe
with Isaiah, c. 1130.
Romanesque expres-
sionism.

Laon Cathedral, facade, early Gothic clarity, begun 1190–95.

Just round its left-hand edge lies a strange depiction of the most troubling incident in the Old Testament. An angel flying directly downwards jams the goat for the sacrifice into Abraham's head. He is about to plunge the knife into Isaac, whose neck he has twisted back. They are all stretched and squeezed by their peculiar situation as parts of a narrow pillar, a transparently contrived excuse for such levels of bodily distortion and psychic stress.

Perhaps the most perverse touch is the inclusion of little colonnettes at the corners of the pillar of creatures, architectural members that might cage them into some kind of order but are instead bent out of shape by their kicks and shoves until these uprights become more zigzags than verticals. It's the final overthrow of architecture and hence of reason.

The sculptures at Souillac may never have taken up their intended roles and locations because of delays in construction of the façade they were meant to be part of. The famous dancing Isaiah on the door jamb, a compelling depiction of prophetic ecstasy, now faces away from the trumeau, part of a portal installed indoors and tamed into a conserved object, as if it were too wild to live with in its natural state.

It can be a relief after the ungovernable energy of the Romanesque to come to the lucidity of Gothic. If one moves forward sixty years to the façade of Laon Cathedral, one enters a world more clear and open. The upper stages of the towers break out into airy pavilions, the last set of them watched over by 24 peaceful stone oxen, perhaps commemorating the animals that hauled the heavy stones uphill. It's as if the old beast life has finally been domesticated and good government has come at last to the Romanesque battlefield.

6
Gothic

Where Gothic began is no mystery. It happened over a short period in a fairly small area in northern France. The process becomes mysterious only if you notice that each of the main components of the style had been around for a while without producing anything much like a Gothic outcome.

Definitions of Gothic put the emphasis in different places. Focillon, the great French art historian, believes in the rib as the generator, which demands the string-like respond, which in its turn seems to dematerialize the system of support and pushes one towards thinner fabric and finally to 'walls' of glass. Ruskin, the Victorian genius who was also a skilled draughtsman, derives most of the story from the tracery and a shift towards viewing the opening rather than the frame as the essential element. The argument between those structural rationalists like Viollet-le-Duc – architect, theorist and violent restorer of medieval buildings – who see cathedrals as machines, and symbol hunters like Lethaby, who arrives via the English Arts and Crafts movement and views all the parts as components of a visionary experience, has been going on a long time. The visionaries seize on the fact that ribs have occasionally fallen out leaving the web intact and holding firm to argue that ribs are mainly pictorial, not functional, giving an idealized diagram of the forces at work in a masonry vault.

The structural rationalists had already pulled off one of the most unlikely coups of interpretation imaginable. To take the great vessels of faith, among the most costly and functionally useless works of humankind and turn them into precursors of nineteenth-century feats of engineering, the great skeletal sheds of railway stations or assembly plants, is a very daring transvaluation of values.

Medieval men, of course, do not talk about structural function. Neither do they acknowledge that Gothic is, as it appears to us, something radically new. Abbot Suger, nearest to a single progenitor of the mode that we can find, seems bewitched by rich materials, not spatial configurations,

Viollet-le-Duc, a design
for a vaulted hall in
iron and masonry by
the leading interpreter
of Gothic as structural
rationalism.

DOUZIÈME ENTRETIEN   (fig. 18)

18

E. OULLHOMME.   MDCCCLXIV.

SALLE VOUTÉE
FER ET MAÇONNERIE.

perhaps because they are easier to point to and everyone can grasp them
and some will object to them.

But to an observer from later centuries the crucial elements are a
striving towards height and lightness in the structure and much greater
amounts of light as well, reaching all of the interior not only via aisle windows but also through large openings high in the main vessel. These
clerestory windows not only provide this extra light; they make you look
up. As time goes on, a disconcerting amount of our attention will become
focused on the vault, but this is a second stage of the story.

Pointed arches are known in everyday usage as Gothic arches and
are by now invested with a heavy cargo of ideological significance. It is
true that they allow one to vary the dimensions of the bay more flexibly
than half-circles do. That leads on to taller proportions and tighter, more

W. R. Lethaby and others, a proposal for an Anglican cathedral, Liverpool, by a leading interpreter of Gothic as visionary symbolism.

compelling rhythms in the piers. So this simple device produces extreme spatial experiences, like the sensation of being pulled rapidly down a vista to an explosion of coloured light at the other end.

Most people carry around such a generalized notion of the standard Gothic interior, which confirms among other things the power of this particular architectural system. No more than any other historical phase, however, is Gothic a unitary phenomenon. The forms we think of as typical were not inevitable, and it is instructive to see how they got that way. Even in logical France, the great instances do not always fit obediently into the story historians want buildings to tell.

It is usual to start the story of Gothic with Suger's rebuilding of the choir of St Denis in the years 1140–44. Part of its prominence arises from Suger's lively account of the enterprise in his *Liber de rebus in administratione sua gestis*, which is remarkable for not noticing that it is dealing with a great watershed in the history of styles. Among the innovations at St Denis was the clothing of the radiating chapels of the apse in an undulating wall of glass.

Suger's choir has been half erased by later revision, so we depend on verbal descriptions and mutilated physical fragments to reconstruct it. An intriguing feature of really detailed histories of Gothic is the occasional appearance of vanished, hence phantom, buildings in the sequence, crucial monuments that have been destroyed like St Nicaise at Reims, St Lucien in Beauvais and the old cathedrals at Arras and Cambrai.

The new attitudes are crystallized with great clarity in a complete rebuilding at Laon, 80 miles north-east of St Denis. The façade at Laon comes later than the interior, and one of the best current writers on Gothic, Christopher Wilson, notes a 'general tendency in Gothic architecture to think of the exterior as a by-product of the interior'. But in spite of later nineteenth-century tampering, Laon's west front remains one of the high moments of medieval building, with its airy towers and large-boned details, its way of keeping the richness under control by wide spacing between the parts and readable plainness in the forms. The towers, which appear to be made of smaller, more fictional buildings set at angles to the wall plane, are inhabited not by the kings who will turn up in later examples but by horned beasts, 24 of them, which some books will tell you memorialize oxen who helped drag stone up the hill. This explanation is too topical for others, who see the animals as part of a generalized diagram of all life. But this story of the oxen fits with the forthrightness that runs through the building, especially in the large scale of details high up on the façade, but also in the clear monochrome consistency of the interior.

At Amiens traces of bright colour, more than traces, have been recovered recently on the portals and prompted a reconstruction (in the form of a light show projected onto the façade after dark) of the whole

Laon Cathedral, two of the 24 oxen that look out from the upper stages of the towers.

Gaudíesque scheme for supplying pulsing life to the enormous crowd of beings who decorate the façade. At Laon no sprawling programme, but three narrow porches contained in barrel vaults. The passages pierced between them were closed up in the nineteenth century to shore up the façade, perhaps at the same moment that restorers were commemorating themselves with craning gargoyle-busts on these very piers. Laon represents a great leap forward but only the first of many, dwarfed by those that followed close on its heels, starting with Chartres, where the nave was begun just as Laon's façade was finished.

At Chartres there is a marked increase in scale made more forceful by simplifying the internal elevation. The structural system is refined by eliminating the gallery, turning it into a skeleton of itself, the lower stage of a two-tier system of flying buttresses that are no longer heavy vanes of stone as at Laon, where they formed almost solid partitions. At Chartres they have become spidery frameworks pierced by little arcades, forecasting the next development at Reims and Amiens in which the buttress starts to resemble a fragile tracery, allowing the walls to do the same and matching them in the other dimension until every solid element partakes of the single striving after height and lightness.

For completeness perhaps we ought to mention important towns of the early thirteenth century that didn't get their cathedrals. It turns out that a crucial ingredient in almost every successful case is a Suger-figure, a powerful and effective bishop who for his own purposes wants a large new cathedral. Sometimes, as at Reims, the coronation church, he can depend on royal patronage. Elsewhere, as at Chartres, he has already made his seat a centre of learning and can raise money on the back of this earlier achievement. Moving stories are told about how the whole community pitches into the task, dragging heavy loads, donating skills, following the century-long saga with baited breath.

There are also the stories of construction halted by popular riots or insurrection, as at Reims, where the grievance was a heavy tax levied to fund the construction. It has been shown that column-figures for the portals at Reims were sometimes carved long before they could be set in place and held over during delays caused by social unrest, so that groupings were revised, and we wound up with the 'wrong' smiling angel in the famous Annunciation group.

While the nave and chancel walls are being dematerialized to admit light filtered through coloured glass, façades and portals are disappearing under sculptural multitudes that far outdo Romanesque schemes in complexity and extent. The west front at Reims is said to contain more than 500 figures in rows of single personages just under life-size near the ground, mounted diagonally to the visitor because they follow the huge flanges of three exaggerated portals, some in the form of demi-figures, or

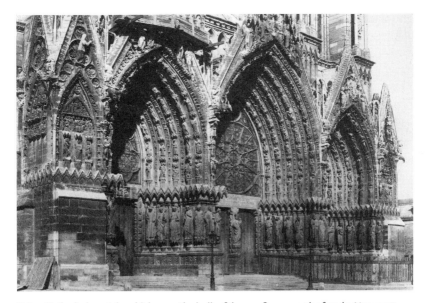

Reims Cathedral, portals, which carry the bulk of the 500 figures on the facade. New west façade from 1255, sculptures post-1261.

Reims Cathedral, central portal of inner facade with walls completely carved with tiers of freestanding figures in niches.

compact scenes, or sets of rulers on little thrones which fit into the hollow of a moulding like left-over traces of the rich vegetable border that formerly filled this space.

As in Romanesque, there is a hierarchy of sizes, and this still produces startling anomalies when big is juxtaposed to small and a giant saint stands on a pedestal covered in delicate little narratives. Higher up, identities become harder to make out and specific narratives simply contribute to a generalized tapestry, ruffled, eaten away in places, but adding to the sense of a teeming whole. So the façade is (in the well-worn comparison) a Bible for the illiterate in the sense that it records more different things than you can keep in mind at once. Unlike the Bible or any book, all these stories are present simultaneously and only simultaneously.

On top of everything there is a carved back to the front at Reims. The reverse of the façade has been hollowed out in a series of niche-like openings, in each of which appears a single figure in the round. The effect is less three-dimensional than the other side of the façade, and more consistent, a regular honeycomb of spaces that respect the wall plane, only embellishing spandrels and borders of all the pointed openings with neatly carved leaves in low relief.

Such unencompassable multiplicity is the aspect of medieval buildings that most attracts and disconcerts us. If the parts are less wild and insistent than in Romanesque assemblages like Moissac, there are more parts in more different mediums. And in spite of greater control of the shape of the whole project, the details have in some sense slipped away. How often in large Gothic buildings is some of the richest intricacy beyond the reach of normal vision, especially in the mode that represents Gothic perception most distinctively, stained glass. Not much Romanesque stained glass survives, generally clearer in its way of telling stories than anything that comes after. Thirteenth- and fourteenth-century narratives are more interesting and more difficult to follow.

What does one say about a fantastic programme like the huge east window of York Minster, 108 scenes in a field of glass the size of a tennis court, so large it needs a second layer of stone tracery located a few feet inside the plane of the glass for stiffening? The narrative is carefully if lopsidedly planned: 27 frames covering Genesis, followed by 81 frames on the Apocalypse, the Beginning abutting the End with no middle in between. Even the more compact Old Testament part finds room for such peripheral episodes as the meeting of Abraham and Melchizedek, in which Abraham, clothed in medieval armour and half again as tall as the king, resembles Goliath.

Much ingenuity went into prescribing and interpreting all these scenes. John Thornton and his assistants spent four years from 1405 to

York Minster, great east window of 1405–8 divided below the top tracery into 108 scenes depicting Genesis and the Apocalypse.

1408 painting them, and then they took their place far enough from human eyes that until the invention of modern lenses it was guaranteed that few would see enough detail to know what they were about. One whole row of scenes is hidden by the double tracery and visible only from far away in the choir.

It is often hard to take seriously the intellectual coherence of medieval narrative schemes. Stories are needed to fill up spaces and there is a limited stock of them. So scenes you've already seen on another side of the building are repeated, like the baptism of Clovis, which occurs at least three times at Reims. Appropriately, some will say, like Wagnerian leitmotifs or reappearances in Proust. Not precisely like them, of course, but apparently there was room for retellings and no rigorous overall editing of the whole.

The single medieval principle that goes furthest to lend unity to variety in narrative is the idea of types or foreshadowings, a system of correspondences worked out between Old and New Testaments in which events in the former are interpreted as occult intimations of the latter, not singly or always very literally, so Abraham's sacrifice of Isaac and the return of the spies from the Promised Land both prefigure Christ's crucifixion.

This is a device that can be abstruse and intellectually demanding or irresponsible in performing an easy levelling of all difference. At their best, typological interpretations work like metaphors in poetry, creating surprising unions. Perhaps the most astonishing instance occurs in a rose window in the south transept at Strasbourg. These two rose windows

Strasbourg Cathedral, central feature of one of two rose windows in the south transept, Moses and Christ as one person with two heads.

represent respectively (and eccentrically) the Old and New Testaments. At the centre of the New is a double figure, two torsos growing from a single trunk. One of them is Moses, the other Christ, and their monstrous overlap expresses the doubleness of Christianity, which subsumes Judaism, not obliterating but transcending the original. Rose windows, a favourite form in France, often look like the outline of an argument, at least in the thirteenth century when made of neatly laid-out rings. In later curvilinear times when intervening spaces fill up with glass, the radiating forms begin to resemble large petals, but earlier, when roses are broken into distinct parts, they are not earthly but celestial flowers, like Dante's model of Paradise, which express hierarchy calibrated by distance from the centre. Here is a form of organization free and tightly controlled at once, where the Zodiac (Reims north transept) or the Tree of Jesse (Châlons-sur-Marne north transept) takes more satisfying shape than elsewhere. Such orders are Romanesque hold-overs, though, and the balance is soon tipped by conceits like that ensconced in the south rose at Amiens, whose round becomes the Wheel of Fortune with figures falling off or clambering on as it rotates. This occurs in sculpted form on the outside, while from within you see a ring of single figures radiating from the centre, half of them with heads pointing downwards.

Amiens is not remembered for elaborate narratives, but for focus and consistency of architectural intention. The nave seems to strive for a single effect, exaggerated height, achieved by tall narrow proportions and vertical emphasis in stone details. Capitals are suppressed on piers of the arcade and eliminated entirely at the crossing. Transepts seem to exist here to provide surprising vistas and change of direction; the symbolism of the cross has been forgotten. Oddly enough, the height of the nave is experienced most powerfully from within the aisle, where the view out is constricted without lessening the sense of a great jump upward.

French chevets or apse complexes are among the wonders of Gothic for the way they make a crescendo of diverse elements. At Amiens the vision is more perfect than usual and resembles a spindly celestial city made of many hollowed-out architectural fictions perched on the upper reaches of buttresses and walls, like destinations unattainable but at least imaginable. Like the interior it is a tiered vision, which illustrates the climb to sublime heights in a set of stages.

The movement towards higher narrower proportions was very compelling, but it came to an abrupt end soon after the nave at Amiens, in Beauvais, whose choir was begun five years later in 1225. The nave never got built, so Beauvais' great height looks more freakish than if the building were complete. Its excesses have been compared to Mannerist exaggerations of Renaissance models: here the tightly spaced cage of flying buttresses finally resembles a complete other building somehow

122

Amiens Cathedral, interior at crossing showing the soaring height and slenderness of the fabric, begun 1220.

extruded in skeletal form by the fragile central mass. At Beauvais the designer was indeed pushing hard against the limits of structural possibility, and his high vaults collapsed 24 years after completion. In rebuilding the vault the number of bays and piers in the choir was doubled, keeping the original vertical proportions but thickening the density of the elevation considerably.

Amiens Cathedral, chevet, a concentrated vision of a heavenly city in miniature.

In the sixteenth century this fragment was given a large and un-orthodox portal, a south transept clothed entirely in a web of tracery. To Gothic purists such irresponsible elaborations of rich surface are anath-ema, and they view it as belittling that the late Flamboyant stage of Gothic so often appears only in addenda to larger structures, porches at Albi or towers at Rouen. But these instances simply indicate that enough large churches had already been built, and at its end the long-lived Gothic is best understood through such juxtapositions. The later addition carries enough detail for a much larger building, miniaturized to fit the space allotted, but suggesting equivalence with the parent who got there first.

Perhaps one does not need to turn to theories of decadence to account for the fact that in later stages of Gothic the energy shifts from structure to surface effects. Effects, it is true, that seem to speak – delusively it sometimes turns out – of unnerving structural novelty.

Beauvais Cathedral from the south-east showing the exo-skeleton of flying buttresses that makes the high walls of glass possible, choir rebuilt 1284–1338.

From the beginning the creators of English Gothic had been more interested in rich and diverse spatial effects than in those rigorous structural demonstrations dear to the French. The 'crazy' vault in St Hugh's choir at Lincoln is an early instance of breaking away from the rules, later pursued more emphatically. Interesting contests have been staged over where the great innovations of the fourteenth century sprang from, inspired by vanished royal masterpieces like St Stephen's Chapel, Westminster, or half-vanished ones like the Eleanor Crosses, which resembled pageant-architecture in their slimness and arbitrary placement.

Already in the octagonal chapter house at York Minster, English restiveness and thirst for surface richness appear in embryo. Wall arcading behind the seats for members of the chapter usually lies flat against the wall, but at York it has begun to break free into a series of small roofed structures protruding into the room with mini-vaults overhead.

Fifty years later at Ely the disruptive potential of wall arcading to break down the solidity of the structure reaches fruition. In the Lady Chapel, almost a detached building angled out from the main body, walls become layered membranes in the lower stages and then turn abruptly to glass above. Such spatial discontinuities are welcomed, and the walls are eaten into by niches both inside and out, not to provide settings for sculpture – they are too shallow – but simply to suggest variable thickness in defiance of all the norms of construction. At lower levels decorative elaboration is unimaginably rich. Arches set within straight-edged gables take on nodding ogee shape, starting with a double curve and twisting it until it leans outward and appears on the point of falling forward. These writhing forms are all encrusted with foliage that seethes with continual movement.

Ely Cathedral, arcading in the Lady Chapel, where nodding ogees are crusted with foliage and figures, 1321–49.

Overhead lies one of those complex patterned vaults, less purely mathematical in feel than Islamic designs, far from a clear indicator of structural principles, more a deceptive mask of these and a theoretical excursion that thrives on multiple readings and deliberately presents itself in contradictory guises.

A more famous novelty at Ely, the Octagon, built to replace a collapsed crossing tower, is an archetypal one off, without obvious ancestors or successors, unless one looks to Spanish *trasparetes* or Baroque domes. It marks a radical departure from what it replaces, taking a simple square opening and making it an octagon by cutting off the corners and building most of what appears to be a stone vault of novel form that does not quite close the opening and creates a star of conoid ribs punctured in the middle by light. Closure is achieved by carpentry instead of the expected masonry. Wood permits a complexity of spatial effect impossible in stone. Views into towers are notoriously disappointing in their scale-lessness and lack of variety, but at Ely the hybrid form achieves a layered mystery, as of a marine organism, equalled only by certain Islamic vaults.

Elsewhere, unorthodox spatial effects sometimes have an ad hoc quality or were brought on by technical failures or unwelcome necessities. The first pair of strainer arches at Salisbury Cathedral occurs in the crossing under the tower with its stone spire, a final embellishment not foreseen in the original design. Perhaps it came as a surprise that these obstructions called forth by fears about the stability of the structure produced rich spatial effects, acting like screens that both conceal and reveal the spaces beyond. By marking off the divisions of structure more emphatically they multiply the spaces and complicate the vision. By raising a spectre of difficulty, they send the eye on a more anxious quest.

When we come to the second 'crossing' at the eastern transepts, structural necessity presumably plays no role at all. Here the strainer arches mirror themselves: an upside-down version sits on top of the initial arch. The result of this doubling is even closer to a Baroque effect, since rectilinearity is abandoned and ovoid openings created, closed at the top by the curve of the vault. Some will doubtless think these untoward vistas were unintentional.

With the east end of Wells Cathedral (rebuilt and extended 1320–40), the intentions of its rich, surprising and inconsistent spatial sequence are less debatable. The English preference for rectangular east ends rather than curved apses as in France looked in earlier stages like a lack of both structural and spatial ambition. But at a certain point the simpler starting place led to an adventurous branching out. At Ely the extension further east is displaced from the main axis and forms a rival to the choir. At Wells (as later at Gloucester) the new spaces are further stages in a single sequence, now visible from the new choir, but formerly screened off.

The Wells sequence culminates in a Lady Chapel springing partly free of the host building. Its shape distorts to an elongated octagon under the stress of pulling itself free. From afar it looks even more elongated, but at moments of your approach you wonder if it might be a centralized figure after all. The intermediate zone is an ambiguous forest of columns, a disconcerting cousin of the wide space with pencil-thin piers at Salisbury.

Another eastern addition to an existing older carcass at Tewkesbury Abbey shares some of these features, including innovative patterns in the vault. At Wells patterns from the choir vault are carried over into the window tracery. At Tewkesbury one realizes with a start that the tracery of rose windows has been laid out on the ceiling. Ribs that one had trusted, even in exfoliated forms where many members never make it to the edge of the vault, to give a sense of the push and pull of structural forces have gone bendy and even cusped.

The Tewkesbury designer grants himself a disturbing freedom to make decorative play absolutely anywhere, even in the last bastions of gravitational necessity. Looking at the twisted ribs at Tewkesbury, if they even are ribs any more, like gnarled knots of branches high up in trees, who does not feel we may have gone too far toward tropical profusion? At this point in the choir of Tewkesbury we are not far from the next great English Gothic invention, the fan vault, a picturesque derivative of the pointed rib vault that set the style on its feet three centuries earlier.

Tewkesbury Abbey, chancel vault whose rib pattern resembles window tracery, after 1288.

Slightly later developments at Gloucester could be seen as a bold extension of the idea of tracery to new parts of the fabric. The problem facing the designer at Gloucester was what to do with an outmoded Romanesque carcass too large and valuable simply to tear down. His solution was to set the new work inside the old, inserting a cage of stone and glass that disguises the heavy Romanesque original by screening it with an entire elevation made of tracery, some of it glazed (like the clerestory that towers above the old building), some left open, allowing partial glimpses of discordant elements beyond, and some of it blind tracery covering the intervening parts of the wall. The overall effect is both consistent – the whole space follows a single grid and culminates in the largest of all medieval windows, a complete wall of glass – and extremely rich: in spite of sparse figural ornament it feels as if the entire structure has turned to ornament or is indistinguishable from ornament.

On the external elevation of the huge east window this is expressed even more clearly. The whole gigantic surface is fused into a single unit by relentless verticals – protruding stone ribs that start as window mullions, then cross onto the pale stone of the gable, where they become ridges on its surface, and finally emerge above it as the uprights in a balustrade.

Gloucester Cathedral, fan vault in the cloister, an important English innovation, 1351–64.

They are finished off by a rail and filled with tracery that turns them into a row of unglazed windows. The giant window is continued in a huge ogee finial in stone, invisible from inside, and the most powerful demonstration of forms crossing the boundaries of different materials.

The cloister at Gloucester is ordinarily credited with the earliest example of a fan vault. From a distance the cloister vaults look like ramifying branches meeting overhead. Close up, you find the 'branches' are not properly attached, but form a surface pattern that violates the truths of structure while creating the most delicately graded play of shadow known to building. The disquiet remains: what looks like arching vaults and spreading branches is really something else. Here lots of raised veins of stone look like ribs, but when you trace them you find them each dissipated in an ogee-fork. The rib, universally regarded as the determining element in Gothic structure, has become a plaything, a surface pattern practising deceptions about what lies underneath.

Romantic enthusiasts derived pointed arches and the general effect of Gothic interiors from branches of trees meeting overhead in the gloom of Northern forests. As they did not know, the origins of Gothic were not Northern in the specific, German sense they had in mind. It is strange to find near the end of Gothic in England and Germany a seizing of this vegetable metaphor, binding architecture to rude truths of tree growth. Disconcertingly, the idea leads to some of the most fanciful results of all.

In the territory between Strasbourg and Prague such fantasias on the idea of the rib are combined with the metaphor of vegetation to produce some extraordinary versions of tree canopies and hedge thickets in stone. At Strasbourg the pulpit is a vase-shaped tangle of branches, graceful but confusing and the kind of web more likely to be the work of a woodcarver than a stone mason.

The priest mounting the pulpit climbs up into a tree. The north porch of the cathedral is an even more extravagant rendition of natural wildness in stone. The person entering the portal looks up at overarching branched forms closing in on him. Inside this thicket large figures are trapped as if in a thorny bower, whose canopy is partly branch-like and partly a decayed tent of Gothic masonry like the roof of an imaginary church. Among the tangle of ribs that form the underside of this structure, many are sliced off abruptly. This idea also appears in many German vaulting patterns and even more gorgeously in a balustrade on the south side at Strasbourg.

In a real forest one meets more broken than perfect branches. Perhaps the carvers want to come closer to the raggedness of the world as against the perfections of art. The effect is quite contrary, of course; chopped-off forms read as strange conceits. We sense the artist grown impatient with completeness and now expressing his need to diverge from the course prescribed by his drawing implements. So the interruptions are in their twisted way like the miracles of natural growth, an infusion of the unexpected, but also like the moment on a building site before the bare frame is filled in.

Strasbourg Cathedral, north porch, pierced canopy looking something like a work under construction, by Jakob von Landshut, 1495–1505.

The last of the Lady Chapel extensions on great English churches follows long after the others. Though it imitates their teasing detachment from the main body and intensifies their jewel-box character, it carries little sign of its dedication to the Virgin. Henry VII's chapel at Westminster Abbey was conceived as a shrine to an English royal saint, King Henry VI. In the event Henry wasn't canonized, so the project lost some of its sacred character and became instead the funeral chapel of its projector, Henry VII, more like an item of personal adornment than the intended reliquary rivalling Edward the Confessor's at the other end of the bridge to the main body of the abbey.

Henry's chapel is among the most magical of all structures, yet it sits uneasily. Partly this follows from its parasitical relation to the abbey, to which it is linked by a tunnel-bridge. Partly it derives from the extremely unsacred character of the architecture. Externally it is the apotheosis of the Perpendicular, appearing like a city of faceted tower-like forms inscribed all over with vertical panels, and ringed at the bottom with a welter of deep-carved heraldic badges, roses, portcullises and so on, like a hedge. It only begins to resemble a Gothic church in a series of buttresses joined to the clerestory by flyers. This system is somewhat miniaturized, as if one were trying to fit a Gothic cathedral into about a quarter of the required space. So between the richness of detail and the squashing of recognizable cathedral features, Henry's chapel ends looking almost more like a table ornament than a church. This impression is increased by the turret tops carved to look like overlapping tiles, more palace than church. These towerlets are now missing their apostle figures but have lately been given back their gold wind vanes, bits of frivolous display. If the missing sculptures shared the spirit of those myriad saints ranged around the walls inside, they would have added little to the sobriety of the building, for a more secular society is hard to imagine. It is as if the sculptors set out to register every eccentricity of dress known to a worldly court.

The crowning effect of Henry's chapel is its fan vault, apparently unique in being constructed of continuously bonded masonry only 4 inches thick. Like other fan vaults but more so, it performs gravity-defying feats, allowing pendants to drip down so startlingly far from the major ribs that it makes some viewers think of arcades of columns missing but conjured into mind by the abruptly terminated verticals. The ribs disappear into a beguiling web of stone lace, which has disguised heavy masonry as insubstantial froth. It is an apotheosis of familiar Gothic spatial formulas that refashions them as worldly display, creating a perfect meeting place for imaginary knights, but an unlikely resting place for a saint.

This is not quite the last gasp of Gothic architecture in churches, but after this they have a decidedly secular air. Even its designer must have

St Eustache, Paris, begun 1532, view of choir vaults, Renaissance detail in a Gothic carcase.

regarded the cathedral-size parish church of St Eustache in Paris as a weird hybrid. That was presumably the point of it, to take a pure Gothic plan, of enormously high vaulted nave and aisles ending in a curved apse with chapels off an ambulatory, and to cast all this in Renaissance classical detail. So some piers are fluted and most of them carry Corinthian capitals at absurdly ungrammatical heights above the floor. France in the early sixteenth century had seen a peripheral infiltration of classical forms, which, unlike the ones turning up in Italian churches a century earlier, camouflage themselves by imitating Gothic clutter. St Eustache is not an episode, however, but an entire schizophrenic narrative.

Nor is it the last. Still in the seventeenth century in places like Cambrai and Arras (both of which had lost their Gothic cathedrals), Gothic spatial formats were employed for large churches in pure classical style. By this time the new vocabulary is presumably not so thrillingly pagan and unsacred, and before long will not require reminiscences of the previous church-style, Gothic, to make it safe for churches.

By telling the whole story of Gothic through church architecture, of course, one loses something, as devotees of castles and burghers' town houses would hurry to point out. There is an even more serious omission. In England especially, cathedrals as they are now would hardly be recognizable by those who built them. Not only is lots of colour missing, but also in some real sense the heart has been ripped out of them with the disappearance of shrines to local saints.

The main reason most people had for visiting York Minster no longer exists. A window in the north-east transept tells the story of St William of York in a hundred scenes. This is a life so boring in ordinary dramatic terms that papal audiences, and disputes over titles, have to be bumped out with twice as many episodes after William's death, in which his influence keeps people from being trampled by horses, killed by falling stones or put in prison.

His window is still there, but his shrine is gone, a gorgeous little building of grey marble whose sides contained rows of alcoves where pilgrims could kneel. On top of this perched the glittering reliquary with his remains, hidden most of the time by its wooden cover shaped like a house. The shrine was thrown out at the Reformation and the broken bits buried in the grounds of the Minster, where they lay undiscovered for four hundred years. In the 1970s large pieces were dug up, including the beautiful vaults of the niches and some exquisite carving. But there is no place for them, no thought of re-erecting them in the choir with its complete set of Victorian equipment, or even of showing them at all.

7
Renaissance

The idea of the Renaissance remains compelling – a decisive break with the past inspired by an older past, a dramatic series of innovations disguised to look like imitations, perhaps only to slip them past church authorities under the cover of the other, older authority. Jacob Burckhardt, the Swiss professor and lover of the South, is still one of the most persuasive propounders of the expansive form of the idea, a revolution in consciousness that tore off the veil of medieval superstition once and for all and let the individual appear in arrogant and inquisitive fullness for the first time (since Athens).

Burckhardt's range of reference is daunting. He emulates those Renaissance all-rounders he describes with a nonchalance that isn't always tolerantly received by his successors. The scope of the subject as Burckhardt imagines it is so large in time and mental space that it catches up both the minutiae of antiquarian researches – coins, gems, etymologies, inscriptions – and the brave new worlds of science and technique. By a long development rich in irony, humanism leads to the scientism we are stuck in now, whose model for every being and process, in nature and in man, is some form or other of machine, a kind of thought seen at its most attractive in Leonardo's drawings.

The Renaissance is more contentious territory than the Gothic, largely because of our imagined relation to it. Medieval man (this is how Burckhardt talks) is clearly not-us, while Renaissance man is proto-us and thus immediately engages our ideas about where we are now. We may look on with newly awakened foreboding at fifteenth-century enthusiasm for the untrammelled exercise of human powers.

Recognizing our kinship occasionally means mistaking our object, with an artist like Giotto, for example, who is sometimes presented as a kind of proto-Cubist. But we are not the first to practise distortions of this kind: Giotto had already been singled out as a precursor of Renaissance discoveries by Vasari, himself not first but following Ghiberti, who was in

Scrovegni Chapel, Padua, frescoes, where Giotto sometimes seems proto-Cubist in his radical simplifications, 1305–10.

his turn famous as a compiler of other people's views. The fifteenth century was already writing the story of a progressive revolution in art and thought, of which they formed the culminating stage.

Modern historians sometimes kick against the artificial eminence given to a few great figures in the history of art in Florence at this time, always the same ones. But this traditional version is at least true to how the Florentines themselves saw things. Architectural history now for the first time becomes the record of the projects of named architects, including unbuilt ones or projects watered down by clients but propounded in their unaltered purity by the geniuses' biographers. Artists', including architects', lives now appear, to establish the individual career as one of the most meaningful forms in which art happens.

Manetti, Brunelleschi's early biographer, has had a determining influence on how we see his subject and hence all the later stages of the Renaissance. For he sets up Brunelleschi as a great innovator and the restorer of ancient forms of building, which the architect studied first hand in lengthy visits to Rome, often in the company of Donatello (who wasn't interested in architecture, according to Manetti). These visits, measuring, studying, excavating, may be fictitious, or are at least enhanced, with an eye on Alberti, the unmentioned rival, an impressive theorist who writes better Latin than Vitruvius.

Sometimes Manetti is making Brunelleschi into more of an intellectual than he was. Elsewhere he shows him as technician or scientist (in a narrow sense of the word). The main excitement and talking point in Brunelleschi's greatest project, the cupola of the cathedral in Florence, is a feature finally invisible because dismantled or even largely absent in the first place. Brunelleschi proposed to vault this huge space without centring, that is to say, without scaffolding resting on the ground. He had devised a method – still not fully understood – by which the masonry would support itself as it rose and leaned out over the space before finally meeting in the middle. So he would need only a light movable platform to support the workers and their materials.

The continuing mystery over how the structure actually works, mystery that survives after centuries of intense speculation, arises in part from Brunelleschi's famous suspicion that others would steal his ideas, so that he preferred rough to detailed models and depended on explaining things on site rather than writing anything down, and in part from the hybrid nature of the solution, theoretically impure, practically enduring. So there are spiralling brickwork, small vaults binding inner and outer shells to each other, carefully formulated mortar, wooden, stone and iron chains

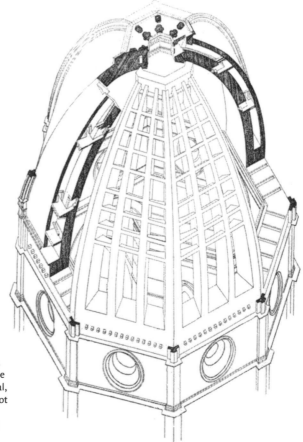

Filippo Brunelleschi, structure of the dome of Florence Cathedral, showing some but not all of the devices in this complex, hybrid solution, 1419–36.

Brunelleschi's dome from street level, looming over its surroundings, taken before the completion of the facade in the 1870s and '80s.

circling the space – all of these cooperating in unknown proportions to produce the required stability. This work, more a feat of engineering than a free-standing piece of architecture, which still dominates views in surrounding streets and the skyline of Florence, embodies only part of Brunelleschi's new conception of the act of design.

At this point in his career instead of whole buildings he was offered mainly adjuncts or embellishments to existing structures, like the sacristy at San Lorenzo and the chapter house at Santa Croce, both of which were intended to pack in other functions and include tombs of the donor's family. In spite of this congestion of purpose, Brunelleschi glimpsed the opportunity to make these spaces into perfect little *tempietti* suggesting more embracing harmonies.

The Old Sacristy is the first integral and enveloping realization of the new vision, formed of the purest geometric elements, a series of circles and squares that assume body as cubes and spheres of air, practically uninterrupted by any obstructing furniture. The transition between the cube and the sphere happens in a zone where circles and parts of circles are traced on flat walls and also on curved spandrels under the crowning dome, pierced in all its segments by round windows.

This is the richest space Brunelleschi ever made, because all the roundels in the middle zone, which jump over and sit under the large curves in turn, are inscribed with perspective spaces in shallow relief, and doors on the altar wall are given decorated frames sloping inward as if towards a vanishing point. All this figured embellishment was designed by Donatello, apparently without consulting Brunelleschi, who even wrote verses voicing his displeasure with the tampering. Now for the first time the architect's design becomes something to which nothing can be added and nothing taken away without spoiling the conception. Even the austere rationalist Brunelleschi gains a reputation for personal rivalries.

And yet even in a world of rampant individualism architectural forms look more and more generic as the initial innovation slips further into the past. No contemporary document connects Brunelleschi with the Pazzi chapel. His first biographer doesn't even mention it, and recently it has

Old Sacristy, San Lorenzo, Florence, detail above cornice level, Brunelleschi's first architectural commission and one of the first spaces in the new style, begun 1421.

been conclusively shown that its porch, a crucial feature of the design, was added later, after Brunelleschi's death. Defining the chapel's relation to Brunelleschi's other work can be pursued, leaving the question of attribution unsettled. And it is not unthinkable that a clever follower could have taken Brunelleschi's ideas and given them an enlivening twist.

It has been a matter of some surprise that Brunelleschi, who wasn't a painter, though a goldsmith and sculptor before an architect, should be credited with the invention of pictorial perspective. At least he produced a couple of demonstration pieces, panel paintings you could hold up in front of views, testing their mathematically precise shrinkages against reality to confirm that the system worked. When you stand in one of Brunelleschi's spaces, the relevance this might carry for architecture is not hard to see.

Major and minor orders are related in ratios pleasing in themselves, but also suggestive of the effects of distance on how the world appears. Some of the pleasure in Brunelleschi's very bounded spaces comes from diminishing series of similar forms traced in the air or on walls, making you feel you're seeing further than you actually are. There is more scope for this in larger spaces like naves of churches, but the most intense effects occur in the more unlikely spaces, like the squeezed side bays and blank arched 'openings' marked out on the Pazzi chapel walls. It is not necessarily an affront to the idea of the importance of the individual to think that a talented follower like Michelozzo could have done a variation on the Old Sacristy that took it further in certain respects.

Brunelleschi is one of those figures in the history of architecture who seems to offer a repeatable formula, thereby spawning a numerous progeny. The idea of the stark contrast between white walls and grey *pietra serena* orders, mouldings and ribs was taken up by a hundred imitators and repeated until it reached seemly blandness. In Brunelleschi's hands the juxtaposition is usually electrifying, because every line written in the darker medium justifies all the surrounding emptiness by its tautness. Like Mies van der Rohe he convinces you that his sparseness is enough.

By imposing mathematical regularity on vision, Brunelleschi made some bold translations between architecture and the universe more plausible. The consonance between his little circles and squares had cosmic implications and could legitimately represent the larger reality of which they were a reduced model. Although the perspective system and the Brunelleschian space put man in a privileged position, they simultaneously belittled him: underlying it was a de-individualized view that sought escape from figuration and focused on something more basic than persons.

In both his theory and his practice Alberti's conception of architecture seems more romantic. There are the coloured marbles that look Byzantine in Rimini and Gothic in Florence, a kind of historical richness that Brunelleschi had no time for. Throughout his treatise on architecture,

Alberti's name for sacred buildings is 'temple'. And for what goes on in them – 'sacrifices' to 'gods', whose different characters give openings for architectural variety. Is it forgetfulness or affectation that makes such absence of Christian reference possible? Or have we entered a separate realm with its own laws? Occasional signs of nervousness appear, as in the subtle justification of the basilican form for churches in De re aedificatoria. Before the onlooker knows what is happening Alberti has modulated from justice (the basilica as a law court) to religion (justice the highest form of God's presence in the world) and the sacred connotations of this architectural type.

Apparently it was thought that covering the Tempio in Rimini with tombs – donors in front, poets and scholars on the sides – would

Leon Battista Alberti's Tempio Malatestiana, Rimini, where he modernized an existing building by referring to antique precedent: side wall furnished with sarcophagi, echoing pagan shrines, from 1450.

Christianize a blatantly pagan design. The remains of a famous Greek scholar were even brought back from Mystra in the Peloponnese to establish a more ancient pedigree. Escaping from superstition, modern attitudes repeat the forms of the earlier veneration of saints' relics. Or it could be a meeting of the collector's instinct with the spirit of parody.

Renaissance humanists didn't invent the clash between sacred and secular: tombs of brutal princes had jostled those of gentle saints before this. But the pope thought something new was going on in Rimini and excommunicated Alberti's patron. Motives for this expulsion may have been mixed, but didn't any of the stigma attach to the architect, or could it have seemed a badge of honour to him or anyone else?

Presumably Alberti had little if anything to do with the far stranger goings on inside the Tempio Malatestiano. Here a series of shallow marble reliefs by Agostino di Duccio give a much richer, more populous version of the pre-Christian cosmos than Brunelleschi's purified domed spaces. Pagan gods and heavenly bodies, including those of archaic, superseded stages like Saturn, are shown with appliances like chariots that suggest at least processions if not forbidden rituals.

Tempio Malatestiana, Chapel of the Planets, zodiac relief by Agostino di Duccio showing a large crab, the astrological sign under which the patron was born, looming over a landscape. One of a series of suspiciously pagan subjects, 1453–6.

Superstition can be liberating if it is the right kind. Is this the thinking in the even more elaborate astrological sequence in the Schifanoia palace in Ferrara of the same date? There entire walls of the largest room were covered with frescoes representing the months through obscure rituals rendered by sophisticated artists using modern perspective techniques.

The overall effect is like the rich jumble of medieval tapestry, but here the parts are hard to read, not because the medium is unsuited to telling stories like tapestry, but because different worlds collide. In the top tier classical gods ride on triumphal cars with fluttering hangings and animal escorts. These allegories are framed by aristocratic activities proper to the god, performed by crowds of big, well-dressed people. Underneath in the middle band three widely spaced figures are silhouetted against a night sky. Under the central figures, gigantic zodiac animals. How could you guess that these personages come from as far away as Egypt and India, and each represent a fixed star that oversees ten days of the month? It remains the most rigid, inscrutable symbolism, which brings together two distant inter-translated ranges of Renaissance thought, the individual and the cosmos, the single body and the overarching scheme.

Below this in the final band, activities of the court so densely crammed that the plan disappears in the detail. These scenes are littered with classical ruins, as if to say that the local family can call upon an ancient pedigree, or that the present is dwarfed by the past, or that the world contains a Babel of tongues, not half of which we can comfortably converse in.

But every ingredient increases the sense of richness. The colliding belief systems – pagan, Christian, Egyptian, Indian – are not intimidating or anxiety-ridden but a playground for the liberated mind and senses, which can now regard half-grasped obsolete beliefs as a kind of cultural depth, to be relished and explored for the light they throw on the universal character of man.

At the same time the elaboration borders on pedantry, not a charge anyone levels at Alberti in spite of his mania for correctness, avoiding solecisms like Brunelleschi's plopping of arches straight down on columns without intervening entablature. But if not a pedant Alberti can at times seem a dilettante, relishing the scope for architectural variety provided by the different characters of the classical gods, guilty of a purely academic exercise. His command of classical sources is impressive, even more impressive that he isn't cowed by them, frequently showing them contradictory in their conclusions and putting them aside at last in favour of his own solution. It's as if they are brought in to show that his thinking doesn't happen in an empty space, but in the midst of something like a family gathering.

Palazzo Rucellai, Florence, Alberti's facade like a textbook illustration of the classical orders, rendered graphically like a drawing, yet with subtle indications of depth, c. 1455–58.

Even now the Roman triumphal arch seems a bizarre design source for the façade of a church. In Rimini it takes on the fortuitous appearance of a ruined arch (it was left incomplete) carried out in rich, obscure materials, not Brunelleschi's neutral stucco but coloured marbles inlaid like gems. The triumphal arch turns up in more three-dimensional form in Alberti's last church, Sant'Andrea at Mantua, but in the meantime he retreats to more delicate and illusionistic effects in his work for Giovanni Rucellai in Florence.

The façade of the Rucellai palace is famous for its meticulous grading of the classical orders, from Doric at the bottom to Corinthian at the top. Even more remarkable are subtle suggestions of depth in the shallow recessions of the plentiful carved detail. A wealth of imagery makes a first appearance in the friezes between floors – flying sails, quills and rings – the Rucellai emblems. The sails especially are so carefully rendered that the effect is like inlay, yet they are shown in slightest diagonal protrusion, trailing little ropes in fluttering movement. Juicy oak garlands are crammed into narrow crevices over the doors. *Bifora* windows, familiar in Italian Gothic, now acquire three tiny classical columns framing and splitting the openings, capped by a tiny entablature, which completes a separate little architectural universe.

The lower ranges of the façade are rich in mouldings and rusticated elements (one set of panels shows stones turned at 45 degrees) that jut out at the right moment to form an integral bench like a cornice. From a little way off this rich façade looks like a drawing. Encountered closely, it is full of teasing illusions, token depths that stand for more, miniature forms that demonstrate ranges of architectural effect that would not easily fit full scale in a narrow street.

In the space between the cathedral and the baptistery where Brunelleschi first demonstrated his mathematical perspective there is now a virtuoso display of the system's potential by his rival. Ghiberti's second set of doors suggests depth miraculously where there is no room for it. Here the principal agent in the illusion is fictional architecture, enclosing the little figures in steeply receding geometry. On the Rucellai façade Alberti has applied the effect more extensively to an entire street frontage, absorbing the lesson that for maximum intellectual power actual depth should be kept to a minimum, approximating the clarity of a drawing.

Once again for Giovanni Rucellai, Alberti carried out another project that remains semi-conceptual, hovering between a model and a building. Instead of travelling to the Holy Land himself, Rucellai sent a deputy to take careful measurements of Christ's sepulchre, a spiritual meditation turned into an archaeological undertaking, like those that serious designers now carried out in Rome on classical ruins.

When the measurements came back to Florence, Rucellai engaged Alberti to build an exact replica which assumes the form of an exquisite little building fitting neatly inside a specially built chapel in Giovanni's neighbourhood church of San Pancrazio. It is a cross between a small church and a tomb, as if reflecting the emissary's uncertainty over whether he was to measure the enclosing building or the sepulchre by itself. More likely it is Alberti's free interpretation of a building as a body, derived from the proportions and organization of a human figure.

But there are plenty of anomalies. The building is dominated by an inscription in large Roman capital letters, which fills the frieze over a series of small Composite pilasters attached to walls divided into square panels, each inlaid with geometric roundels or those familiar sails, quills and rings. This building inside a building is apsed and crowned by carved marble battlements of stylized lilies like peacock plumes. And the whole conceit is carried out in dark green and white marble harking back to Tuscan Romanesque. The little temple is unroofed and empty: its inscription warns us that Christ's body is not here. So the project is an elaborate architectural hoax, the model of a structure somewhere else whose secret kernel is a glaring absence. Alberti's response to the puzzling brief is to combine cultural flavours into an eccentric hybrid, a synthesis as difficult to give a rational accounting for as the astrological exegesis in Ferrara.

Alberti's replica of the Holy Sepulchre, Jerusalem, in a Florentine church, St Pancrazio, which combines Gothic and Renaissance flavours, completed 1467.

In *De re aedificatoria* Alberti promulgates more balanced, less eccentric views than in architectural projects like this where the particular synthesis between sacred and secular must sometimes have seemed decidedly alarming. For the fullest embodiment of Alberti's notion of how thoughtful architecture houses and gives expression to a whole decorous way of life we might turn, not to his own completed projects but to a state of modest scale like the little duchy of Urbino, where the focus falls naturally not on the architect, who keeps changing over the long gestation of the palace, but on the ruler, who evolves from military to cultural hero as the favoured building type moves from fortress to meeting place of the muses.

Federico da Montefeltro, the ruler of this little state, has been portrayed in a couple of memorable images. In his study he is shown reading in a full set of armour, perhaps a ritualized presentation of the interests he combined rather than an exact record of how he lived. In another idealization, a contemporary account of how he spends his days, we see him first inspecting an outlying part of his domain, then moving to civic discourse listening to his subjects in town, and only later turning to private study and self-cultivation.

The palace at Urbino, built piecemeal and never fully aligned to any grand design, is another portrayal of this tension between public and private, monumental and intimate. Like the town that surrounds it, the palace is made of brick, underneath tentative and incomplete stabs at marble coating, and thereby never forgets something humble, even rural, in its roots. On the two-sided courtyard that faces the town the palace looks like a medieval carcass partly classicized, still showing its two different identities, a perception reinforced by finding that the symmetry in the street doesn't match what lies behind – the right-hand door leads to the centre of an internal courtyard. A possible motive for leaving the façade incompletely transformed is its resemblance to a Roman ruin, like so many classical hulks now brick with sparse travertine trim.

The internal courtyard by contrast is one of the most perfect ideal spaces of the Renaissance, where pale Roman bricks set off carved detail. Among other things the court is bound together by two tiers of large but exquisite Roman inscriptions applauding the ruler in the moderately obscure classical tongue.

Ducal Palace, Urbino, internal courtyard, with its notable inscriptions in revived Roman lettering, from 1468 onward.

This courtyard was meant to lead to another that would have held Federico's tomb, a circular structure like the great imperial mausolea in Rome. The whole effect would have been less modest and ingratiating if it had culminated like that. Instead, we ascend to a graduated series of public spaces, including a kind of throne room for the most outward-facing sort of event, and to the private quarters, which include a tiny chapel lined in coloured marbles that gives a highly introverted idea of devotion. This space is paired with a Temple of the Muses, again small and private, for matching devotions to other, non-Christian powers.

And finally the space to which the most intense artistic attention has been devoted, a scholar's study where the book cupboards are disguised by doors inlaid with exquisite marquetry in perspective, depicting doors half ajar or fully open, revealing books tumbled together or scientific instruments or statues in fictitious niches, and finally a view onto a terrace through a loggia to a distant landscape, all depicted in wooden inlay. The illusions would have been even more lively when this room was in use, when doors inscribed with doors ajar, half revealing fictitious books within, stood ajar revealing real books within, in dizzy overlays of perspective. And this little haven with its intarsia views lay right next to an open loggia looking onto a sweeping panorama of ducal terrain.

The most famous image of Federico, by Piero della Francesca, shows him silhouetted against such a landscape. It forms a heraldic pair with a portrait of his second wife. They face but do not see each other, like people who will soon turn into graven commemorations of themselves. And on the reverse, as if on medals that have come part-way alive, they sit stiffly on little triumphal cars, ministered to by Virtues like ideal citizens and drawn by pairs of mythic beasts. Here the landscape is nearer and very beautiful, but the whole set of four images makes one uneasy as Piero is peculiarly able to do.

His *Flagellation*, in Urbino now, as the ducal portraits are not, is one of the most disturbing expressions of the mental power conferred by the new attitudes of the fifteenth century. The problem is a disparity between the two sides of the picture, which do and do not inhabit the same space. Perhaps for our comfort we need another scale between these two, which the painter has deliberately left out. There is a disjunction between figures and architecture, the figures inhabiting a flat wafer of space, the architecture zooming back into the distance. The beautiful calm that settles on everything in Piero's pictures is so unsuitable for what is going forward here, and the disparity remains an unfinished business we cannot resolve. This hypnotic picture makes us wonder how central to the Renaissance it is, this technique of turning every situation into an experiment, in which certain possibilities, geometric, mechanical, proportional, are coolly tested.

Piero della Francesca, *Flagellation* (c. 1455–60), an unnerving application of rational perspective to a violent subject.

Interiors at Urbino like the little chapels belong to the richer Albertian interpretation of antiquity. Certain works of the 1480s in Venice also bear superficial signs of kinship with this approach, but probably derive their liking for rich materials and surface effects from different sources, particularly the old Venetian connection to Byzantium. When the Venetians pilfered precious marbles and carvings from Constantinople in the thirteenth century, they did it as the inheritors of the New Rome who shored up an imaginary version of their city's antiquity as founded by Byzantine refugees.

Santa Maria dei Miracoli, a miniature building like a shrine that was built by Pietro Lombardo to house a wonder-working image of the Virgin, could actually draw on the stock of looted marble panels in the masons' yard of San Marco. The casket-like exterior of the church is entirely coated in rare marbles, as if someone had turned the little chapel in Urbino inside out. The background colour is creamy white laced with saffron veins. Panels that have no windows in them are bisected by mullions of grey marble that give the idea of folding doors. The façade is diversified by porphyry inlay in decorative patterns that suggest at one and the same time the cross and female adornment. The circular gable outlines both a barrel vault and the shape of a coffer.

The whole exterior is substantially devoid of imagery, relying on varied colour and veining full of linear incident to take the place of narrative. But Lombardo, primarily a sculptor, was soon after this involved in elaborate three-dimensional illusions on the Scuola Grande di Santi Giovanni

Pietro Lombardo, Santa Maria dei Miracoli, Venice, 1481–9, Renaissance geometry viewed through the filter of Byzantine richness.

e Paolo, where coloured marbles are no bar to layers of carved illusion. And inside the Miracoli the equipment of the raised sanctuary – elaborate railings, benches, altar and candle-stands – is covered in classical motifs carved in relief on luscious, soft-seeming marble.

The attitude to materials, classical imagery and architectural scale calls up the *Hypnerotomachia*, an architectural fantasy in prose by the Venetian friar Francesco Colonna. In that interminable or deliciously languorous book, depending on your view, rare materials carrying exotic geographic pedigrees are treated as incitements to sensuous indulgence.

Two woodcuts
from the
*Hypnerotomachia
Poliphili* (1499),
illustrating
a classical
triumph that
employs as its
main motif the
Rape of Leda by
Zeus in the form
of a swan.

And a state of aroused desire is stretched out by turning it into an antique triumph with a beautifully constructed car covered in enigmatic scenes pulled by six odd beasts attached by special ribbons and ridden by girls in flimsy dresses playing archaeologically correct instruments, while on the car sits a beautiful girl being raped by a swan to the delight of the accompanying throng of young lovers.

The narrative is slowed by careful descriptions of how clothes that both reveal and conceal the body are constructed, and by piles of classical parallels that work in a backwards fashion. They are always belittled by comparison with the present maiden or garment or ceremony, but they provide validation after validation. The goal is always a crowd of maidens or a wealth of contexts and the effect of these intervening numbers of similar things is endless deferral.

Christian references are noticeably absent from the *Hypnerotomachia*. Santa Maria dei Miracoli is laid out like a church, but when empty feels like the setting for pagan ritual, a classical pageant that would be slow moving and lovely to look at, giving life and meaning to the rich materials. A secular building of the same period on the Grand Canal has been connected (not plausibly) with Lombardo and the Miracoli. It's called Ca' Dario and has a documented connection with Byzantium: its patron Giovanni Dario was Venetian emissary to Mehmet the Conqueror. Like the Miracoli it is a complete tissue of coloured marble, at least on the canal side. Like the Miracoli's, its mind is divided between Renaissance orders, geometry as a plaything and a game, and the building as a surrogate field for personal adornment.

Ca' Dario's architect is unknown, if it had one, and something about the workmanship makes it seem ramshackle in spite of the luxurious materials. The strong asymmetry, based perhaps on a simple vernacular model, seems careless at first, until one notices conflicting local symmetries, especially the one centred on the 'jewellery' of porphyry roundels that are framed by single arched openings on either side, openings finished off at their outer edge by thick pillars, the inner set not quite in the middle of the façade. The composition goes on producing puzzles that are live issues but not resolvable. The last one is made by the nineteenth-century iron balcony jutting out on the far left. Perhaps this too just repeats an older dislocation, for it hints at a system that would divide the whole façade into quarters.

Ca' Dario is only playing with the idea of a classical building, in a spirit that has wrecked from the start any hope of simple consistency, and thus remains truer to the spirit of ruins, to classical remains as they actually are in the present world of the senses, than the works of Brunelleschi.

Not in the Roman works for which he is now mainly remembered but in his first documented work produced in Milan, Bramante shows himself a follower of the richer, more pictorial Albertian conception of antiquity. His early development is obscure, but he is known to have begun in the court at Urbino as a perspective painter, and perhaps as the designer of illusionistic interiors, which may include the marble-clad chapel and the study enclosed in wooden scenery in the Ducal Palace. Bramante's first absolutely certain work is even more fruity and heavily flavoured than these two, an architectural print engraved by someone else, the design prominently credited to Bramante on a pedestal in the foreground, which supports a classical column emerging from an urn and finished off with a cross, the only Christian, though not the only contemporary, reference in this overripe and derelict interior called *Ruined Temple*.

In *Bramante architetto* Arnaldo Bruschi finds Brunelleschi, Alberti, Byzantium and Rome all taken up and transcended in the fictive building

Ca' Dario, Venice, a more nearly vernacular example of classicism with a luxurious Byzantine flavour (an earlier building remodelled after 1486).

intimated in the print. The space shown is apparently about half of the interior volume of an entirely regular cross-in-square structure, a standard Byzantine format. But its ruination, an abundance of surface detail and the exceptionally melodramatic lighting make it practically impossible to notice this regularity. We are placed off-centre in an area where the structure has broken down and the arcade is now missing, giving us the equivalent of a cutaway view of a side-arm and corner vault that we would not, standing in the complete building, be able to see. It's not for information that the extra vista has been opened up, but for multiplication of confusing pictorial richness.

Spatial elements like oculi, blind oculi, wall niches, split capitals, inscribed reveals of arches – all characteristic of Bramante's architecture in the immediately ensuing period – are combined here, it is true, yet it takes great persistence to ferret them out in the maelstrom of Romantic shadow. The *Ruined Temple* is a further stage in the perception of classical architecture as loaded with an overpowering weight of cultural baggage, inspiring the collector in us, who assembles every possible motif in a single confined space, where the wood is lost in the trees.

Bramante's first actual realized architecture appears in Milan at Santa Maria presso San Satiro, where the extent of his contribution remains disputed. The finishing touch was a fictional extension to the actual structure, the portrayal of a matching apse arm, needed for liturgical and aesthetic reasons, which there wasn't room for on the site. So Bramante contrived the three-dimensional illusion of a coffered vault, not just a painted deception like the later ones of the Baroque, but an actual space drastically shrunken and thus functioning more like a painting than a building.

Bramante may have continued in the romantic theatrical way in occasional designs thereafter, but under the influence of Roman remains all around him and the preferences of new patrons his architecture sobers up, beginning with his very first Roman work, the cloister and convent at Santa Maria della Pace, based on a regular grid though operating in a tight urban site that isn't regular.

His attempt to manipulate pure, pared-down elements in these circumstances throws up lots of anomalies and contradictions. Perhaps this residue of struggle is what makes the space so fascinating, in spite of the lack of elaborate content. Most of Bramante's dilemmas will not even break the surface calm for most observers, but there are hints of quirkiness underneath the general severity, especially at the corners where the ruling Ionic order virtually disappears into the wall, leaving only the merest vestige of itself. This has been labelled a 'thread' pilaster, ugly considered in isolation and a reminder of the sacrifices entailed in observing consistency in the widths of bays.

So the most expressive element, deriving from the human figure, must die in order that measure may be preserved. What is left of the Ionic pedestal is even less comfortable, hedged as it is on both sides by Tuscan pilasters, while on the floor above, the merger at the corners produces not loss but increase, since all three pilasters were Composite in the first place, so partial crowding out just looks like blurring of parts.

So you could proceed, taking apart this small composition step by step, finding out in the process how many decisions are hidden in it, how much more variety than first appears, how many more deviations from perfect consistency than one ever suspects. Bramante has managed to fit all four orders into the tight space. On the lower level he combines the two main forms of courtyard – arches resting on piers and spaced vertical members supporting an entablature directly – by applying a larger order of pilasters to the piers of the arcade, an order that splits all the pier capitals in two. Seen head on, these tall Ionic pilasters are the dominant element. Seen in raking view, they become thin and delicate, almost a kind of scenery. At their base the floor of the cloister finds itself co-opted as the last protruding moulding before a plain wafer of plinth sitting on the ground. Elements featureless and pure in themselves act metamorphically and impart to all this stone the feeling of organic life, of substance that moves and changes.

Very soon after this, Bramante was asked by other non-Roman clients, the king and queen of Spain, to commemorate St Peter's crucifixion with a building on its supposed site. He saw the opportunity in this largely symbolic commission to fill the largest ambitions of a typical Renaissance architect on the smallest scale.

Bruschi sets his imagination loose at San Pietro in Montorio, seeking parallels between classical and Christian forms and meanings. Circular temples had been declared suitable for Vesta, Diana and Hercules: Vesta the earth, Peter the rock, Diana the moon, Catholic chastity and the round building; Hercules and Peter as strong brave heroes, for whom Doric is the correct order. But the sixteen granite shafts from an antique source came with the commission, and perhaps told you already by necking and proportions that they needed to be Doric.

Anyway Bramante made them the occasion of a very correct exhibition of the order with triglyphs and metopes filled up with twelve different types of liturgical implement, inspired by a pagan series surviving on the Temple of Vespasian. The columns circle the little cylinder of the temple and were to be circled in their turn by an enclosing taller colonnade whose entablature would line up with that at the top of the temple's drum. A circular building in a circular court would have created the sense of radiating rings, not a static but an active model of the regular cosmos and the God who designed it, immemorially associated Himself with the perfection of the circle. Bruschi adds a further layer, the expansive Catholic Church spreading evenly into the world from the martyrdom of the first bishop of Rome, which made Rome a centre and gave impetus to endless further conversions. So Peter stands for all his successors, especially the last.

But Bramante's main attention seems to be focused elsewhere, on the attempt to erect every part of a complete and perfect building on the smallest feasible scale, thereby combining the intellectual delights of the

Donato Bramante, Tempietto, San Pietro in Montorio, Rome, 1502–10, a miniature that realizes the Renaissance dream of a completely centralized structure.

model with the practical convenience of a structure you can actually walk the whole way round and into.

The parts have been ingeniously multiplied. Each column possesses its own corresponding pilaster attached to the curved temple wall. They are not so far apart that you in any way need this reminder, all the more wonderful to have such consonance, like a kind of companionship where the two could almost reach out and touch each other. Overhead a miniature coffered vault, precipitously curved, which causes continual shrinkage towards the implied centre. The pilasters, however, do not shrink, neither do they curve, and the meeting of their bases with the moulding of the wall is consequently full of incident. On the inside, where dimensions are even smaller and pilasters are bunched in pairs, they do curve and the proportion of the intervening wall drastically shrinks.

Every element that has to fit into the external system – windows, niches, doors – is pushed very near to the limit of compression at which it would cease to be usable or recognizable. One element finally cracks, the main doorframe, whose mouldings, though not the opening itself, spill onto the framing pilaster as if to say 'See, I am operating at the absolute limit of smallness and must stretch the rules so that people of normal size can enter this building', which is in some sense the last necessity. The project would have ended in true uselessness if at the last moment it had denied us entry, which it comes up to the edge of doing, as you are reminded every time you pass the threshold.

The space inside is not painfully constricted, though, because of its height and the light admitted by four windows in the drum, an effect of early Christian provenance it is said. A dome clearly holds the meaning for Bramante that it held for many of his contemporaries, the fulfilment in another dimension of the cosmic implications of the circle. When, at St Peter's, he came to tackle the challenge of the largest church in Christendom it was practically inevitable that his solution should be a centralized domed space, this time on such monumental scale that though it won great admiration and had long-lasting influence it hadn't progressed far when construction was halted by non-architectural causes.

A strange coda to Bramante's career: his only piece of theoretical writing concerns the completion of a Gothic building, the cathedral in Milan. Instead of a dome over this crossing (used by Brunelleschi solving a similar problem in Florence), Bramante recommends a solution that follows Gothic principles of structure and composition, which, judging from his practice, would not necessarily rule out radical invention within the framework.

The culmination of the thinking that propelled the centripetal order beyond the centralized building in widening rings was the ideal city radiating from a single central point. Filarete and Leonardo were among those who projected these cities as single organisms, conceptions that existed on paper for almost a century before anything much like them was actually built.

The fullest surviving realization, at Palmanova in the Veneto, was built in 1593 as a military outpost to oppose anticipated Turkish invasion. Palmanova is centralized and radial, but angular and crystalline, not curved or circular. Circling its streets is like being indoors, and also like

Palmanova, near Udine in northern Italy, late projection of a centrifugal design for a whole settlement, placed here for military reasons in 1593.

changing your position continually without leaving the starting point. Much more than any centralized structure it gives one the uncomfortable feeling of being always in the same place, with the result that in outlying streets you don't really know where you are. To some this will seem the fulfilment of an important philosophical concept, to others a nightmare, as the perfectly logical place turns out to be highly disorienting and appreciated best from the air or on the pages of an atlas.

For a number of reasons the rationality of the Renaissance had begun to pall on contemporaries long before the 1590s, a reversion brought on by political changes that led to cultural disillusion, pushed still further by subversive personalities like Michelangelo, who is merely the most unclassifiable of many. The shift was noticeable enough to attract a new style-name in the following century that has stuck ever since, Mannerism, a term that suggests unfairly a trivializing decline into hollow artifice. Though Mannerism's characteristic vice may be complexity for its own sake, at its best the new mode represents an intensification rather than a decline from Renaissance achievement.

8
Mannerism

There's a version of the progress of art, and of culture in general, mod-elled on the life of creatures, which begins in childish clumsiness and goes through phases of youthful vigour, followed by healthy maturity, leading to decline into effete and decadent stages, and on to extinction and perhaps even a drawn-out aftermath like putrefaction.

The earliest version of the sequence in Western art is the development from fifth-century Athenian purity to Hellenistic overscaled bombast. The pattern is repeated in Roman history in the transition from Republic to Empire, and later appears in the development from Romanesque to Gothic (early, high, late), ending with Flamboyant or Perpendicular etiolation. In some accounts of the next phase the shift from Renaissance to Mannerism is the whole story. In others the sequence continues from bad (Manner-ism) to worse (Baroque) to a nadir of empty triviality (Rococo).

Dividing lines are hard to agree and depend on what the observer wants to see. One of the best critics finds plentiful Mannerist tendencies running through Bramante's work, and it is common to label Michelangelo proto-Baroque. We can agree that Mannerism is a motion of discontent, impatient with the harmony of the earlier Renaissance, achieved at great cost but now seeming too easy. We are not likely to agree on the source of the unease. Is it spiritual anguish following war and upheaval, the sacking of Rome in 1527 by the emperor's mercenary armies above all? Or a process internal to art, the familiar itch for novelty that has become so much more insistent in the last two centuries that we read it back into many states of society where it must have been the faintest undercurrent? Or is it down to Michelangelo's unquiet character, which had dispropor-tionate influence on his successors' choice of subject and approach, freeing them as Vasari thought from one bondage to saddle them with another even more capricious?

Perhaps Michelangelo's first architectural commission, for a fu-nerary chapel, was bound to lead to perversity. It put him in direct rivalry

Michelangelo, New Sacristy, San Lorenzo, Florence, side wall with blind niches, crowding and other Mannerist subversions of classical harmony, 1520–34.

with Brunelleschi, who had designed a matching space on the other side of the nave of San Lorenzo a hundred years earlier. According to Vasari, Michelangelo was conscious of this rivalry. He used a version of Brunelleschi's materials and even of his wall elevation. But Michelangelo's darker stone contrasts more starkly with the plaster walls and creates a more forbidding effect. To the elevation he added an extra storey, changing the proportions, which are no longer comfortably adjusted to the body. The corner treatments are particularly revealing: there, a superfluity of elements appear that crowd and even overlap each other. Blank niches push against giant Corinthian pilasters that are creased and trapped by them in the corners. These empty, functionless marble niches are among the most mesmeric features in the history of architecture. There are hollows where there should be mass, blankness where we expect ornament, protrusion where the surface profile should be flat and general mystery over which element of the established classical system we are dealing with at any particular moment. A powerful urge to deny or alter the nature of the familiar parts operates repeatedly, but pure arbitrariness would never hold our attention like this. The result is a whole series of discords but also of concords, as new (and strange) relations are set up. The breaks in the segmental hoods of these niches, for instance, line up with the corners of the missing rectangular solid carved out of the centre that leaves behind the impression of its body.

Even at its most rigidly straight, the geometry feels bodily, the incisions painful, like lacerations of the flesh.

Michelangelo's designs for the fortifications of Florence made around the same time exhibit a similar translation of muscle and skeleton into the vocabulary of abstract Renaissance ornament. Or you could say that these two ranges of discourse are fused. He always thinks as a sculptor, for whom geometry is anatomical in the first place, who can adapt ideas arising from the organization of the body to surprisingly remote contexts. How else explain the visceral tensions created among those neutral materials in his chapel in Florence?

His other great architectural project at San Lorenzo, the library vestibule, also operates in a tall tube of space and crushes the entrances down to the bottom and into the corners. But here there is no glistening marble, no detachable sculpture with its rich narrative.

The library is on the floor above, a safer place for books, and the function of this introductory space is just to get us there. This simple brief leads to an extremely dramatic space where an anti-architecture is enacted like an absurdist play. We meet a few motifs familiar from the earlier interior: frames that look like windows but are blind, denying access. And crucial elements that appear trapped or imprisoned. In this case it is giant two-storey columns that, instead of quietly supporting the upper parts of the structure, have been depicted as lodged in or half excavated from

Michelangelo's staircase in the vestibule of the Laurentian Library, Florence, a room-size piece of sculpture that fills its function uneasily. Executed by Bartolomeo Ammannati from a clay model, 1559.

the interior of the walls. There are also parts that appear upside down or in the wrong plane: powerful volutes hang free on the walls instead of taking their proper places under the columns.

The only truly useful piece of equipment here, the stair, is the most freakish of all. Michelangelo couldn't come from Rome to supervise its construction, so he sent a clay model for Ammannati to interpret. The built result is certainly sculptural, and treacherous too. It engorges the space, leaving little room at the sides. The central stair flows down in confusing curves on each tread. The rail is too low to use. On two further sets of uneven-looking steps alongside, the rail has been left off. So the simple function is repeatedly denied and a host of uncertainties set in motion.

These rooms of Michelangelo's feel like spaces to study rather than inhabit. The vestibule, which we regard as an independent sculptural piece, was intended to form an element in a three-part composition, two small, intense spaces separated by the long narrow library full of reading desks running down either side, whose end elevations form miniature colonnades in the middle of the room.

At the other end was a triangular closet for rare books (never built), Michelangelo's version of the Mannerist *studiolo*, the ultimate introspective space where the learner communed with his most personal thoughts. Here Michelangelo specified an interlocking labyrinth of shelves in which the reader would have sat immured.

In the next generation Ammannati and Vasari designed a couple of such spaces in corners and crannies of the Palazzo Vecchio for Cosimo and Francesco de' Medici. The older, more cramped version communicated with the world outside via hidden stairs and a window onto the street below, masked by a door that looked like another cabinet full of rare stones and coins. The later version, from the 1570s, is windowless, covered in exquisite painting and sculpture tending towards the scale of manuscripts or jewellery, and sealed off from the huge public room it abuts.

The forms remind us of those in Urbino a century and a half earlier, but there is now a more awkward conversation between public and private and a new enthusiasm for secrecy, either a kind of game or a prompting of genuine paranoia. A parallel move in the game was the construction of an elevated passageway leading from the Uffizi along the river and hence across the old bridge, through the western gallery of a church, and then the upper spaces of private houses requisitioned for the purpose, to end in the Pitti palace. Thus did the Florentine duke communicate with his subjects, reminding them constantly that he had secret means of congress between his two main spheres of activity, a far cry from Urbino's informal engagement with rural and civic affairs.

In the next generation at the Casa Buonarroti in Florence, Michelangelo's *pronipote*, known as Michelangelo the Younger, created his own modest *studiolo*, part of an elaborate Mannerist shrine to his great kins-man that turned Michelangelo's life into ritualized images and embedded a few small pieces of his work in the exquisite setting like flies in amber.

It was inevitable, no doubt, that Michelangelo's innovations, the fruit of fervent searching, should be turned to something less disturbing by even the most fully attuned of imitators. The proportions of the Sistine Chapel ceiling, where the border takes over from the centre and energy is diverted from biblical scenes to contorted nude figures who have no place in the action, which had their particular causes in the artist's temperament and the physical form of the vault, later became a standard decorative for-mula in a variety of other situations. The most famous instances are two long galleries at Fontainebleau, and the most entertaining, a miniature version that took Giulio Clovio twice as long to produce as Michelangelo spent on the Sistine ceiling.

In this arch-Mannerist manuscript, the Farnese Hours, biblical scenes are dwarfed by borders full of struggling nude figures of all ages and bits of classical decor that are energetic too – grinning monsters, rams' heads, masks, all pretending to be made of gilt bronze. Much play with scale: cameos are depicted inset in these borders at full size, while around them living babies of more minute scale sit astride bronze horses they are taming. The whole effect is agitated but not anguished in the least, an amaz-ing example of workmanship, not a remarkable piece of expression.

Giulio Clovio, double-page illumination from the Farnese Hours showing ideas from the Sistine Chapel ceiling transferred to a less than architectural scale in a medieval format, 1537–46.

Almost anyone will come off badly in close comparison to Michelangelo. Maybe none of his contemporaries rivals him in seriousness and depth, but there are interesting architects of that time whose work is recognizably Mannerist, like Giulio Romano. Giulio is known for prolific designs for luxury appliances like ewers and wine coolers that play with the possibility of turning them into monsters, harking back, whether he knew it or not, to the art of primitive peoples.

Something similar could be said of his deviations from the norms of classical architecture: he aimed to animate the building by destabilizing its familiar elements. Some of his distortions are so unexpected that you might even wonder for a moment if the building is falling down. Giulio's most striking work is in Mantua, above all in a pleasure complex called the Palazzo del Te, which was converted from a rustic predecessor into a grandiose version of a suburban villa. The quasi-rural setting provides the excuse for employing a sophisticated grasp of architectural form in the task of undoing architecture to arrive at wildness and finally at chaos.

The villa consists of four long low ranges around a courtyard; it appears to occupy an island reached by a bridge across a token body of water like a moat. The courtyard offers a parody of enclosure, wider and bleaker than the others we have seen, as if the sides fled from each other. The walls are punctuated by generous openings, all blocked, and niches, all empty, like architecture before or after the sociable stage in which people live in houses.

And these walls transmit small but disturbing messages. In the centres of the irregular bays between unfluted Doric columns the

Giulio Romano, Palazzo del Te, Mantua, studious disruptions of classical norms, including dropped triglyphs, blind windows and pseudo rustication, 1527–34.

Palazzo del Te, a grotto-like entrance passageway with roughened columns and rugged coffering.

triglyphs drop down maybe six inches from their proper place in the frieze and hang there, suspended. You don't immediately notice that this is impossible, or isn't what it seems. If they fit correctly in the first place they couldn't have shifted and besides they can't move now, so there's nothing to worry about. You don't think this, but take the little displacement as the initial tremor of an earthquake that will shake the whole structure; the tiny sign makes it all feel unsound. Yet your disquiet isn't really the practical kind. You don't plan your escape, but ponder the deliberate use of well-worn motifs to convey the idea of their own dissolution.

The masonry surface between the columns raises similar questions in the most stylized way. Individual stones are presented as separate, jutting forward several inches of anything like mortar joining them together. Most of them are smooth, but a few are extremely rough, as if unhewn. These are not scattered randomly but always appear in the same symmetrical layout.

On top of this, underneath all this, the stones are not stones but representations of stones. A smooth ashlar wall has at some earlier stage been carved to look like a rougher kind of masonry. The channels between the variegated 'stones' are a kind of decorative carving, not primitive unfilled emptiness.

Can anything so calculated really give insights into the roots of architecture? The vaulted passage leading into the garden may provide the answer. The vault is supported by four bulging columns with a surface like boiling lava or rock in a molten earlier stage. The bulge, though regular like entasis, suggests geological pressure, a weight too heavy to bear. And overhead, the cave-roof consists of rugged coffering making gloomy shadows but obeying an intricate geometry of big octagons and small squares.

Giulio dedicates his considerable learning to turning our perceptions inside out. An ingenious ceiling pattern summons up the world before man. In the Room of the Giants illusionistic fresco suggests the place is coming down around our ears and returning us to primal chaos. The

Palazzo del Te, Room of the Giants, subjective architecture: fresco that instills unease about the reliability of the structure, 1532–4.

Pirro Ligorio, Bomarzo, park of monsters, a wooded garden haunted by phantasms in stone, mostly 1557–63.

clinching stage in this argument lies beyond the passage to the garden, the place where forces of nature and art meet in an even freer variety of ways, where those like Giulio and his patron in search of the primitive, both as the earliest and deepest human stages and as the pre- and non-human, have the best chance of finding what they're after. The goal, as devotees of alchemy like Francesco de' Medici also realized, is finally psychological, not geological or botanical, and that is why the answer will be found in the studio or the garden, not outside the walls in the wild.

The most compelling Mannerist experiment in calling monsters out of the self in a garden is found in Pirro Ligorio's mythic landscape at Bomarzo, developed over thirty years from the 1550s. It includes a few wholehearted portrayals of architecture as demonic or at least hostile to human needs, such as a room purporting to be the mouth of a monster where you sit on his teeth and take your food from his tongue.

Another little two-storey building in terminal decline leans at 50 or 60 degrees, taking away one of the basic reassurances of social life, while all around the landscape erupts in unfriendly creatures or forgotten myths, a terrain polluted by bad thoughts and unpleasant dreams. These were always liable to be understood in a contrary sense, and the present owner has added fibreglass dinosaurs to the sixteenth-century stone population to turn the Freudian phantasmagoria into childish pranks that will increase Bomarzo's appeal to modern children.

When we come to diffusion northwards of Italian architectural innovations, fascinating inequalities in the development occur, like bunched-up fabric. Especially in England but also in France in the most interesting cases, we seem to jump over the clear, rational phases of the early Renaissance straight into deviant, eccentric forms.

Unlike his English contemporaries, Philibert de L'Orme had spent considerable time in Rome in the 1530s. Apparently he felt a need to distance himself from these sources or to transmute his borrowings into something rich and strange, barely recognizable. Thus the elaborate tombs for François I at St Denis, especially one for his heart, a cross between architecture and jewellery. The most exquisite features of the château built for the king's mistress at Anet are hoisted out of reach to animate the roof. These look like sarcophagi on tall pedestals but are actually chimneys, exorbitant instances of imparting high meanings to base necessities.

The chapel at Anet takes its place in the series of small round temples of the Renaissance. It knits together the space by matching the spiralling coffers of its little dome to a spiral pattern in black and white marble on the floor, three- and two-dimensional versions of the same pattern, one flattened by distance, the other creating the spectre of an abyss.

For equally sophisticated illusionism in England perhaps one needs to turn to Shakespeare's gorgeous, baffling and claustrophobic poems, written while theatres were closed by the plague. *The Rape of Lucrece* and *Venus and Adonis* turn people into jewellery and grisly murders into occasions for figurative language pushed to the verge of logical collapse.

By comparison, English architectural effects are crabbed and amateur, like Thomas Tresham's Triangular Lodge at Rushton, not apparently a

Philibert de L'Orme, Anet, château gateway, where sarcophagus chimneys are just visible in front of the chapel towers, 1547–52.

Thomas Tresham's Triangular Lodge, Rushton, Northamptonshire, an architectural meditation on the Trinity worked out by an amateur while in prison for his Catholicism, 1595–7.

trivial conceit but a passionate intellectual construction thought up by an imprisoned Catholic to show his devotion to the Trinity in safely coded form.

Strangely regular forms in the plans of prodigy houses by Robert Smythson like Hardwick in Derbyshire and Wollaton near Nottingham are not arcane expressions of religious fervour. But they seem an almost superstitious harking-back to the crystalline layouts of medieval defences.

George Gower (attrib.), the 'Armada portrait' of Elizabeth I, the Queen turned into a cosmos by her clothes, c. 1590.

Robert Smythson, Wollaton Hall, Nottingham, 1580–88, an Elizabethan 'prodigy house' that borrows motifs from Continental engravings never meant for outdoor display.

He clings to these obsolete historical forms the way courtiers cling to tourneys and jousting armour. Portraits of Elizabeth I, much cruder and much livelier than comparable renderings of Florentine rulers by Bronzino, make the queen a kind of monster or machine whose animating force has gone out into her clothes, until she represents a whole cosmos. The owners of Wollaton, while commissioning a house like a fantastical model of a feudal castle, were becoming rich by mining coal on their estate. For a last brief moment they were able to combine the idea of a ruler and his building as divine constructs fallen from heaven with the beginnings of industrial entrepreneurship.

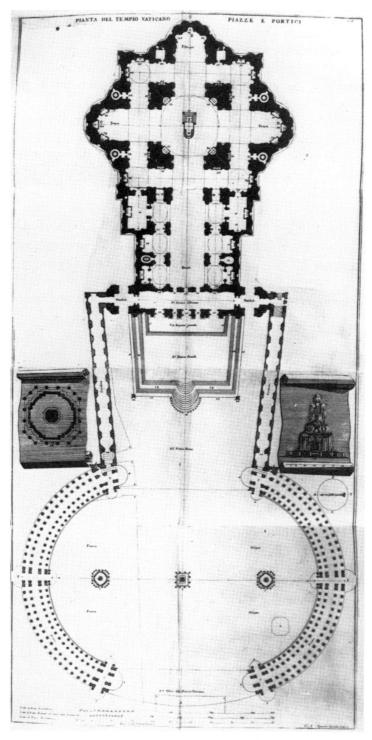

St Peter's, Rome, plan showing Bernini's colonnade of 1656–67 that creates a huge elliptical piazza (misrepresented as segments of circles in this engraving by Fontana).

9
Baroque

It seems fitting that the origins of the word *baroque* are in dispute. It isn't entirely at home in any European language and has been derived from widely different sources: a philosophical term for a twist or reversal in Scholastic argument, or a misshapen natural form, the baroque pearl. Both the incompatible sources imply deviation from a straight track, and distorted movement.

The architectural origins of the style in Counter-Reformation Rome are not in doubt. It is Catholic, expansive, absolutist, and Gianlorenzo Bernini was its first, most brilliant exponent, though not so much an architect in the Renaissance sense as the orchestrator of a mixing and blurring of mediums. The ideal Baroque composition storms and over-whelms the senses; one submits almost before one knows what is happening. At least that is how one imagines that Bernini's improvements at St Peter's were meant to work.

The order in which a visitor meets them is not the order in which they were built, but they form a connected experience described here as the perceiver encounters them, because the Baroque puts a new empha-sis on subjective fervour of response. Bernini's interventions magnify the scale of St Peter's by adding a huge outdoor room in front of the church. This consists of two stretches of colonnade – travertine columns planted four deep crowned by a giant entablature with a balustrade, on which parade a whole troop of agitated figures, one per column. Bernini likened this shifting expansive effect to a maternal embrace, on a scale that would terrify the heretic and astonish the infidel. The colonnades form a porous oval, open at a point directly opposite the façade of the basilica and enter-able at many others from surrounding streets.

By contrast with the circle favoured by Renaissance architects, the oval is a molten, unstable form, preferred in the Baroque for its animat-ing force and the multiplicity of viewpoints it generates. Bernini employs it at different scales: gargantuan at St Peter's, more intimate at Sant'Andrea

St Peter's, Rome, diagonal view of church from the Piazza, showing the colonnade as a producer of spatial fluidity.

on the Quirinal, where the viewer enters on the long side and feels the space swirl sensuously round him, the heated effect increased by rose-coloured marble coating on the walls.

At St Peter's Bernini orchestrates the whole progress of the worshipper and overpowers Michelangelo's structure without actually erecting anything very solid himself. With a gigantic altar canopy he creates powerful turbulence that affects the surrounding space. Though this construction is coated in metal, its forms are fluid. The whole twists and vibrates, starting from Solomonic columns and ending in an open canopy hung with fluttering cloth fringes rendered in gilt bronze.

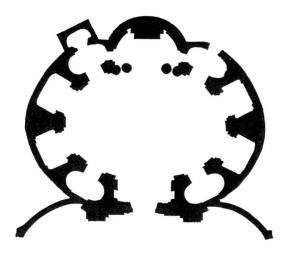

Gianlorenzo Bernini, Sant' Andrea al Quirinale, 1658–70, plan, the oval favoured by the Baroque on another, more intimate scale.

Gianlorenzo Bernini and Francesco Borromini, St Peter's, baldacchino, 1624–33, an altar canopy of twisting open form and unexpectedly solid, luxurious materials.

The movement does not stop there, for the canopy is also a frame, allowing a glimpse of a more sublime reality beyond. This ecstatic vision is actually the papal throne: surviving bits of the wooden chair of St Peter (now thought to be the coronation chair of Charles the Bald dating from 877), the most literal basis of papal power, are held aloft, as if in a reliquary shrine, by oversized Doctors of the Church in bronze. Clouds of infant angels surround the shrine and metal rays of light shower down upon it, issuing from an oval window of yellow alabaster like the sun emerging from clouds and representing the power of the Holy Spirit to inform the pope directly. For this is not just the gorgeous transformation of a few bits of old wood into a focus for prayer. It incorporates a functioning throne into which the pope can be lifted, and from which he can beam down on the faithful like the king bee at the centre of the ramifying hive (which is how Satan is shown in Milton's *Paradise Lost* in a space clearly modelled on St Peter's).

Bernini had had a practice run at such an orgasmic conflagration of sculpture, painting and architecture fourteen years earlier in a side altar at Santa Maria della Vittoria in Rome. There he interpreted a passage in St Teresa's autobiography in a novel fashion, turning it into a scene in a play. The saint and an angel appear in a recess lit by hidden sources. The young male angel pierces the languid female saint who levitates but threatens to slip off the cloud in the intensity of her delirium. This quintessentially intimate moment is observed by an audience of craning marble spectators, recognizable portraits of the donor's family, including members long deceased.

Bernini was apparently aware that he had employed sexual excitement as a metaphor for spiritual illumination. His piety went mainly

Bernini, St Teresa in Ecstasy, 1644–52, Santa Maria della Vittoria, Rome, a sensuous religious allegory.

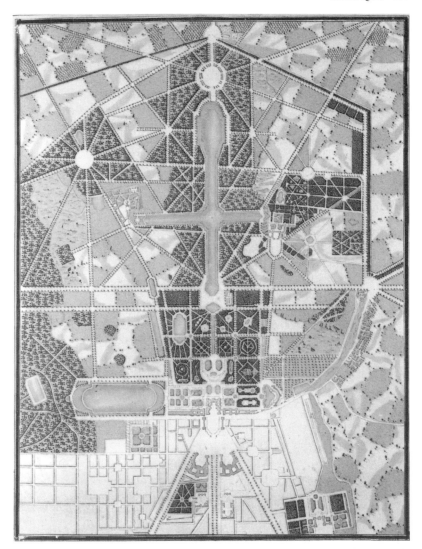

Versailles, plan of palace and gardens, a prime instance of the enormous scale and masterful geometry of the Baroque of rulers. Le Nôtre's involvement in gardens at Versailles, 1661–87.

unquestioned by his contemporaries, and his filtering of religious truth through a haze of expensive materials apparently expressed sincere devotion. But Bernini's is the Baroque of rulers, the right mode for authoritarian power at places like Versailles, where the canal in the figure of a cross measures three miles on its long axis, where thousands died of malaria digging artificial water features and turning the landscape as far as the eye could see into a single work of art.

There is another Baroque, represented best by Bernini's rival Borromini, whose presence in Rome is less conspicuous than Bernini's, though he built nowhere else. In Bernini's hands the oval is an expansive, easy form. In Borromini's it is difficult, recondite, obscure, and he arrives at it only after a struggle, or at least a sinuous sequence of thought. He collaborated with Bernini on the Baldacchino for St Peter's, eventually felt used and cheated by him, and found his first independent commission building a Roman outpost for poor Spanish monks on a cramped site near Bernini's later Sant'Andrea, built for the more prosperous Jesuits.

Working for such clients, Borromini couldn't afford expensive marbles, but they wouldn't suit him anyway. His natural inclination points towards architecture as a practically colourless medium, from which the thought shines forth unimpeded. Partly because of its scale and complexity of detail it is tempting to include San Carlino in the series of centralized *tempietti* of the Renaissance, following Bramante and De L'Orme, followed by Guarini and Santini.

But if San Carlino started in a centralized plan you can hardly tell that now. The central core of space has been so crushed and distorted by fitting itself to the narrow site that even the oval to which the circle obligingly adapted itself is barely recognizable below the level of the dome. The walls undulate irregularly, held together by piers now almost notional in the corners, marked by closer spacing of columns and the only straight stretches of wall, the shortest sections of all.

Borromini made drawings explaining some of the underlying geometric principles of the space. They seem to say that this room that is all curves was projected from two equilateral triangles. Whatever the truth of this bizarre suggestion (the clients were Trinitarians and would presumably appreciate having the ruling symbol of the order so deeply embedded in the fabric), it doesn't begin to describe our experience of the space, which incorporates incompatible hints at forms that aren't actually there: four arms of a cross, for instance, strongest in deep, eccentric coffering above the entablature that fills stretched lateral and pinched axial lobes, which would expand if they weren't held in by some perverse rigour. The old classical compulsion to harmonize the circle and square, the sphere and the cube, makes a last-ditch appearance in these foreshortened and contracted apses. How else can one explain the angular gable forms, corresponding to the columns beneath but made to follow the curve of the apse, their two halves shrinking and leaning towards their meeting in a complete travesty of their original form?

Overhead the oval at last becomes perfectly clear at the base of the dome where the plain classical moulding is finished off with an emblematic balustrade like that on Alberti's sepulchre in San Pancrazio. This one is different, though, visible all at once as a complete crown of martyrdom and marking the inside not the outside of the sponsoring form. The dome is wonderfully lit by the lantern and entirely covered or rather carved with coffering. Apparently there are late antique or early Christian

Borromini, San Carlino, Rome, 1638–41, facade completed after the architect's death in 1667; this was Borromini's first independent commission, carried out for a poor Spanish order of monks.

Borromini, San Carlino, view into the oval dome, whose coffering includes the emblem of the order.

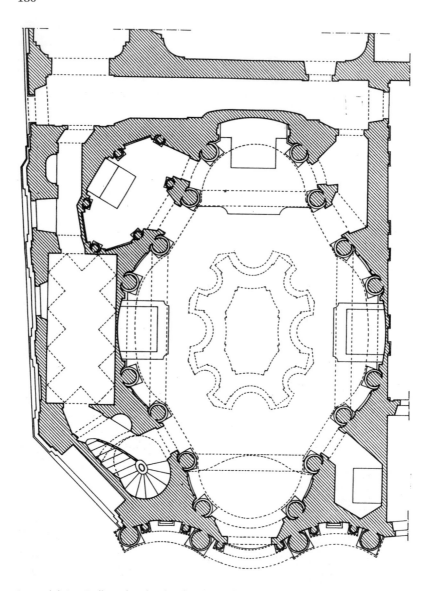

Borromini, San Carlino, plan showing the extremely individual forms Borromini arrives at, having started from ordinary triangles and ovals.

precedents for the bewitching pattern of these coffers, but like De L'Orme's transfer of classical mosaic designs to three dimensions on intensely curved surfaces, these interlocking crosses and octagons become something else when implanted on this hollow form like the inside of the skull. We are staring into negative, conceptual space, the final triumph in the attempt to turn sluggish masonry into pure thought.

Students of Borromini's work persist in the face of much contrary evidence in the belief that his work remains hidden, overlooked, a secret.

The summit of his career, Sant'Ivo della Sapienza, a chapel for the university, followed a tortuous course over the reigns of three popes and looked doomed to incompleteness at different stages. Instead of an expansive public square it inhabits a pinched court, from the end of which it springs up like an apparition, the convexity of its dome fighting free of the concave storeys beneath. The dome does not resemble a dome but

Borromini, Sant' Ivo della Sapienza, Rome, 1642–60, a university church hemmed in by a relatively narrow court and bursting forth in an extraordinary display of unplaceable elements.

another bulging solid, periodically confined by a sober order. The cornice here is one of the oddest details in all of Borromini. What looks like normal egg and dart turns out to be a little row of winged and grimacing heads, not *putti* but bald men of a certain age, looking in different directions, too uncomfortably individual to allegorize as stages of learning.

There have been many attempts to account for what comes next, a sequence Borromini called the *tempietto* on the *tempio*. It is a disguise for the lantern that starts with concave arcades *à la* Baalbek (not that Borromini knew the temple of Venus in the Lebanon) and then turns into a spiral ziggurat like a smaller version of the big minaret on the oldest mosque at Samarra. Unlike the minaret it is encrusted with baubles like the horns of a snail and dotted with oversized jewels in stucco. On top of this a flaming laurel wreath in stone. To cap that Borromini devised an airy three-dimensional crown of iron that he made the smiths cast and recast many times until the profile was just right.

Such a rush of disparate forms, such a dizzy ascent to lift them out of reach – it seems a final move in a game of hide and seek where no one is meant to follow. The exclusion wasn't literal. According to Joseph Connors, the most determined and imaginative student of this architect, climbing the spiral for the view was a popular pastime when it was new, but the symbolism is so heterodox and so congested we cannot expect to solve it and had better just enjoy our mystification.

Borromini, drawing of the plan of Sant' Ivo della Sapienza, which began from two intersecting triangles forming a six-pointed star, the points of which are then manipulated to create two contrasting geometries.

Borromini, Sant' Ivo della Sapienza, view into the dome showing the two geometries of the plan in their clearest manifestation.

The plan of Sant'Ivo is a landmark in the history of architecture and takes the Renaissance fascination with geometrical overlay that packs multiple figures into the same space to new and never surpassed heights. While it was under construction the story got about that the plan was based on the Barberini emblem of the bee, an idea that is certainly barking up the wrong tree, but starts from something real, an extreme complexity of outline with jutting features that people assumed were trying to look like some recognizable bit of reality.

In fact the plan is abstract but extremely complex. Two equilateral triangles are overlaid to form a perfect six-pointed star of wisdom. Since among other things this would make an unattractive space with six unusually sharp corners, the arms are treated as two sets of three and systematically truncated and enlarged until superficial resemblance to triangles is lost. They become alternating concave and convex crimpings of the space carrying the system of the dome down to the floor.

Looking up inside the dome is one of the strangest and most twisted of spatial experiences. Nothing holds still, and window frames alternate between concave and convex. Instead of Renaissance stillness, ceaseless broken movement. The star hidden to the point of invisibility in the plan breaks out in profusion in this shattered heaven. All the steeply arching ribs are lined with large eight-pointed and less-large six-pointed stars in deep relief, all in plaster and all in tones of white. The restoration of Borromini's monochrome interior has proved that the detail in his enigmatic ornament is emphasized, not lost, when colour is removed.

Guarino Guarini, San Lorenzo, Turin, 1668–80, view into a dome that is like a mathematical puzzle which fractures space by allowing bursts and slivers of light to illuminate the fabric in a variety of ways.

The vault of Sant'Ivo was completed while Guarino Guarini was studying in Rome. Apparently the record one would love to have of conversations between these two men does not exist. Perhaps they never met. The line connecting them remains one of the most compelling links in all of architecture. Guarini was a priest and mathematician who came to Rome to study theology, not architecture, whose early work in

Lisbon, Messina and Paris exists now only on paper. Until 1997 one could study the culmination of his bold spatial experiments in Turin. Then the more complex of these two extraordinary works, a reliquary chapel added to the cathedral, was badly and perhaps irreparably damaged by fire. But Guarini's church of San Lorenzo still survives intact. The leitmotif of this space is piercing or hollowing out. Walls are turned into filigrees of columns and arches in order to reveal spaces beyond them, half seen and mysteriously lit from sources only partly visible. Spaces of ambiguous form open up in series, a special room for the chancel and a further one for the altar. It feels fictitious or hypothetical, like a mathematician's breaking of motion into moments in order to understand it.

The experiment culminates overhead in a series of domes, domes like puzzles, which have been dissected into tissues of ribs more like the vault in front of the mihrab in the mosque at Córdoba than Brunelleschi's serene simplicity. The greatest novelty is that the web has been pierced in every conceivable manner to admit light from many directions, but also to create voids and discontinuities in the fabric, as if to show how much can be taken away leaving the building standing, hence closer to late Gothic than to Renaissance attitudes to structure. Again, as on the ground, the sequence continues in further stages, and the dome opens into another dome beyond with a further system of ribs and two rings of punctures letting in still further bursts of light. The simple colouring scheme husbands the light in little prismatic receptacles that are painted lighter colours than the surrounding walls.

Trickery with light is an old Baroque device. Bernini employs it to increase the seductive pull of dying saints, while Guarini uses it to make geometrical truths appealing to the senses. His most demanding project is the chapel attached to the altar end of Turin Cathedral to display an important relic, the Holy Shroud. The relic was a dynastic prize, only recently arrived in Turin, owned by the royal house but authenticated by the Church. A plan from around the time of the consecration shows this complicated position clearly. The back wall of the cathedral has been removed and the cylinder of the chapel intrudes marginally but forcefully into the apse. Externally, of course, the new chapel dominates the skyline, towering above the smaller dome over the crossing. On the plan the new building entirely fills the space between church and palace and the two jurisdictions are colour-coded: palace walls are yellow, church walls purple. The Shroud chapel, including the altar displaying the relic, is shown in yellow, and the interlocking between the two colours is a complex entanglement.

The Shroud has been compared to an electrical phenomenon, a picture impressed on Christ's grave clothes by an immaterial force radiating

Guarini, Chapel of the Holy Shroud, attached to the Cathedral, Turin, 1667–90, a further development of the dome broken into segments and lit in many increments to create effects of baffling complexity.

from His divine body and leaving physical traces that can be picked up by human eyes and interpreted as a ghostly presence. To house this unusual optical phenomenon Guarini devised a very tall space of circular plan lightly impinged on by two circular vestibules at the ends of umbilical passageways. The entire space is coated in black marble that has acquired a dusky richness over time. The shock comes when one looks up and sees what has happened to the favoured termination of such spaces in the Renaissance. Instead of the continuous surfaces of a dome, diminishing imperceptibly to completion, above the drum the curves have fractured into a staccato series of angles and the single fabric has become a precarious tower of separate layers.

The substance of the walls is so thoroughly eaten away to make windows that only a staggered pyramid formed by their flimsy frames remains. At the top in place of a lantern, the cut-out pattern of a giant star-burst, electrified at the edge by bright light coming from beyond what we can see and filled in the centre by a gold sunburst higher still. As we expect with Guarini, there are multiple unseen light sources in this final theatrical space far above.

As at San Lorenzo and even more so, the accepted terminology of domes does not fit. You could describe these parts very differently: the curved lower surfaces are part of a truncated dome, cut off to admit the telescoping hexagonal tower, which performs the role of an oversized lantern (a second storey as tall as the first) that is then closed by a further dome with a spire growing out of it. The trouble with this analysis is that it is derived entirely from studying the printed section and does not correspond at all to one's experience of the space.

Yet the whole effect is as much a diagram as it is a picture. Guarini has gone even further than he did at San Lorenzo in alienating his most concentrated meanings from everyday reality. The illumination in this dome, which bears uncanny external resemblance to Borromini's Sant' Ivo, is defiantly unnatural. But this is Baroque theatre deflected in an unaccustomed direction to say that miracles cannot be made smoothly continuous with normal vision.

The fire of 1997 has brought to light previously unknown features of the building, like the crucial role played by metal chains and belts in holding the dome together. Apparently the tiered arches form no part of the system of support: sizable gaps in them have no effect on the stability of the fabric. It was also confirmed by examination just before the fire that ocular as well as structural deceits play a crucial part in the effect made by the dome. The stone used varies in tone from black to much lighter grey and the tones are graded from top to bottom to make the ascent appear steeper and longer than it actually is. Illusory effects in fresco now destroyed had recently been discovered and would have been revealed by cleaning.

The period of study required before Guarini's construction is so thoroughly understood that it can be accurately rebuilt has turned out to be extremely long. The works of Borromini and his heir Guarini do not reveal themselves at once or even at last. San Carlino is small, but the two little hexagonal chapels at opposite ends of the main space are much smaller. San Carlino is relatively austere, but its crypt is barer still. And yet even these smaller or barer, inferior or left-over spaces are so densely packed with thought that the most devoted study will not exhaust them.

The divergence between the senses and the intellect exploited by Guarini becomes more grotesquely evident in the most interesting work of Jan Santini Aichel, an architect from an Italian family naturalized in Bohemia who was sometimes given the task of re-Catholicizing churches wrecked in the religious wars, where he was apparently instructed to keep them Gothic. So he evolved the idiosyncratic hybrid style usually called Gothic Baroque, which is to say Baroque structures made out of residually Gothic forms like pointed arches and rib vaults.

Such descriptions do not prepare one for the fractured reality of his pilgrimage church of St Jan Nepomuk near the monastery connected with the saint displaced to Zelená Hora in Moravia. Santini had earlier built a cemetery nearby, dedicated to the Trinity, in the form of a three-leaf clover with a pavilion in the middle of each lobe. Before long an abbot wanted it bigger and added a fourth, wrecking the symbolism but enlivening the plan. The pilgrimage church has been confused with the earlier project, possibly by those who haven't been there and who therefore get the scale wrong of this church, which can hold 2,000 pilgrims and thus cannot reasonably be called a chapel, as it has been in some surveys of the Baroque.

Like the cemetery compound concretizing the Trinity, the pilgrimage compound based on a five-pointed star of martyrdom reveals itself most clearly from the air. The church makes a beautiful crystalline figure and sits inside another starburst or ten-petalled flower formed of cloisters at a distance, like an exhalation from the core. These geometrical phantasms are reminiscent, first, of Jan Nepomuk's torture and death – five stars appeared over his floating corpse, thrown from Charles Bridge in Prague by his torturers – and, second, his devotion to the Virgin whose stars have ten points. To the pilgrim all of this is evident as multiplied concavities in the perimeter wall, like martyrdom perhaps in jagged incompleteness, materializing voids more powerfully than solid forms.

The church itself, serene in plan, resembles in its immediate presence a body broken on the rack. It is framed by disjointed backward-facing prisms that turn out to be stairs. Over the entrance a distorted gable sticks up like a twisted tongue, pierced by a sword-shaped window. When Jan Nepomuk's body was exhumed in 1719 as pressure grew for his beatification, his tongue, cut out by his tormenters because he wouldn't reveal the secrets of the confessional, was found uncorrupted.

So the two emblems of different vintages, the tongue and the stars, are incorporated differently in his building by Santini, the stars most powerfully in the plan, though bristly little stars also stick out all over it, the tongue more locally, though the stair extensions that come between the five star-lobes look like tongues in plan. By convention, five five-pointed stars appeared over the river, so five chapels ring the central space. Large five-pointed figures are superimposed on one another in at least three tiers in the plan, each time rotated 180 degrees, like Sant'Ivo carried a few steps further. Like Crashaw's ultra-Catholic English poems of the century before fixated on tears and blood, the building incorporates the pain of martyrdom in an elaborate intellectual structure, not actualizing the

Jan Santini Aichel,
St Jan Nepomuk,
Žd'ár nad Sazavou,
Moravia, 1719–22,
detail of facade,
Gothic forms in
Baroque arrange-
ments that refer to
particular parts of
the saint's martyred
body.

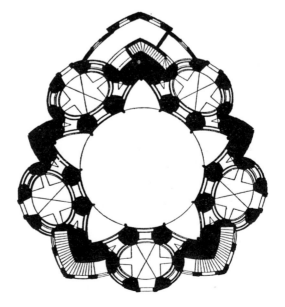

St Jan Nepomuk,
Žd'ár nad Sazavou,
plan, incorporating
the saint's emblem in
an exfoliating design
that looks like a
botanical study.

gore but converting it to geometrical solids heavy with meaning, meaning that suffered only a trivial setback when the fabled tongue turned out in later scientific tests to be a piece of brain tissue.

Baroque expansiveness that had its beginnings in Renaissance enthusiasm for centralized structures portraying the cosmos, which came in later stages to embody serious hagiographic visions, reached attractive fulfilment in large but unserious playgrounds like the Zwinger complex at Dresden. On one level it is no more than a festive tabletop on which toy soldiers could perform manoeuvres to amuse a provincial prince and his court. It was inaugurated by a royal wedding at a time when many of its galleries and pavilions were ready to be looked at but not used: the interiors had still to be fitted out. Looking from one side to the other of the unfilled space, it seems loosely enclosed with mostly light and flimsy elements. The tallest piece, the Kronentor, is delightfully complicated but useless, an oversized table ornament that serves as a gateway and viewing platform and carries dynastic emblems and references of absurdly inflated size. The beauty of the Zwinger, as opposed to truly pompous works like the palace at Versailles, is its lightness and transparency. You can see straight through its most imposing structures. The main sculptor, Balthasar Permoser, is better known for little ivory figures, and the frilly detail of the cavorting stone throngs in Dresden takes no notice of their actual scale, with the result that everything here is intimate as well as huge.

What got built is only the first stage of a complete new royal palace, in part doubtless prompted by the Elector's position as King of Poland from 1697. Pöppelmann, the architect, claimed that this garden-like outdoor room was inspired by a Roman theatre as described in Vitruvius. Was he hoaxing his royal patron and perhaps himself as well? Some parts of this garden-architecture were assigned more substantial contents: corner pavilions held the growing ducal library and other pavilions his collections of art and curiosities, making a rich and fantastic world and leaving the ways in which all of it was really grand or finally little forever in doubt. It was the ultimate Rococo act to start with the most amusing rather than the most necessary parts of the new palace.

In the Rococo, boundaries are deliberately blurred, between inside and outside, between sacred and secular, between one art and another. Thus stone carving imitates more temporary materials, fluttery cloth or flimsy papier mâché. Thus water is incorporated in un-static forms. If you have a steep slope you can engage in long drawn-out play coaxing a rivulet downhill, pretending it wants to stop along the way, or that it gets lost and is found again.

There are Portuguese penitential routes along which water provides the connecting thread, like the stairs of the shrine at Bom Jesus near Braga, where Fountains of the Five Senses mark stages between little dioramas of

Matthäus Pöppelmann, Zwinger, Dresden, Kronentor, 1713, gateway in the courtyard that held the Duke's library and collections of art and curiosities in corner pavilions.

the Passion in fictional pavilions punctuating the climb. Putting religious instruction outdoors like this almost inevitably makes it a more subjective, perspectival experience. How can the devout mind not stray to the peripheries? Hasn't the instructor given up the pretence of control and set the learner free in the wider natural world, which everyone is coming to see as the province of increasingly secular science?

A compelling parallel to the Rococo taste for outdoor rooms is the vogue for bower-like interiors. Strangely enough, the most light-hearted designs occur in churches, like those based on varieties of oval plan by Dominikus Zimmermann in southern Germany. At both Steinhausen and Wieskirche a double-wall system – tall piers supporting the vault not far in front of the outer wall – is used to confuse the boundary. At

Wies the inner layer of wall comes apart in quasi-natural sprays of water and foliage. In the chancel the arcade merges with the ceiling in cloud effects, and whimsical punctures give views through to further punctures in different planes.

All these forms are at one and the same time rather bulky and verging towards non-existence. The paradox is achieved by effects of light, hard-to-pin pastel colours enhanced by splashes of gold and silver leaf, shined on from loopholes in the walls like openings in clouds.

Correspondence between inside and outside is often slight in these buildings. Zimmermann favours nondescript envelopes in which strange window shapes make arbitrary incisions. Such contrast only heightens the explosive effect of interiors whose 'naturalism' is luxurious artifice. The grotto-pulpit at Wies presents a garden feature in wood and plaster, glittering like a jewel but simulating simple things like water and rock. Water translated into silvered plaster suggests a spontaneous effusion of wealth that is now pouring toward the spectator.

The root experience at Wies seems deeply at odds with such engaging architectural devices. This church was built to accommodate floods of pilgrims coming to worship an unattractive but miraculous image of the Scourged Christ, which had been despised like the Being it represents and banished to a peasant dwelling, whose occupants began to notice real tears glistening in its eyes, after which the crowds started to appear. The church is the exotic flower that springs up in the remote meadow watered by these tears, exorbitant and unwarranted in proportion to the miracle. It is a kind of garden in a landscape, whose unexpectedness is its point. At the same

Dominikus Zimmermann, Die Wies, pilgrimage church, Bavaria, 1744–54, view of the chancel arcade and vault showing cloud effects in punctures over columns.

time such buildings can be seen as standing near the beginning of the eighteenth-century move towards the simple, the natural and the true, to be found outdoors in a union with non-human elements of Creation.

Another pilgrimage church in a remote location in northern Bavaria marks the spot of another peasant vision, and thus corresponds to this sentimental idea of the roots of religion. The church at Vierzehnheiligen actually raises a sculptural interpretation of this 300-year-old vision as the crucial focus of a magnificent interior. This means that the high altar is upstaged by a powerful concoction that blocks the nave and makes it impossible to enter or be in this church without thinking of the vision that provoked the building in the first place, a building that now becomes much more literally than Wies a container for the vision, placed at its service. It is possible for a visitor to Wies to leave without realizing that the gruesome little Scourged Saviour actually brought into being the beautiful architectural phantasm that now dwarfs it.

By a strange coincidence the disposition of forces at Vierzehnheiligen duplicates or forecasts the new liturgical arrangements of the last forty years in which the main altar is moved from the far end of the space to somewhere nearer the middle, a shift towards a more democratic idea of the ceremony, but also perhaps a return to centralized organizations of ritual space, as embodying a more accessible conception of wholeness and the unity of Deity and individual worshipper.

At Vierzehnheiligen the shrine looks like a momentary occurrence, a state coach that has come to a temporary halt in its progress. But a glance at the plan shows that this arrangement was not imposed on an unwilling architect. The focus has been displaced to the centre by spatial causes deeper than the dislodging of an altar. The swirling of the space and the fraying of its contents are parts of a single process. Lots of subsidiary nodes of energy are set up, in half-open, half-closed side chapels and in circular 'transepts' loosely allied to the central oval.

The shrine is a descendant of Bernini's baldacchino at St Peter's, which expands and at the same time collapses the original idea of an open pavilion under an enclosing roof. It forms a tiered mound whose upper reaches sway in the spiritual breeze. Finding places for fourteen saints has resulted in four perspective series of three figures that shrink dramatically as they ascend. Their lopsided poses make them points of activity, not rest, and the supporting fabric is coming apart. The natural sources of its forms are rocks eaten away by water, and spray colliding with solid matter or spending itself in air. All the bubbling movement of oddly mixed materials – stone, metal, plaster, and each of them imitating the others – suggests both decay and an outpouring of insubstantial wealth. The cyclical movement depicted hints at the paradoxical wastage in all expenditure, generating melancholy.

Balthasar Neumann, Vierzehnheiligen, pilgrimage church, 1743–63, view of the nave with a tiered shrine to 14 saints in the middle of the space.

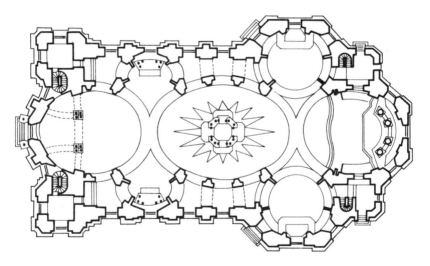

Neumann, Vierzehnheiligen, plan, a version that emphasizes the sequence of elliptical and circular vaults.

The Rococo stucco workers of south Germany produced wonderful transfigurations of heavy architectural matter into archetypally momentary form, but it is an intensity that carries its own dangers within it. In Watteau's paintings there's a similar turning to the natural world, which deepens and makes numinous the most casual human acts. But the pleasure-seekers seem to know already, even as they set out, that these joys will end in disappointment. The most fervent expressions of colour and

Giacomo Serpotta, Oratorio del Rosario di Santa Cita, Palermo, 1685–1718, teeming with figures that hang from, or burrow into, walls; sculpture turning itself inside out to become a container.

brushwork occur in women's clothes where satin and silk turn to water and cloud, beautiful transformations that cannot last. Raptures in plaster share the same fate.

The Baroque ambition to set every atom of the fabric in motion, and do away entirely with the fixity and permanence of walls, reaches un-heard-of heights in regional outposts, of which there are so many that no account can include them all. It is an expansive style in that sense too, spawning local variants in Naples, Catania, Porto, Goa, Andalucia, Mexico, Peru and St Petersburg. A strong instance of peripheral Baroque as the most extreme of all is the work of Giacomo Serpotta in Palermo. He starts with altarpieces in large churches but his most original composi-tions are transformations of nondescript boxlike rooms, oratories for confraternities of devout laymen, into teeming environments like altar-pieces you can walk into and stand encased in.

It is as if a complex sculptural work had turned itself inside out and become a container instead of a free-standing object. The walls now pullulate with figures, mostly infants, who are able to cling to swags of rumpled fabric or to perch unsteadily on jutting frames enclosing dioramas where tiny adult figures enact pompous scenes. Babies, because their movements aren't controllable and because their weight makes the whole gravity-defying spectacle a little less improbable. There is a saving austerity, essential in keeping the commotion from descending into chaos – this vision is practically colourless. Except for an occasional lute or trumpet or wall sconce picked out in gold, all the plaster is off-white, polished to simulate marble. One of Serpotta's cleverest discoveries was a method of incorporating marble dust in the last coat after the light frame of wire and cheesecloth had got its stucco covering.

Sicilian Baroque is notable for pushing out the boundaries in other ways too, putting things in the street that would normally stay indoors, whole populations of grotesques on the façade of a palace in the main street of Scicli, for example. A favourite architectural motif is the balcony, a kind of indoor–outdoor space, the inside billowing into the outside, a cornice bulging into a balcony, then subsiding back again.

Baroque in a whole series of towns in south-eastern Sicily was stimulated by an earthquake in 1693, after which they rebuilt in flamboyant forms of the new style. Most of the energy in the churches of Noto, Modica and Ragusa goes into elaborate façades, spurred on perhaps by the play of shadow in the strong Sicilian sun.

For the most elaborate of all Baroque façades, though, one must go to Spanish colonies in the New World, where native carvers carrying out European instructions created the liveliest and most illogical of all Baroque deviations from classical norms. Apparently the forms were first devised indoors in wood and stucco as extravagant backdrops for altars called *retablos* that eventually took over the whole wall, even creeping round corners and spreading onto the ceiling. These constructions typically marshall armies of columns that stretch the whole height of the space and collide with their neighbours on both sides. They are barely recognizable as columns, having put out shoots like living things and generated ledges, scrolls, hollows and bulges that destroy all continuity.

At some point these complicated visions in gilded wood migrate outdoors and turn into stone. Here they are free to grow even taller and expand sideways so their components can become larger and more numerous. In the most extreme manifestations, like La Compañía in Guanajuato and the Sagrario attached to the cathedral in Mexico City, by a mysterious reversion the last word in artifice resembles a natural form all over again, something dredged up from a coral reef or discovered where trees have plaited themselves together in the jungle.

The later stages of European Rococo are often striving after natural effects indoors. Such disruptive impulses shattering the stolidity of architectural form reach an unexpected fulfilment in England, which had not been hospitable to standard forms of either Baroque or Rococo. This fulfilment comes not in architecture strictly speaking but in constructed landscapes that alter radically the idea of a garden by seeking effects of artifice that can be mistaken for natural.

These result in some of the largest and most unbounded of all works of art, which incorporate the surrounding countryside by employing the ha-ha or sunken fence to conceal where the boundaries in the land-

Lorenzo Rodriguez, Sagrario, Mexico City, 1740–68, the parish church attached to the cathedral, view of side facade; though based on classical elements like columns, each unit is multiplied or subdivided until no longer recognizable.

owner's property lie, but are still recognizable as single compositions because grouped around focal features like irregular bodies of water created artificially by damming streams.

At Stourhead in Wiltshire there is a preferred direction for one's circuit of the features, many of which have by now disappeared, strung

Stourhead, Wiltshire, landscape garden, 1740s, the surprising apotheosis of Baroque expansiveness in a Protestant country generally unsympathetic to the style.

out around the lake. Some critics have found the hidden key in a single literary text, Virgil's *Aeneid* in this case, in spite of the fact that vanished episodes included Moorish tents, Chinese umbrellas, monkish hermits and rooms made of twisted roots.

Paintings like Fragonard's *Swing* portray a much vaguer and more sweeping symbiosis between Nature and man, Nature like a large emblematic orifice that might swallow one's daytime self entirely. Unlikely as it sounds, such constructions were actually built. The Grotto at Stourhead contains a series of pebble and rock-lined rooms that culminate at the nymph guarding the spring that feeds the lake. This is read by some as another literary episode, a bit of Virgil set in a reassuringly familiar Underworld, and by others as the plumbing of momentous new psychological depths. However serious or trivial one takes this probing of roots to be – akin to Marie Antoinette playing shepherdess in her rustic hamlet, or leading on to reawakened interest in Gothic architecture in the Protestant North and the whole Pandora's box of Romantic subjectivism – we have arrived by a clear progression at the furthest point from the style's origins in Bernini's Rome.

10

Historicism

In the nineteenth century the work of contemporary designers recapitulated in a disorderly way the entire history of architecture. This phenomenon, called 'historicism', is often seen as an uncreative dead end, the resort of those without ideas of their own who turn to copying others. But the most imaginative revivalists point the way beyond imitation and reshape our view of the past in the process.

It is true nonetheless that the nineteenth century gave a history to many aspects of reality that hadn't had one or had at least been satisfied with legendary accounts of where institutions and other cultural forms came from. In this transformation of perception first language and then texts were historicized, including the most venerable, which entailed a similar decomposing analysis of belief. Along with social forms and the natural world, architecture too acquired a more detailed and scientific picture of its own development.

Interest in historical forms was not new – the Renaissance is often described from this perspective – but the nineteenth century added an important new ingredient. Eighteenth-century Gothick as practised by Horace Walpole and his friends is not entirely inaccurate, but to later, more scientific eyes it looks random. A well-observed tomb recess becomes a mantelpiece and is watched over by a delicate fan vault in plaster. The designer borrows piecemeal and recombines the parts picturesquely to give a Gothic flavour at once more intense and more superficial than the real thing. Incidentally, when this approach is superseded it does not therefore entirely disappear. The picturesque and the scientific can occur conjoined in the much later Gothic revival of designers like Ninian Comper.

But this is not the main route followed by nineteenth-century historicism, and the crucial divide between Walpole and later Gothic revival is marked by works like Thomas Rickman's *Attempt to Discriminate the Styles of Architecture in England*, which established distinct phases of development within previously uniform fields like 'Gothic', gave all of these their own names (Norman, Early English, Decorated, Perpendicular) and began the process of assigning to each a distinct meaning. Architecture was on the way to becoming a specialized academic subject with a historical as well as a technical vocabulary, so that the practitioner needed to know more than he had just a moment ago.

The Gothic Revival is the great catalyst in the historicizing of nineteenth-century architecture, at least in England. But it doesn't enter an empty field; rather, it sets itself in opposition to an earlier revival, classicism in various guises. From here, both of these historical styles look like bulwarks against the style-less explosion of industrial buildings and related structures like bridges and train sheds that accompanied the Industrial Revolution, but this isn't how the revivalists saw it.

An earlier historicism, the reaction against the Rococo in the final years of the old regime, took the form of a cooler, pared-down classicism, which might still be delicate and 'feminine' like Marie Antoinette's Petit Trianon, but embodied a turning away from moral and aesthetic licence in search of a kind of purity. At the same time much more radical forms of this search appeared, marked by unbuildable grandiosity of scale and virtual absence of ornament. In the proposals of Etienne-Louis Boullée for museums, libraries, legislative halls and mausoleums, architecture becomes philosophy, grappling with the infinite and other concepts that aren't amenable to structural solutions.

Boullée is often paired with Claude-Nicolas Ledoux, another translator of Enlightenment ideals into ambitious architectural projects, who actually got some of his manifestoes built. He began by designing a series of imaginative town and country houses for aristocratic clients, which led to two important public commissions that gave him the scope to realize his frightening supra-individual dreams.

Although Ledoux's two schemes are vastly different in scale and type, they are obverse and reverse of a connected vision of architecture as it entwines itself with social life. The more visible scheme is a series of city gates in a new wall around Paris whose purpose was the collection of tolls. These ceremonial entrances would function primarily as barriers, where all of those entering the city would be searched, and taxes collected on goods brought in. For these structures of clearly repressive character Ledoux devised a rich vocabulary of simple geometric forms so purified to essentials that they looked gigantic – cubes, cylinders and arches more rudimentary than anything ever built before.

The other, more obscure project was a new town in the wilds of eastern France, an installation serving the government salt monopoly and placed in such a remote spot because this particular industrial process required plentiful timber that was converted to charcoal for drying the salt, a technology that had been replaced before Ledoux's vision, interrupted by the Revolution, could be realized.

The vision included Rousseauist idealization of the forest setting. The spacious layout of projected buildings, presented in persuasive bird's-eye view, does not look like a town. Through the power of rudimentary classical geometry all the empty space conveys not freedom but control. Distances between buildings are intimidating and suggest that design is a superhuman activity.

Only half of the projected circular core at Chaux was built, two matching saltworks framing the bristling Director's House, a central eye surveying the ring of dwellings that ray out from it. None of the strange public buildings instructing the populace in civic duties and sexual mores got built, nor did the dwellings that would have moulded people to their occupations and accompanying social roles. Ledoux had amused himself devising a complete alphabet of shockingly clear forms that would represent the lives lived inside them, architecture as definitive prescription.

Like other sweeping ideal schemes, Ledoux's has made critics wonder if he really meant it to be executed, but the forms are hard-headed and the architectural primitivism is followed out in compelling detail. Like many later projectors of vast schemes, Ledoux had a good grasp of architectural possibility narrowly defined and a poor one of political likelihood or human need. His designs remain a high-water mark of returning buildings to pure mass, unpenetrated stone solids that are sometimes so recalcitrant they only show part way above the ground they are pushing their way out of, or trying to return to.

The most imaginative English classicist, John Soane, also favoured radical reduction of surface detail. He attacked the survival of classical

Claude-Nicolas Ledoux, Chaux, 1774–9, the Director's house framed by saltworks in Ledoux's half-built ideal industrial community in the wilds of eastern France.

motifs like sacrificial altars and skulls of oxen as distasteful reminders of pagan rites, long discarded except in art. But he is not the literal-minded functionalist that such strictures might lead one to expect.

Detail is not missing entirely from Soane's buildings but appears half erased, as if rubbed off, and light filters in from hidden sources, increasing the sense of a dissolving fabric. His most complete surviving work, his own house in Lincoln's Inn Fields in London, was an exception originally in its small scale and extreme intricacy. Soane's collection of antiquities and curiosities has taken over the building as perhaps it did his life. Taken it over, leaving few of the blank surfaces that he otherwise favoured, but been subordinated at the same time to a controlling vision.

Soane's house can be described to sound like a Renaissance cabinet of curiosities, but this would be a blinkered view of these Romantic interiors, where individual objects are swept up into a compelling narrative, not samples itemized in separate cases, but vehement particles of connected discourse. They are inseparable from the architecture – intermittently one feels that they *are* the architecture, the parasites that have so overgrown the host they become it. So by a method remote from pastiche Soane has constructed a ruin that is alive, a series of reminiscences that constitute a space and become historical in a completely original way. He performs a merger, through architecture, of the development of a single sensibility and the history of a culture.

Soane is modern in the provisional character of his ideas and the temporariness of the personae his house asks one to assume. The visitor is successively an archaeologist, a Gothic hermit, a connoisseur. The thread that binds them is the idea of psychic space, which the house encourages us to see as deeper than previously suspected. Soane provokes the building's users into embarking on such journeys by playing with scale – small things presented as large – the gigantic rosettes on the hall ceiling, casts from a huge Roman basilica – or large as small – Soane's biggest projects implanted in model form in tiny spaces – tricks that loosen perception and encourage us to view architecture as taking place in the mind.

The museum became one of the great nineteenth-century building types, not as private treasure house, but as the commandeering of culture as part of the apparatus of the state. At least this is the way the cultural monuments designed by the greatest German classicist of the early nineteenth century seem to function. K. F. Schinkel's Altes Museum in Berlin makes a connection between antique architectural forms and Prussian political assertiveness. Like Soane, Schinkel is no slavish imitator. He takes the classical idea of peripetal columns and stretches it to the breaking point in the long horizontal façade, a consistency with little apparent focus. But the severity of the museum's façade is punctured and the

Sir John Soane, his own house, Lincoln's Inn Fields, London, where the fabric is sometimes so perforated and encrusted that it feels more like a ruin than a building. Soane's alterations began in 1792 and continued through the 1830s; this corridor dates from 1824 when the Picture Room was constructed.

experience transformed as soon as you enter. Now the building becomes scenographic, and you ascend behind a double screen of columns as in late classical temples like Apollo's at Didyma. These shifting perspectives remind one that Schinkel got his start as a designer of stage scenery and in later life went on painting theatrical architectural views like the

Karl Friedrich Schinkel, Altes Museum, Berlin, 1822–30, a long unpedimented front like the side elevation of a Greek temple.

famous 'Installing the Frieze of the Parthenon', which conveyed the mason's eye view, now repeated in the Altes Museum vestibule via stairs that take you virtually to the level of the capitals where all the details grow larger, the viewpoint is turned inside out and you look out on the city through an intervening frame of classical architecture. Schinkel has made us participants in the world of classical forms by means of a theatrical encounter that is almost filmic in its carefully worked out series of views.

Earlier in his career Schinkel had lost a battle over styles. He argued strongly that Queen Luisa's mausoleum should be a Gothic shrine enclosed in a little forest, but eventually found himself supplying classical details for the design actually chosen. Both Schinkel and Soane designed in Gothic mode when seeking certain gloomy, historical effects. For them it is a cue for a particular range of emotions.

This flexible attitude came under attack from the 1840s as Gothic forms took on heavy moral significance. England was the earliest European country to undergo traumatic industrialization, and naturally became the place where vehement opposition to these changes first occurred. Thus it happened that the Middle Ages came to represent above all a contrast with the present. Seeking a counterweight to the mechanized world conjured up by modern industry, designers and writers like Pugin and Ruskin veered violently backwards to pre-modern times, before canals, turnpike roads and standardized manufactures.

The Reformation had stripped English religion of much of its sensuous texture and variety. Dissenting sects that gained ground with the working class in towns went even further than the Established Church in rationalizing the outward aspect of religious observance. So it was in the beginning an evidently quixotic project to try and reconnect modern Britain with its Catholic past, as if the last three centuries could simply be wished away.

Pugin was a Catholic convert who started as a conventional antiquarian but came to imagine practising the rituals that went with the spaces and appliances that he studied and collected. So a conception grew up of an organic relation between one's aesthetic preferences and one's whole style of life. To be a medievalist might come to include living a medieval life in the present. One by one all kinds of outmoded apparatus of Catholic worship was resurrected – vestments, vessels, lights, screens and images of all sorts. Floors, walls, windows and roofs began to be inscribed with pattern and picture until hardly a blank surface remained.

Pugin's attention is usually more firmly focused on interior fittings than on the envelope that holds them. His most influential works were even more condensed, books not buildings, modelled in part on medieval manuscripts. So he crowds a lot of miniaturized detail into powerful bird's-eye views of medieval hospitals or monasteries or cathedral closes, without worrying that the analytical tool of the comprehensive dissected view couldn't be less medieval in spirit. Contrasts (1836), his most persuasive publication, even sets up a series of detailed visual comparisons between rooted medieval existence and sterile modernity bereft of the consolations of both art and the natural world.

To most people Pugin's name summons up an idea of restless patterns on every surface, stained-glass windows teeming with bright colours, and spaces subdivided by wood and metal screens. His theories about construction seem at odds with this profuse aesthetic. In his designs for household furniture ornament is unexpectedly subservient to construction, which Pugin takes pains to make clearly visible. Supports and joints are not concealed. Finishes do not hide the grain of wood or the presence of metal. The user can easily visualize the process by which the object was made. But it is an approach to design more evident in his furniture than his buildings, and in his vicarages than his churches. In these domestic projects artificial symmetries give way to irregular compositions dictated by pragmatic disposition of internal features. Materials also obey something more like functional imperatives, brick with modest amounts of stone trim that can be justified structurally, not simply by a liking for visual variety.

To be sure, Pugin arrived at this position by degrees. What began as a conventionally picturesque lack of system gradually traced its origin to

THE SAME TOWN IN 1840

1. St Michaels Tower, rebuilt in 1750. 2. New Parsonage House & Pleasure Grounds. 3. The New Jail. 4. Gas Works. 5. Lunatic Asylum. 6. Iron Works & Ruins of St Maries Abbey. 7. Mr Evans Chapel. 8. Baptist Chapel. 9. Unitarian Chapel. 10. New Church. 11. New Town Hall & Concert Room. 12. Wesleyan Centenary Chapel. 13. New Christian Society. 14. Quakers Meeting. 15. Socialist Hall of Science.

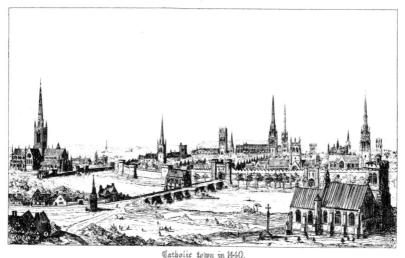

Catholic town in 1440.

1. St Michaels on the Hill. 2. Queens Cross. 3. St Thomas's Chapel. 4. St Maries Abbey. 5. All Saints. 6. St Johns. 7. St Peters. 8. St Alkmunds. 9. St Maries. 10. St Edmunds. 11. Grey Friars. 12. St Cuthberts. 13. Guild hall. 14. Trinity. 15. St Olaves. 16. St Botolphs.

A.W.N. Pugin, a plate from Contrasts (1836), showing the same English town in 1440 and 1840, with spires replaced by factory chimneys and devotion by greed.

a deeper kind of cause. Requirements of the life lived inside the walls overrode the wish to observe certain formal niceties. And so in pursuit of seamless wholeness of the resurrected medieval style of life, Pugin, the fervent believer who had a lavish chapel in his house right next to his private cathedral-scaled church, verged oddly near the greatest French student of Gothic, Viollet-le-Duc, atheist and structural rationalist. Yet it is a convergence more apparent than real. For Pugin, visible construction led to an interest in the mind of the worker and finally to the spiritualization of the whole process of design. In this phase at least the English Gothic Revival strove towards a sacramental view of labour rather than a simple style change.

Ruskin couldn't easily acknowledge a debt to Pugin because at that stage he was fiercely anti-Catholic, but he found it deeply congenial to regard the worker's effort an integral part of the meaning of the building. Architecture was stone that had become instinct with human feeling, a process that occurred not by remote transmission from tyrannical overseer to salaried employee but through the imagination of the carver in physical intimacy with the material.

Ruskin's relation to religion was ambiguous from the start. In his diaries it occasionally seems that for Ruskin Italian churches are simply the places where the most interesting paintings happen to have washed up. It is an important feature of the whole experience that looking at them isn't easy or comfortable. Services interfere and rouse him to fury, as cold and damp do not. Although writing home from Italy he frequently complains that no one now values these treasures properly – the obscurity in which he finds them confirms this neglect – we may well feel he relishes the role of discoverer. Interpreting disregarded marvels is tantamount to bringing them into being, and resembles the crystallizing act of fixing an especially complex rock face in a drawing.

When Ruskin describes the medieval workman he is describing himself and giving privileged place to the waywardness of his own character, capable of concentration so extreme it is like a kind of religious devotion, but applied so unpredictably that it results in the most eccentric picture of the reality it describes.

Of course, Ruskin's personal qualities did not come straight through into buildings designed by all those who were influenced by him, but there is an uncanny connection between Ruskin's attention to sensuous texture, which could lead one extremely far from codifiable system, and the route followed by the Arts and Crafts movement, starting in idiosyncratic varieties of historical imitation to end up in an aesthetic that had freed itself from resemblance to a model but clung even more fervently to an idea of authenticity with its roots in a scholarly approach to the history of styles.

An unusual number of nineteenth-century English architects wrote books about aspects of medieval architecture, usually focused on one country or even one region. Connections between such researches and their authors' own buildings were not always easy to pick out. Sometimes they were doubtless equipping themselves to deface more confidently the surviving medieval buildings of Britain, for there were always Revivalist architects who took a notably high-handed attitude to precedent in their independent commissions, like William Butterfield, who used modern materials to approximate Gothic effects more or less freely.

Butterfield occasionally covered the interiors of his churches in large easily read tile pictures of biblical subjects that abutted abruptly on

William Butterfield, Keble College, Oxford, 1868–82, view of chapel and buildings along the street front, inexpensive industrial brick used in variegated patterns as an analogue of medieval carved detail.

stained-glass stories of completely different scale. Framing the pictures were jittery patterns in coloured marble or brick and glazed tile. Bolder forms and harsher finishes than any medieval precedent were carried out in garish chemical colours unknown to earlier centuries. Butterfield was sometimes called on to justify these excesses by pointing to Gothic precedent. But to us he is most interesting for the ways he found of diverging from strict historicism towards a truly contemporary style that would reflect the pace and texture of modern life where printed advertisements shrieked for one's attention and mass production poured floods of coarse goods at the feet of a growing public. Instead of three-dimensional carving Butterfield often substitutes more easily laid patterning so bold it leaps from the walls. For all that he denies it, he is moving towards a mechanized equivalent of medieval ornament.

The street elevations of Keble College are as lively as anything in Oxford, but achieve their effects entirely in cheap, durable brick glazed in different colours and laid in wild patterns reminiscent of the spots on an animal's skin or the sequence of electrical impulses that make up a message in Morse code. Butterfield has made an ingenious halfway house ambiguously poised between the present and the past, which solves the problem of the unreality of the Gothic dream by disrupting it himself.

More delicate issues arise when nineteenth-century architects tackle the question of what to do with surviving medieval fragments, manhandled in the meantime by an unsympathetic eighteenth century. This seems an unlikely proving ground for the first shoots of a new architecture that was radically modern, but so it proved to be. Butterfield's solution to this particular dilemma was to signal the presence of the new work by using materials or finishes that couldn't be mistaken for medieval, in forms relatively sympathetic to and congruent with what was already there. Thus his metal screen on a heroic scale that closes the high arch of the central tower at St Bees in Cumbria. This screen obscures the wound left by the chopping off of much of the eastern arm of the building when the priory became a parish church in the sixteenth century. Butterfield's insertion makes an appealing mystery of an awkward amputation, and the clash of metal against stone is softened by the muted earth colours, as of fresco, that the metal is painted.

But there is a less flamboyant, nearly invisible style of resolving these design questions that is even more fruitful and prescient for the later history of architecture. It arises from the practical twist that William Morris gives to Ruskin's fantasies about medieval workmen. From Ruskin's powerful urge to personalize art comes a new appreciation of anonymous vernacular forms, handmade but generic. Perhaps the new appreciation surfaces first in the house Philip Webb designed for Morris at Bexleyheath on the south-east edge of London, a version of pastoral embodied in no-nonsense materials and forms of barely detectable Gothic flavour, whose excesses take the form of asymmetries and deliberate crudity of execution. Webb is a designer for whom simplicity entailed a difficult struggle. Every element of his only completed church design at Brampton in Cumbria is carefully thought out, with disjointed results of great integrity.

Philip Webb, Red House, Bexleyheath, Kent, 1859, in rustic vernacular with a few Gothic traces.

Different roofs cover matching aisles, dormers on one side and not the other. Suddenly near the altar an entirely domestic window pokes through high in a blank expanse of wall. Old hierarchies are violated and the building sometimes feels as much like a barn as a church.

In his own independent designs Webb produces something odd without strong personal flavour. In the corresponding treatment favoured by Webb and Morris for old buildings, the restored structure comes out looking more primitive and rustic than before the improvement. Floors and walls are returned to their ancient unevenness. Discarded but venerable appliances like Romanesque fonts or old altar slabs are put back in their traditional locations. Roofs replaced with old stone slates, ceiling woodwork re-exposed in its old rusticity – in short, the building encouraged to reveal its piecemeal character as a witness of diverse historical moments.

These ideas were codified as the programme of the Society for the Protection of Ancient Buildings (SPAB), an organization founded in 1877 in opposition to high-handed Victorian restorations, like Sir George Gilbert Scott's proposals for Tewkesbury Abbey. The Scott method aimed to raise the whole structure to the level of its best parts, leaving a consistent building ready to play the grandest possible part in the history of architecture. The SPAB method aimed at a new kind of authenticity, based on the idea of a building as a creature that has grown up over time, suffering reverses, recording conflict and giving a sense of bumpy passage. It also expresses a suspiciously socialist appreciation of the humble against the grand, the regional against the metropolitan, the unlettered against the sophisticated. Yet appreciation of vernacular forms was at this moment in these hands a sophisticated preference, rebelling against meaninglessly profuse or generally unthoughtful Victorian ornament. Morris designs are often almost as crowded as those they replace, but founded on firmer intellectual foundations.

And Morris and SPAB were not trying to escape from history completely, only to make a more discriminating choice of flavours. Morris began renting Kelmscott (a seventeenth-century Cotswold manor house) in 1871, and Gimson and the Barnsleys moved to the Cotswolds in 1894, followed by Ashbee and his Guild of Handicraft in 1902. The moves were made seriously and for keeps. They came to learn as well as teach, but were in a position something like the anthropologist camping among his tribesmen. They had discovered a vanished historical stage that survived intact in the present through the miracle of the obscure geographical pocket. The initial appeal of the vernacular is that it lies outside the history of architecture with its overbearing styles, but in the end, and in outsiders' hands, Cotswold vernacular becomes a style too, which can be reproduced, watered down or parroted too glibly like any other.

C.F.A. Voysey,
reversible cloth
in silk and cotton,
1898, a more stylized
version of rusticity,
leaves as Rorschach
mazes.

Other British designers like Voysey and Mackintosh were perhaps more successful in leaving historical flavours behind, but fell into aestheticist exaggerations instead, which make one suspect the influence of Continental Art Nouveau. Voysey's fabric designs are generally much emptier than Morris's, with a stronger sense of rigid but attenuated underlying geometry. The same combination of austere blankness broken by patches of untoward lushness crops up in his houses, where it reminds one of similar effects in English or Portuguese late Gothic. One tends to remember Voysey houses as being more stripped down and proto-Modernist than they are. The bold expanses of white pebbledash are interrupted by bay windows – which look more medieval when angular and stretching over two storeys – and even by oriels in designs of the 1890s, as at Colwall in Herefordshire.

The materials look regional – limewashed plaster, sandstone accents, green slates – but it is a Northern idiom that doesn't seem particularly at home in the South or East. Voysey's proportions are often the most compelling features and hard to trace to particular sources. Long, low silhouettes are strengthened by overhanging eaves, by strip windows and wide low doors that make one think of barns. These windows, made

C. R. Mackintosh, Glasgow School of Art, 1897–9, 1907–9, north-facing studio windows along the street facade; a Scottish castle vernacular tending toward Art Nouveau incorporates the British functional tradition of iron and glass.

to resemble slits, are the most perplexing feature, pokey but unyielding, as if the house needs to defend itself against ferocities of climate, yet also highly stylized, a minimalist effect marking a strange kinship with the Modernism Voysey professed to abhor.

Mackintosh pushes much further into pure aestheticism, favouring elongated vertical proportions that often suggest growth become spindly and therefore vulnerable. The two phases of the Glasgow School of Art show this at different moments. In the earlier studio wing Mackintosh goes in for uncharacteristically exposed structure, of factory-inspired bluntness. Iron lintels and window frames butt right up against dark masonry, and large expanses of glazing seem to be held in place by frail metal struts that break into brittle metal blooms at the joints.

In the later library obvious organic references are dropped, but flimsy verticality is if anything increased, this time in wood, inspired by Japanese design or the skeletons of insects. Voysey had sometimes switched axes on urban sites, still elongated but vertical not horizontal, as in the small house in Bedford Park in London, a complete break with the mellow brick consistency of the earliest garden suburb that surrounds it on all sides.

One hardly knows whether to count the garden suburb idea as backward- or forward-looking, as an attempt to turn the clock back to a village past and to pretend that such a mock simple life is possible on the edge of a modern city. Or, taking it as Le Corbusier did, a new idea of community designed from scratch to undo some of the unhealthy features of the historical city. Parker and Unwin, the most successful British projectors of early instances at New Earswick in York, Letchworth and Hampstead, worked out traffic hierarchies and ideal densities that have had wide influence since, while the communal buildings included in their schemes have been jettisoned by most of their descendants. One thing that wouldn't have pleased these early designers of ideal suburbs is the tight connection between their contribution and the car-dependent world that followed close behind.

W. R. Lethaby may occupy an even more precarious position between Arts and Crafts and modernity, between timeless tradition and a bare landscape cleared of every marker except the principles of rational structure. Lethaby wrote a book about Hagia Sophia, sometimes credited with setting in motion the Byzantine revival, and decorated an insurance building in Birmingham with obscure Sumerian symbols. But before many years had passed he turned against historical references altogether and ceased to practise architecture.

His last building, the parish church at Brockhampton in Herefordshire, is often regarded as one of the quintessential triumphs of the Arts and Crafts, but it must have been a humbling experience for the architect, who realized it could never be repeated. Though it incorporates a concrete vault, it disguises this up-to-date feature under a coating of thatch, and even more unexpectedly under an archaic form of pointed arch, almost Anglo-Saxon in its stilted awkwardness. The walls of red local stone are so irregularly laid that they resemble a bumpy weave. Window tracery in the same stone looks like oversized basketry, while the tower is eccentrically finished off by weatherboarding and wooden shingles. All in all, it is the most aggressively handmade building of its own or any other date and required kinds of on-site supervision that made a financial mockery of Arts and Crafts pronouncements about workmanship.

Later Lethaby woke up from the Arts and Crafts dream, but his laments over wasted hours studying cathedrals do not make pleasant

W. R. Lethaby, All Saints, Brockhampton, Herefordshire, 1901–2, a handmade building in local materials that conceal the nave vault in concrete.

reading. In the interval he had entered the competition for a new cathedral in Liverpool with an outrageously exotic Byzantine design capped by a folded concrete roof based on parabolic arches.

At this single point the comparison with Gaudí in Barcelona is very close and might cause one to speculate that in order to build such a behemoth Lethaby needed to be more of a fanatic. For all his radical structural

Antoni Gaudí,
Sagrada Família,
Barcelona, 1882
and still under
construction.
Spindle-shaped
towers of Gaudí's
'last great sanctuary
of Christendom'.

experimentation, it is hard not to see Gaudí as the end of something, the furthest edge of Gothic Revival, who takes the Ruskinian hypothesis of the individuality of the medieval workman further than it will go. Although Gaudí built a surprising amount, his career is also a graveyard of uncompleted projects, above all the Sagrada Família, like Brockhampton times ten thousand, which could never have been completed on Gaudían principles and only goes forward via the kinds of mass production its original designer would abhor. But – a more manageable subject for discussion – also in the church for the textile workers' colony outside Barcelona, a perversion of the ideal-suburb idea devised to save workers from the radicalism of the towns – the church that in ten years of construction never got further than its crypt, before being terminated by the Great War.

This poor fragment constitutes nonetheless the most complete and intense exposition of Gaudí's ideas about the relation between structure and expression, which comes to fruition in the porch under the empty platform on which the main space would have stood. This porch consists

Gaudí, crypt porch of unfinished church for textile workers' colony at Colonia Güell, near Barcelona, the latest, most idiosyncratic Gothic revival, 1898–1915.

of a double arcade of astonishing irregularity within a clear overall plan. The stone columns appear to twist like the trunks of trees responding to weather and forces of growth. The vault into which they branch and merge moves in more agile and unnerving ways, its ribs wrapping themselves in spirals in search of greater strength, the infill between ribs billowing as if moved by air currents overhead.

The materials are an unholy patchwork of industrial tiles, broken plates, odd-shaped pebbles, slag from a furnace, and bricks, no two of which look alike. The result is a fabric alive and changing as architecture cannot literally be, a picture of spontaneous development through natural process that is thoroughly unfaithful to how the building was actually built. But it is entirely faithful to what the building wants to mean. Gaudí uses his powerful rational understanding of structural principles to create beguiling illusions of instability and thus of exhilarating freedom from the laws he had so thoroughly mastered. Architects of the Gothic or Baroque would have sympathized, but in Gaudí's moment this was not the direction in which architecture was about to go.

11

Modernism I: Functionalism

Waking up to the variety and complexity of the past was one of the key developments of the nineteenth century, a time of the discovery and cataloguing of forgotten civilizations and the scholarly recovery of many past architectural forms. But in the end this marvellous weight of history became an overpowering burden from which artists of all kinds needed to escape. So in the decades before the First World War there's a great convulsion in all departments of culture desperately seeking the authentic mode of modern civilization. In this violent break with the past, artists, architects and musicians often drew on traditional sources after all, but ones outside Western fine art inheritance.

At some point in the early years of the Industrial Revolution in Britain, engineering and architecture had come apart, or at least a split had begun to appear (a split that in different forms goes back at least as far as Plato) between two radically different ways of solving large structural problems. Perhaps the attitudes which finally threatened architecture as conceived ever since the Renaissance sprang most immediately out of an interest in a new material, iron, viewed by most architects as profoundly un-architectural, perhaps because its strengths and limitations are so different from those of masonry.

Wanting to span the Severn at a place near Coalbrookdale in Shropshire now known as Ironbridge, and needing to clear the tall masted river traffic, in the vicinity of iron mills whose proprietor could use the project as a form of advertisement, a local architect proposed a single-span bridge made entirely of iron. As finally completed, five years after the initial proposal and intermediate cold feet among investors about the strange design, the bridge must have looked alarmingly insubstantial, composed of an airy web of thin members without heavy masses anywhere near the water. From railings to serious supports the iron bridge seems to consist mainly of air, until you reach stone piers under the roadway that don't actually have their feet in the water.

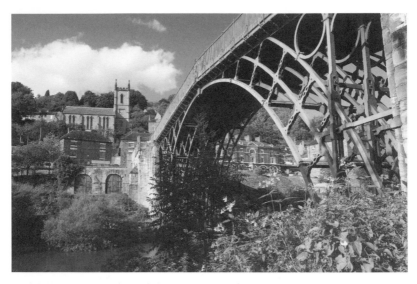

Ironbridge near Coalbrookdale, Shropshire, 1777–80, an early example of iron construction, lighter and cheaper than masonry, engineering edging out architecture.

For someone used to arched stone, brick or concrete construction, familiar since the Romans, this device appeared to defy basic rules and to take little notice of gravity. It is true that the bridge incorporates a few ornamental forms, like ogee arches near its ends. Though these are no more than flimsy tracery, perhaps they seriously deflect the structure towards garden buildings or other flights of Gothick fancy. In any case this breakthrough in construction doesn't seem to have given ideas to architects. Later metal bridges are generally framed by masonry towers and iron is relegated to inessential spanning jobs in greenhouses and conservatories until Joseph Paxton, the Duke of Devonshire's gardener, enters the fray surrounding the stalled competition to design the temporary housing for the Great Exhibition of 1851 in Hyde Park.

The resulting jump in scale is enormous. Suddenly iron and glass are thinkable for the most monumental constructions. Railway sheds had already employed the new technology at Bristol, where the iron structure was disguised as a hammerbeam roof, but the Crystal Palace was a spur to conceive the possibilities more ambitiously. After this came multiple naves (at Paddington, 1850–54, and King's Cross, 1851–2), curved tunnels of iron and glass (at York, 1871–7, and Bristol, 1871–8), and greater and greater spans (243 feet at St Pancras, 1866–8). Still, through all this exuberant development, the new materials continue to be despised or at least mistrusted. They need a veil of conventional masonry to cushion or mediate their entry into urban space. To allow the new scale of the train shed to appear in the street was permitted once, in a façade of brick and glass at King's Cross in 1851–2, and then not again in London for the rest of the

Sir Joseph Paxton, Crystal Palace, built in Hyde Park, London, to house exhibits for the Great Exhibition of 1851; this design by the Duke of Devonshire's head gardener was inspired by greenhouses in the new materials.

Paddington Station, London, 1850–54, a train-shed where new materials make the leap to an important new building type.

Gustave Eiffel, Tower in Paris for the Exhibition of 1889, an eyesore that became a monument and an inspiration to artists.

century, while in Paris Hitorff could get away with a heavily ornamented metal and glass front on his Gare du Nord of 1861–5.

A crucial step in admitting the new materials to aesthetic respectability occurs with Eiffel's design for a monumental marker for the Paris Exposition of 1889. His skeletal iron tower, which did nothing to clothe and little to prettify itself, caused shock and consternation but quickly imprinted itself as an unforgettable icon.

Not long before, Eiffel had spent sixteen years working out the structure to fit inside conventional clothing on the unconventional scale that iron made possible. *Liberty Enlightening the World*, who ended up in New York, had started as a different allegorical personage in a different location, a lighthouse in the form of a colossal Egyptian peasant at the entrance to the Suez Canal. Its allegorical clothing obscured and continues to obscure the Statue's place in the history of technology and its relevance to modern architecture. One could view the tower in Paris as *Liberty* with its clothes off, and get a hint of its pivotal role in promoting the machine aesthetic by tracing its appearance in the work of painters alone.

Some of Picasso's paintings from 1909–10 could be described unsympathetically as the human figure reduced to articulations of fragmented forms like machine parts. Getting to that point had been a tortuous process that began without much warning in 1906–7 in studies of African sculpture and the secretive project of the *Demoiselles d'Avignon*.

Even the super-confident Picasso was hesitant about admitting the direction in which his work was heading except to like-minded intimates. At the same time he viewed the experiment as monumental, not casual, as indicated by the trouble he took constructing the surface he was going to paint.

He reduced organic form to a mechanical construction and did this by a methodical destruction of its wholeness and harmony. The surface and all its constituent forms came apart into bits. Like battlefield explosions this destruction produces a great release of energy. The pieces do not finally remain apart but get fused together in a new set of tense relations, perhaps reaching a provisional resolution only in the mind of the viewer.

The idea of the machine as the modern subject par excellence is not necessarily dominant or even present in Picasso's thinking, who regards the process of form-giving more abstractly. Still, much of the force of these works derives from their subjects – the female figure and even the female nude turned into grey pistons, pulleys and metal plates seemed a frontal attack on basic pieties.

'Cubism', like similar slighting misnomers applied to past artistic phases and movements, is adequate in some ways and inadequate in others as a description of this revolution in painting. It catches the dehumanized strangeness of the results but leads one to expect regularity and stasis that aren't there. The term is a more appropriate name for architectural innovations, appearing around the same time in houses built by the Austrian polemicist and designer Adolf Loos. Looking at his Steiner house in Vienna of 1910, one first notices the absences or what has been taken away. A conscious stripping of the building's clothing of ornament has left an uncomfortable nakedness behind.

So that we cannot mistake the intention, all the rudimentary and in some deep way undetermined or generalized substance is presented in stark white render of hard-edged rectangular forms like enormous sugar cubes. Windows appear frameless, there is no cornice, and the roof is invisible. At least this is our impression of the house from the garden. On the street front, with a polite nod to convention, the vertical of the wall slides into the curve of the roof.

Loos's interiors are another matter entirely. Rich materials create a torpid and comfortable darkness. In the Steiner dining room a preposterous web of wooden beams looms overhead. In later projects like the Müller house in Prague of 1930 the exterior becomes an enigmatic mask, with fewer concessions to symmetry and baffling equations between window openings and 'windows' that are punctures in hollow walls on the skyline. The main interest is now concentrated in the interior and a series of interlocking spaces of different heights. An open stair makes

Adolf Loos, Steiner House, Vienna, 1910. An austere exterior of hard-edged rectangular forms.

the change of level between drawing room and dining room into a kind of mental exercise. These highly theoretical manipulations of volume are thought to have contributed to the free plan in Le Corbusier and Mies, where the design is freed from the constricting tubular envelope and the luxurious coatings that condition the Austrian's spaces.

Loos's move to Paris in 1922 brought him into closer contact with the European avant-garde and resulted in notable projects for the Dadaist poet Tzara (built) and the disturber of sexual taboos Josephine Baker (unbuilt). The early years of the century had been characterized by artistic movements issuing manifestoes like political parties and staging performances that resembled terrorist incidents intended to alarm the public. One of the noisiest and most extreme, at least rhetorically, was Italian, initiated by Tommaso Marinetti, a literary figure, but most substantially embodied by a sculptor, Umberto Boccioni, whose work is devoted to conveying movement in works which don't actually move, through devices like showing successive stages as overlapping repetitions of cavalry charges or careening cyclists.

The Futurists were most literal of all in advocating violence and destruction as purgative and renovative. They didn't manage the trashing of museums or paving over of Venetian canals urged by Marinetti, but their enthusiasm for war led to actual deaths at the front and the effective end of the movement as a result of these losses. One of those who died in uniform was Antonio Sant'Elia, the most impressive architect allied to Futurism, whose grandiose project for a *Città Nuova* of 1912–14 got no further than a set of forceful perspective drawings. These show a dense urban environment oversupplied with power stations and transport interchanges. Futurist dynamism appears as traffic on different levels, threading its way through cliff-like masses of building draped with lots of electrical cable, urban fantasies with more future in set design for film or theatre than construction in existing cities.

In other European centres, worship of mechanical power took more sensible and persuasive form. Architects in Germany had been involved in factory design ever since Behrens's work for AEG, the giant electrical manufacturer, for which his designs included domestic appliances and typography as well as architecture. Like many young architects of the period, Walter Gropius and Adolf Meyer had spent time in Behrens's office while also picking up something from more radical sources. So their design for the Fagus shoe factory at Alfeld flaunts the new materials,

Antonio Sant'Elia, *La Città Nuova* (1914), an ideal city by the leading Futurist architect which emphasizes circulation, transport and – illogically – stolid monumentality.

steel and glass, more aggressively in more anti-structural form than Behrens had done, and their model factory in the Werkbund exhibition at Cologne of 1914 idealizes them iconically in the guise of streamlined function. The part of this factory commonly illustrated in architectural histories is an administrative block that provides a monumental front to the workshop behind, a strange reprise of the division at St Pancras and other Victorian stations. At Cologne the symmetrical façade is framed by a stepped sequence of corner pavilions, first in brick and then in glass, wrapped round the solid core and exhibiting as in an x-ray the metal stair within the transparent envelope. Although this motif is presented clinically, it partakes of the glass mysticism current among the designers around Bruno Taut who formed the Glass Bead Chain. The idea of circulation as expressing the dynamism of modern architecture, a visible sign of its dedication to progress and the future, is a persistent theme in many early Modernist projects of the inter-war years.

By 1925 Gropius had moved on considerably in ideological commitment to the fusion of art and the processes of mass production. His design (with Hannes Meyer) for the new Bauhaus in Dessau carries on the powerful symbolism of exhibited circulation as a badge of progressive intention. Like the School's teaching programmes after the departure of the mystic Itten, the buildings transfer the factory aesthetic to the world of art and clothe the activity of the artist in the garb of up-to-date technology. Different sections of the institution are clearly distinct yet forcefully joined by transparent bridges that give the whole complex the appearance, at

Walter Gropius and Hannes Meyer, Bauhaus, Dessau, 1925–6; glazed corners (walls detached from the system of support) in the workshop wing of this radical art school.

least from the air, of an efficient mechanism whose parts exist in dynamic tension with each other.

The Bauhaus remains the most influential design school of all time, some of whose teaching procedures were still being treated in Britain as new discoveries forty and fifty years after the school was closed down by the Nazis. And the idea of fully glazed corners on multi-storey buildings and a separation between the wall and the frame that allowed apparently weightless transparency of the building envelope have proved such potent overturnings of ordinary common sense about how buildings work that eighty years later they remain among the most powerful of all of architecture's gravity-defying tricks. So it is still too early to calculate the benefits or otherwise of the Bauhaus love affair with technology, but the suspicion sometimes surfaces that the enterprise supplied a sugar coating of attractive formal design to processes and attitudes that have done far more harm than good and betrayed the benign hopes that accompanied the setting out.

Treating the various art movements of the early twentieth century in isolation is false to the material. To take just one instance, van Doesburg, the leading polemicist of De Stijl, a Dutch form of reductive idealism, was invited to the Bauhaus in 1922 and played a crucial part in pushing it towards engagement with the non-individual processes of mass production. But because of the abstract purity of its initial position it is also true to the nature of De Stijl to see it first in isolation.

In fact, the only member who never relented from devotion to a narrow range of primary and universal elements was a painter, Mondrian, who from 1920 produced a series of two-dimensional works based on irregular but strictly rectangular grids outlined first in grey and then in thick black 'lines', among which intervening panels are occasionally filled in with primary colours. The metaphysical purport of the primaries and the reasons why no further colours could be allowed were set out by Schoenmaekers, an obscure Dutch philosopher whose dogmatic mysticism resonated with van Doesburg and the others.

The results are momentarily so freakish that they send critics searching for causes in Dutch Calvinism and produce in one of the best recent histories of art the longest single analysis of a work of art in the whole book, offered in justification of a particularly sparse work by Mondrian. These uncharacteristically tedious pages are peculiar in their anxiety to show that there is more here than meets the eye.

With Rietveld we are on firmer ground. He began as a furniture designer and in 1917 produced a chair that looks uncannily like an exploded drawing, disarticulated into separate parts that don't even touch each other, an illusion created in part by painting the members according to a strict and arbitrary colour code that allows some of them to float and some to disappear.

Gerrit Rietveld, Schroeder House, Utrecht, 1924, the fullest realization of De Stijl in architecture.

In the meantime he designed a couple of influential interiors, but the first full realization in architecture of De Stijl ideas did not appear until 1924. This house of modest scale in Utrecht designed in collaboration with the client has been accorded iconic status ever since. It is easy to see why. Every visible element of the construction has been rendered as abstract form, not conditioned by practical necessity but inspired by pure formulations of the mind. Walls appear as planes floating in an ideal medium, not bound to each other but able to take up positions freely like lozenges in painting. They are attached or seen in proximity to thin uprights into which the task of support appears to be concentrated. But these are so slender they seem no more than lines, barely three-dimensional. So in exterior aspect the house looks like an asymmetric composition of purely geometrical elements in neutral materials, concrete, steel, glass, valued not for their substance but for their ability to represent abstract form instead.

Even more pregnant with the future is the demountable interior, which on the upper floor can be opened into a single interpenetrating space or closed off in conventional rooms by moving partitions, a partial realization of the formal dynamism suggested by the free play of elements on the exterior.

In reality, underneath the appearance of alienated modernity the Schroeder house consists of traditional wood and brick construction. It is also Rietveld's only work of the kind. Like his startling but uncomfortable furniture, Rietveld's architecture from here onwards became more interested in ordinary human need than utopian abstraction and therefore drops out of the history of modern architecture.

Rietveld's conception of the house as a kind of folding toy or device consisting of moving parts finds an echo in those telling pages of Le Corbusier's *Vers une architecture* that line up pictures of contemporary automobiles with images of the Doric colonnades of Greek temples. These pages assert that the two artefacts share certain properties: venerable monuments possess the anonymity and purposefulness of machines and mass-produced appliances now embody an elegance and spirituality equal to the temples'. Or, making allowance for a certain rhetorical exaggeration, one could see in the page an urge to synthesize opposites, a certain ruthlessness of functional analysis with the formality and permanence of classical system, though at times Corb seems bent on stripping this of its aura. So he insists that the marble of the Parthenon creates a world of pitiless steel.

In the house-studio that Corb designed for Ozenfant around this time he took elements that would spell factory to most observers, like the sawtooth roof profile, but transformed them on the interior to produce positively metaphysical effects, far from functionalist directness. So the broken skylights are turned into a uniform grid of light spreading out over the whole ceiling, continuing without interruption the glazed wall towards the street. A regular and largely empty universe opens in front of one like a tremendous invitation to effort, for someone liberated into a new kind of space. It is the first and one of the purest of those famous double-height spaces that introduce the scale of the landscape while remaining entirely

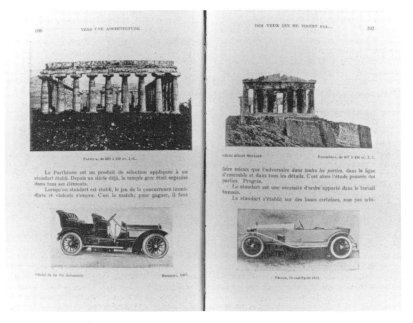

Le Corbusier, spread from *Vers une architecture* (1923), juxtaposing classical temples and modern motor-cars.

Le Corbusier, studio house for Ozenfant, Paris, 1923, the interior an idealized derivative of industrial prototypes.

indoors. In this case the meaning of the jump in scale is conveyed in crucial part by a useless but exciting little balcony like a perch on the edge of a cliff, perhaps later to be used as a sleeping platform but in powerful early photos simply suggesting an abstract vantage point like the figure of the observer in a Friedrich painting.

Corb claimed that at this time he spent the morning painting and the afternoon doing architecture, thus lending to his days that antithetical structure seen on the pages of Vers, of someone looking to synthesize the soft and hard or cerebral and affective or practical and aesthetic tendencies of his chosen profession.

One can read Le Corbusier's paintings from the years of closest contact with Ozenfant for their interpretations of objets-types – books, bottles, Ionic capitals – that are striving towards more universal forms and textures without ceasing to be recognizable. At times every substance approximates architecture, while scales trade places as in Alice, suggesting a world more sensuous and formally free than architecture is allowed to be.

Modernist inversions that in other hands might seem just doctrinaire or shocking here partake of imaginative play, re-conceiving the world in order to put the individual back in touch with forgotten sensory pleasures. Thus the jardins suspendus at the tops of Le Corbusier's houses, an idea fulfilled at Garches and Poissy, which replace the lost ground taken up by the building in the first place – a recovery hinted at by the pilotis' attempt to free the ground at the other end, which remains an abstract or conceptual kind of reclamation – these gardens, coming where they do, at the furthest remove from an ordinary garden, burst on the observer with all the force of impossibility. This is a house that insists on reconnecting you with the earth at the most unlikely moment. Also a house that lavishes its energies, providing entertaining ways of traversing itself, like ramps, that while more elemental than stairs, are a kind of costly theatre as well, costly if one takes a strict view of spatial efficiency.

Le Corbusier, *Still-life* (1919); in his paintings of this period ordinary objects become archetypal and quasi-architectural.

Surprisingly at this crucial point in the process of throwing off the burden of the past, some of Corb's most compelling spaces were made for artists to work in or collectors to display their prizes in. Corb's lifelong ambivalence about untrammelled newness and his hankering to combine it with enduring formulations of order appear in studios for Ozenfant and Lipschitz and galleries like the space in the Villa Laroche with a gently curved wall climbed by a ramp that mimes breaking out of the confines of a room without actually doing it.

This space of 1925 is a kind of bridge hoisted on pilotis as well as a profound resting place. Though the basic spatial subversions of bourgeois domesticity had been worked out ten years before, they weren't fully formulated as *Les 5 Points d'une architecture nouvelle* until 1926, near the moment of their most persuasive realization in the form of individual dwellings. The principles start and conclude with emptiness on the ground and the outdoors on the roof. In between, displacing the structure away from the walls allows eerie effects of floating and of being able to see everywhere at once, which, though only a narrow framed view through strip windows, goes on and on without the normal interruptions.

Corb's drawings of interior spaces sometimes convey his intentions better than photographs. A cinematic sensation of speed is imparted to these horizontal expanses cleared of their internal divisions. The inhabitant is propelled through the space by the visible means of rising from one level to another, pictures of dynamic movement that work whether you are actually using them or not. Le Corbusier was clearly carried away by this ideal of life projected forward and cleansed of debris, but it is amazing that he could have thought these strange formulations would ever replace most people's sense of home as a safe, closed-in place that provides separate spaces – rooms – for different activities going forward simultaneously.

The fullest realization of the ideal, the Villa Savoye at Poissy of 1929–31, isn't urban at all and has been – not unreasonably – likened to Palladio's Villa Rotunda for its geometric purity and perfect situation, commanding a green space radiating from it in every direction. The plan is not symmetrical, but the main elevation gives a disconcerting vision of classical harmony, a cube, hollowed out below, it is true, to an arcade of columns abstracted to sticks, and hollowed out above too by a large 'window' that for a long stretch has nothing but empty air behind it. So this up-to-date villa seems to have some of the properties of those flimsy eye-catchers closing the view in picturesque parks, or of a piece of machinery dangling its weak legs beneath a strangely weightless body. When one finally gets there and inspects it more closely one finds that exactly the working parts – the curved crown one took for a service core – are completely hollow, just a windbreak on the roof, so that what appeared to be a functioning machine is pure geometric ideal, a ghost, like the best room that has no roof. It is sometimes said that Corb's early trip to Greece and Asia Minor gave him the template for turning life upside down like this, but perhaps that just indicates a wish (in the critic) to tie to physical facts ideas that fly so thoroughly in the face of the climate where this architect mainly built.

In some sense the last word on the roof terrace was spoken around the same time in a conversion for a rich client in the centre of Paris. Beistegui was an aesthete who'd inherited Mexican silver mines, and the lavish project provoked Corb's closest brush with Surrealism. The rooftop platform was surrounded on two sides by hedges that could be raised and lowered by electricity, revealing the familiar monuments of the city like the Arc de Triomphe and the Eiffel Tower peeking over the parapet like monsters in dreams. On an upper level reached by a rail-less stair and surrounded by its own secretive shoulder-high wall was a prankish room lacking a roof, paved in thick grass and furnished only with a Rococo fireplace and a flimsy garden chair. Finally the last tacky detritus of European civilization is displaced into a nowhere, like one of those rooftops in Morocco from which, there for reasons of modesty, here of metaphysics, only the sky is visible.

In this period when Le Corbusier thought on larger scales, the subtlety of his work for individual clients disappeared along with all evidence of the past. The results in both the Ville Contemporaine of 1922 and Plan Voisin of 1925 are extremely bold – empty and monumental at once – and crushingly symmetrical. All the problems of Paris, physical congestion and social confusion, are solved by reduction, identical towers in regular grids with a transport interchange at the centre and undifferentiated green space stretching around, under and beyond the buildings without visible limit. From our vantage point eighty-five years later it is practically impossible to think our way into the frame of mind in which this vision of the city reduced to a gigantic and monotonous simplicity appeared as liberation. Corb never built anything remotely like it – Chandigarh in India, whatever its shortcomings, is something else entirely – but the vision had a powerful influence, most baleful in Eastern Europe and the Third World, most benign in Brasília.

The idea of a Modernist building sited on an ideal plane in the middle of empty space provides a kind of starting place for examining another great Modernist architect, Mies van der Rohe, a minimalist who makes others look positively pictorial by what he manages to eliminate, taking a formal vocabulary with humble origins in industrial structures and processes and raising it to sublime heights.

He began like so many others in the classicism of Behrens's office, and under the influence of radical art movements pushed this source beyond any hint of historical flavour. In 1923–4 he designed a pair of ideal villas, one in brick, the other in concrete, that reveal a decisive turn towards abstraction. There was no client, so there need be no services and in some deep sense no specificity about these designs. The Brick Country House is

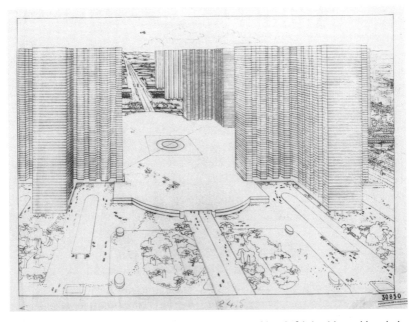

Le Corbusier, Plan Voisin, 1925, which replaces the messy historic fabric with crushing clarity centred on a transport interchange where airplanes land.

Ludwig Mies van der Rohe, plan of the Brick Country House, 1923–4, a radical deconstruction of domestic space.

long and low with a double-height core already hinting at an ideal self of uniform height. From one end of the core a low unpenetrated wall stretches to the edge of the horizontal sheet of paper like a Chinese scroll.

The plan, one of the most telling images in the history of architecture, shows us what to make of this. Here the garden wall appears as a thick line that stretches to infinity. At first this design looks as rigorously organized as a Mondrian, but somehow suggests powerful centrifugal movement. The spaces are all partial materializations, moments of tentative focus that keep coming undone, because here walls do not create enclosure. They seem to slip sideways instead of coming securely to rest, so that the inhabitant is set loose or cast adrift in a world without boundaries, like an atom in the newly expanded universe.

In an important way the Brick Country House represents Mies's wildest moment, where he explores most completely the metaphysical implications of the free plan and its new conception of domestic space. The Barcelona Pavilion of 1928–9 comes nearer than any of his other buildings to realizing this alarmingly unanchored world, because of the honorific nature of the brief and the consequent absence of any function to speak of.

The Pavilion goes beyond the House in refined experimentation with unusual materials – tinted glass, chrome, highly polished marble and the famous Mexican onyx that provided the module by which every other element was proportioned. Mies valued these materials not only for their distracting luxury, but for their various ways of reflecting what surrounded them and thus of partially disappearing themselves. Recalling similar contradictions in Loos, rich materials as employed by Mies sometimes spawn intellectual as well as sensory confusions.

For most of its life the Barcelona Pavilion was not there. It lasted less than a year and was demolished in 1930, but continued to exercise an overpowering influence in black-and-white photographs, taken before the doors were hung, that therefore gave an unusually intense sensation of spatial fluidity. The plan is another work of breathtaking graphic minimalism. Together with the photos it sets forth the idea of walls freed from enclosing and bounding functions that drift through the space like shafts of light or shadows. Pools echo the roof slabs or reflect or glance off each other, producing a general sensation of disembodiment.

The nearest equivalent in the real world to the Pavilion (finally reconstructed in 1986 so that it is visitable again in scrupulous replica after a fifty-year gap) is the Tugendhat house in Brno of roughly the same time. Using different means, it too presents itself as a kind of mirage, something barely there. One should try to see it in snow when the off-white render of nearly featureless walls merges with the sky and the ground until one comes to the main formal accent, a curved wall of milky glass, leading one towards . . . emptiness, an unexplained glimpse of the distance through a gap in the building's substance.

Like the Barcelona Pavilion it presents a powerful silhouette of a special kind, just an emphatic horizontal, reinforcing the ground and the horizon, already-existing datums. The Pavilion could be long and low with nothing in it because it had practically no responsibilities to fulfil. Tugendhat can be so little there through its pervasive whiteness and through a steep slope you can't see, which allows the living spaces to occupy a level below and concealed from the street.

Mies van der Rohe, Tugendhat house, Brno, Moravia, 1928–30, street entrance, where the building seems to open onto a void.

Mies left Germany at about the same time the Tugendhats left Moravia. His designs for public buildings had been commended in a couple of Nazi architectural competitions but were not built. His Reichsbank proposal of 1933 has been depicted as an ideological capitulation to Fascism, faceless and repetitive monumentality, especially on the canal side where three commanding hulks are lined up. Except that they are not lined up, but imperceptibly converging, and the other main façade is subtly curved in response to the street pattern. And like some Baroque plans this symmetrical façade is placed off-centre in relation to its surroundings.

After his move to the United States Mies went back to producing refined derivatives of factory prototypes in major projects like the IIT campus, where the format is horizontal, or the Seagram building and other commercial projects, where it is generally vertical.

In small works like his house for Dr Farnsworth Mies approached an absolute limit of design that sought near-invisibility and immateriality, a paradoxical destination for the enthusiasm over industrial materials and

techniques to end in. The Farnsworth house is built of standard steel components put together with such formal stringency that the proportions agree in all three dimensions and thicknesses are all reduced to the same minimums, so that this assemblage of massive members gives an appearance of practically weightless membranes suspended without strain above the earth. All the steel is finished in white enamel, applied in seventeen coats with hand finishing between the applications. So the resultant simplicity is achieved by methods that recall Japanese lacquer trays or boxes, treating the whole building like an exquisite craft object and recalling, in its deceptions, the furthest excesses of the Arts and Crafts.

An undignified coda could be added that would show the ideal stubbing its toe painfully against tedious reality. After devising her solution to the complete lack of privacy created by glass walls, Dr Farnsworth still found that she couldn't afford to heat or cool the space to a tolerable temperature, so she sued the architect, and lost.

Mies van der Rohe, Farnsworth House, Plano, Illinois, 1945–51, where modernism initially inspired by industrial prototypes comes closest to immaterial vision.

12

Modernism II: Expressionism, Constructivism and Deconstruction

Early in his career Mies had been pulled in another direction entirely. In the early 1920s he shared an office with Hugo Häring, famous for the bulgy organic farm buildings at Gut Garkau, and in this period Mies produced designs that from certain perspectives resemble fractured organic forms, buildings as gigantic crystals. Expressionism in architecture is a very German phenomenon, defiantly un-French, its model an organism – or at least a form taken from nature – rather than a machine. Architects like Häring thought the shape of the building should emerge from deep intuitive sources inaccessible to reason.

For the most uninhibited realization of this tendency in architecture we could turn to film sets for the good reason that film, a medium in constant motion, can more easily find forms for transitory moods or emotions. Windows, doors, walls and railings in *The Cabinet of Dr Caligari* are given raking, non-rectangular shapes, suggesting a world distorted by strong feeling. The inhabitants are caught off guard by something viewers have guessed from the first frame – that the violence barely contained by these fractured shapes is bound to break out eventually. In such settings murders will be attempted or committed.

There is limited scope in ordinary reality for buildings that provoke extreme behaviour, so the archetypal Expressionist works all fill specialized institutional functions, like Bruno Taut's Glass Pavilion of 1914 at the Werkbund Exhibition in Cologne. It has a faceted crystalline form that can be read as cumulatively curvaceous like a flame or large fruit. It advertises a modern material, glass, of which it seems entirely constructed. This little building is heavily inscribed with slogans proclaiming the mystical capabilities of its own substance. Taut went on to publish if not to build less discreet versions of the idea, including a cathedral-like implantation of glass sitting among snow and ice high in the Alps.

A recurrent pattern appeared in the mid-1920s – most Expressionist architects came down from the Alps of fantastic projects to the flatland of mass housing. Taut was responsible for 12,000 new dwellings in Berlin in the late 1920s, yet he didn't completely abandon the intuitive strand of architectural thinking. A villa design of 1926–7 at Dahlewitz south of Berlin of bold quarter-circle plan is touted as a giant sundial, colour-coded to signal its responsiveness to the movement of the sun through the day, its heating pipes picked out in primary colours as well.

Hans Poelzig had been building Expressionist works earlier than the others, in obscure eastern locations now in Poland – Posen (Poznań) and Luban (Luboń). The most radical are industrial, a chemical factory and a gasworks; in photos they look like Expressionist film sets, based on narratives of ore travelling along snaking railway viaducts. His Upper Silesian Tower of 1911 for a fair in Posen, later converted to a water tower, is filled with over-scaled intestinal stairs and walkways in sheet metal. Before sobering up for good he did film sets for *The Golem* and a theatre interior in Berlin (destroyed in the Second World War) reminiscent of sea-cave effects in the Alhambra.

Erich Mendelsohn's career mirrors the others, another story of wildness tamed or relinquished, and of disruption and movement in the designer's own life. Mendelsohn surfaced in the First World War as the producer of a voluminous series of fantastic sketches on extremely small scraps of paper sent back from the Russian front, a translation of the violence and imagined violence of the war, in which the fixed world of architecture becomes the scene of controlled explosions. Though tiny they are conceived on vast scales, not that of the person or the dwelling but the industrial installation or the transport network. They show architecture breaking free and able to move easily, antidote to the stalled war going nowhere and the society on hold until it is over.

They strike us as among the most purely fantastic of all architectural ideas, likely to remain mental explosions or bursts of energy, drawn as solid but imitating showers of sparks, jets of water, clouds of mist. Once and once only Mendelsohn got the chance to build one of these passing outbursts. The brief for a hard-headed scientific institute had nonetheless its inevitable cosmic dimension. In conversation with his astronomer friend Freundlich, an admirer of Einstein, Mendelsohn became captivated by the equation that converted mass to energy and discovered a world in flux at the heart of matter. So his observatory in Potsdam resembles a moving body whose contours are changing as it plunges through space. The details that look like streamlining – window shapes and parapets on the entrance terrace – have deeper significance than the conventionalized sweeps of Art Deco or of Mendelsohn's later department stores.

Two incompatible versions of the process of construction are in circulation: that lingering wartime shortages forced Mendelsohn to

Erich Mendelsohn, Einstein Tower, Potsdam, 1920–21, architecture that aspires to embody a new theory of matter in its form if not its construction.

substitute brick for the reinforced concrete he would have preferred. Or, that the Tower is a deliberate concrete-brick hybrid like the Luckenwalde hat factory that followed. Mendelsohn used concrete for base and crown and brick for the more sculptural mid-section, believing the materials stronger in combination than separately. If one adopts this version, one perceives the architect as an Expressionist in the Baroque sense – the impression the building creates and its overarching meaning are separate from the technicalities of its construction, which interest only a few specialists.

In some ways Hans Scharoun is the most interesting of the Expressionists who joined to form the Glass Bead Chain and then came apart after the war. Like most of the others his work modulates formally from jagged explosions and curvilinear lumps to hard-edged Modernist regularity, except that Scharoun never gives up the curves entirely, or even more importantly, the suggestions of energetic movement that the curves stand for. His model house for the Weissenhof Siedlung, soberest of all his works, still shows cubes wrapped in curves. Internally it is full of chamfered corners, the least disruptive intimation of curvilinearity. Not long after, in the Schminke house in Saxony of 1930–33, Scharoun disrupts the composure of the plan by shifting Modernist volumes like a deck of cards to produce one of the most compelling images of changefulness in the whole history of architecture.

Scharoun lay dormant in the Nazi period to emerge afterwards having converted Expressionist ideas from a language of extravagant external forms to new and deeply rooted kinds of spatial organization welling up from inside the plan. That afterlife is another story, but Scharoun's career exhibits striking parallels to that of another architectural maverick who likewise appears to undergo two developments, cut off from each other in his case by Depression, not war.

Frank Lloyd Wright's first career was inspired by craft ideas; he assembled a team of workers in various decorative media whose contributions quickly evolved away from separable decoration. Not for long do Wright's designs bear much resemblance to English Arts and Crafts, except in their enthusiasm for traditional materials, wood, brick, stone – and glass conceived poetically, not as a radical solvent of architectural solidity as it was in Europe. In the Prairie houses Wright found his way to open-plan domestic space that flows continuously because screens have replaced partitions. His motivation was radically different from Mies's and Corb's, though. Rather than a separate man-made device set against the natural world, the house is something like a feature of the landscape, generated by the hearth, a lump of rock at its centre. The fireplace was fetishized in the Arts and Crafts until the inglenook became a secluded little dwelling within the larger dwelling. Wright pushes the idea and the space further than anyone else, towards a mystical reconnection of the individual with the land.

The hearth is the element most obviously carried over from Wright's early to middle phase. In Fallingwater of 1936 craft quaintness is dropped for the modern materials par excellence, reinforced concrete and metal-framed glazing, while the hearth idea and the rootedness it signifies become even more primitive. Like Scharoun Wright adopts Modernist forms and materials only to push back to a more radically romantic idea of man as part of nature. For Wright concrete seems to represent above all the possibility of bold cantilevers, that is to say of spaces working their way free of supports. So although Fallingwater looks from a distance like an abstract rendition of a geological formation, rock shelves made of something else, the spatial sensation standing on the balconies attached to every room is that of floating over the stream, released from gravity to swim in air.

Frank Lloyd Wright, Fallingwater, Bear Run, Pennsylvania, 1935–7, vacation house inspired by Japanese interfusion of nature and architecture.

Wright had the crazy idea of coating the concrete lips or rails of the shelves in gold leaf, vetoed by the client, who perhaps did not appreciate what a convergence this would have achieved with the Japanese aesthetic Wright had been inspired by. Fallingwater is a compelling approximation in a new architectural vocabulary of those fusions in seventeenth-century

Japan of buildings and their surroundings, as in Katsura Detached Villa on the edge of Kyoto. To a degree these interpenetrations are always illusory, or rather they depend on suggestible subjects: you have to want them for them to work their magic.

Gold, used non-naturalistically on screens depicting scenes by moonlight or on lacquered shrines deep in pine forests, does not break the spell but magically furthers one's absorption. With its vertical surfaces picked out in gold, Wright's villa would have become a celestial vision, raising the landscape to a higher power.

By a strange whim Scharoun wanted his late masterpiece to be sheathed in a metallic gold final coating, a plan finally carried out after a fashion after his death. Like other Scharoun buildings of the period, the Philharmonie in Berlin makes a gawky effect externally, which the anodized aluminium doesn't soften. Scharoun's attitude to materials is puzzling. A lot of deep thought about the spaces is materialized in the end with a certain deliberate crudity, as if to say that refined attention to detail is a distraction from the essential purposes of building, providing for human possibility or growth.

The Philharmonie fits into its setting, for long a no-man's land between East and West and one of the most devastated areas of the ruined city. So the shard-like forms of the concert hall and its unsoftened overlaps with other Scharoun buildings nearby make the painful effort of reconstruction permanently palpable. But Scharoun's exteriors aren't

Hans Scharoun, Philharmonie, Berlin, 1956–63, designed from the inside out, so that the external forms sometimes seem gawky and ill assorted.

exactly planned, rather they happen, as the consequence of internal spaces pushing their way outwards.

Wright's last great urban project, his only building in Manhattan, ignores the city and plants the most unrectangular artefact in the most powerfully orthogonal setting on earth. The Guggenheim Museum, designed during the War and finally built in the 1950s, is a gigantic spiral in concrete that imposes a wholly different scale on the city that exists, which, of course, there is no hope that the city will adopt, except that the Whitney Museum nearby is an obvious descendant. So, because it can afford to, because it almost needs to, this building turns inward and withdraws into its single unified space that follows different rules from all other buildings. The rare architectural analogues include the spiral minaret-towers of Iraq that Wright's museum turns inside out and upside down, and, its unwanted descendants, a certain kind of parking garage.

Where Wright's form is closed, Scharoun's is open. Where Wright's is perfect and complete, Scharoun's is ragged and incomplete, like an enclosed landscape unsure of its own boundaries. The plans of the concert hall give it in the most exciting graphic form. In the spaces of the entrance hall and stairs to different areas of seating, levels do not break off distinctly but overlap, flowing into each other and back, in more than one set of movements.

There is a painting of a funeral by Max Beckmann that conveys the excitement and confusion of such reversible conceptions of space. The picture presents at one and the same time two incompatible views of the event, so that you can't find the right way of looking at it. Some parts of the picture are upside down, some right side up, but the two are inextricably tangled. Scharoun would doubtless have appreciated those stories of early twentieth-century painters learning from the accidental sight of their work upside down.

Most concert halls are uni-directional, rows of seats all facing towards the narrow end of a rectangular box. Scharoun's hall isn't rectangular or flat, nor is it raked in any simple fashion. He describes it as a landscape – it is a valley and its broken slopes are vineyards, comfortable-sized patches held at various angles to the light. The tent-like canopy overhead is a form of sky. And the stage . . . is at the bottom of the valley, nearer one end than the other, fully visible from every part in the hall, but not set apart in another world.

Scharoun shares with the earlier Expressionist phase the likelihood that buildings arrived at in this manner will be too individual to be easily assimilated by other architects and thus to play a nameable part in the history of architecture. There's a European Modernist whose peculiar history puts him in a better position to bridge the gap between organicism and strict Modernism. Alvar Aalto began in Nordic classicism, which always

Alvar Aalto, Paimio sanatorium, Finland, 1928–32, with clearly distinguished functions and elements dictated by methods of treating tuberculosis, like the long south-facing flank.

had latent vernacular tendencies, and found his way to stripped-down white-rendered forms with which gatekeepers like Giedion and Le Corbusier could be comfortable. Except that even at his most severe Aalto was softening the edges and disorganizing the geometry. In Paimio sanatorium, a complex institutional project in a forest location, Aalto wreaks havoc with the idea of an axial plan, ostensibly because tubercular patients need to be oriented differently to the sun in successive phases of their treatment. As at the Bauhaus different functions are separated, given tailor-made accommodation and then tenuously re-joined. Except that the final effect at Paimio is comfortable relaxation of the rules, not analytical rigour. And Aalto's obsession with detail – special breathing chairs, heating and lighting adjusted to inhabitants who spend their lives horizontally – has practical and social as much as aesthetic goals.

Aalto did not stop at this partial violation of Modernist principles, but moved further from uniformity and easily read organization in projects like Villa Mairea, a relatively lavish one-off dwelling where he was given his head to rethink the house in contemporary form. The Expressionists had earlier moved from lurid irrational blobs to colourless hard-edged Modernism. Aalto moved in the other direction, partly a function of his coming on the scene half a generation later, partly of his location on the fringes of Europe, in Finland, where the problems of the congested metropolis did not exist.

Alvar Aalto, Villa Mairea, Noormarkku, Finland, 1938–9, where modernism is strongly tempered by vernacular motifs and materials.

Villa Mairea is so powerful because it is working its way to a new synthesis, not just mechanically overlaying one thing on another. The ingredients are Corb's villas of the 1920s, Fallingwater – whose integration with its setting prompted Aalto to look for a stream he could build over, a search he was deflected from – and Finnish homesteads grouped loosely around courtyards. Aalto's attitude to materials is changing too, as if he is opening up to memories previously regarded as not architectural enough.

Now the plan is basically rectilinear, if somewhat lopsided and sprawling. But internally regularities are concealed by varying the rhythm of supports, occasionally clumped like trees, or wrapped with dramatically natural materials like cane or rattan. Sometimes the Modernist accent, one concrete column among the wooden ones, is the exception, the allowable quotient of disorder.

At times Aalto merely flirts with the vernacular, as in the grassy roof of the passage to the sauna by the pool. But the ambiguity of the project runs deep, and who can say whether this house is camouflaged Modernism or Modernism as camouflage of the more basic forms of our life, or can be sure which is the frankness and which the concealment?

Towards the end of his life one of the arch-Modernists began to have his doubts and shocked many of his followers by a dramatic turn towards the irrational, most dramatically in a religious building, of all things. Before Ronchamp Le Corbusier had shown signs of a different attitude to materials and even played with the idea of grass roofs at Maisons Jaoul at Neuilly, but at Ronchamp the Modernist geometry comes completely unhinged. Walls slope dramatically and then pull themselves upright again only to curl back from the other wall they seemed about to join, leaving a sizable gap between. When you look closely you see that the slit is glazed, but the impression remains of a building that is coming apart. Corb claimed that the twisting and bulging roof form was initially suggested by the upturned shell of a crab he found on a beach in Long Island. From inside it looks like a tent, from outside like a lump of thatch.

Aalto had soon replaced smooth white render on external walls with limewash over brick, not smooth and not evenly white. At Ronchamp the strongest trace of the old Modernist palette is the stark whiteness of the walls, but now they are rough-cast, not an industrial finish, but an echo of Mediterranean vernacular. The flank that meets the pilgrim toiling up the hill goes further into the primitive than any authentic vernacular. Small and irregular punctures, glazed sometimes in clear and sometimes in colour, dig their way through thick walls to cast mysterious and uncertain light. Perhaps the most unnerving feature of all is a little sliver of daylight that runs along the joint between the wall and the ceiling the whole way round the interior, interrupted seldom, by pillars supporting the roof concealed in the walls, which few will recognize for what they are.

Ronchamp poses a conundrum hard to resolve: can one ever forget that one is viewing an imitation of a numinous space by an extremely ingenious architect? Now the pilgrims are all pilgrims of architecture, but why is coming to Ronchamp any different from visiting Borromini?

Le Corbusier, Notre Dame du Haut, Ronchamp, 1950–54, modernist geometry and design sources substantially abandoned.

Except that it is, for Borromini at his most outlandish is still part of something, working in a recognizable genre, and Le Corbusier is inventing everything out of his own head, or happy for us to think so.

The strand of early twentieth-century avant-garde that I have kept till last, Russian Constructivism, is in many ways the most extreme, and remarkable most of all for the strong responsive chord it struck with designers forty to sixty years later in radically different social and political circumstances. Forms devised in chaotic times by designers intent on connecting with the world outside art are picked up in contented times and put to work in some of the most alienated architecture the world has so far seen.

It is easy and perhaps also appropriate to tell twentieth-century architecture as a fragmented history. The proliferation of avant-gardes around the time of the First World War looks like a great cultural centrifuge in which a unified culture flies apart in many pieces. Certainly in Russian Constructivism the fragment gains a kind of centrality, comparable to the place of the machine for Rationalists or the organism for Expressionists, and similarly positive, an intimation of unrealized possibility.

Even before the Revolution a tendency is observable that became stronger after it, for the work of artists to engage, sometimes aggressively, with the world outside the studio. Vladimir Tatlin's corner reliefs, for example, have an ambition to influence space beyond their own boundary. Rather than a safe resting place, the corner of the room is treated as a dynamic point of departure from which one can strike out in various directions at once. Tatlin's constructions are dynamic in another sense as well – a sophisticated geometry is embodied in rough materials, suggesting that something so crudely assembled could be taken apart or rethought. The lack of fine finish implies that the thought is not entirely finished.

In later phases of the Civil War many painters and graphic artists were pushed into three-dimensional design, as if under pressure to engage actively in social change and to have immediate, visible effect. So Alexander Rodchenko designed a newspaper kiosk like a materialized Suprematist painting, a tower of flimsy, clashing forms. It appears to be a demountable construction, or even better, to suggest erection and de-erection continually. Its energetic pieces barely cohere, like a collage that hasn't decided whether to join up or separate, or a portrait in miniature of a society in flux.

In this chaotic period the energies of real architects like the Vesnins got deflected into more achievable kinds of construction like stage design, where the results often look like unfinished buildings or the x-rays of buildings. A powerful iconography is being worked out of architecture as process, something newly underway with most of its life still ahead of it. At the beginning prosaic obstacles even furthered the development of

Alexander
Rodchenko,
Biziaks, 1919,
newspaper kiosk,
an architecture
that looks flimsy,
demountable,
in flux, like
the society
around it.

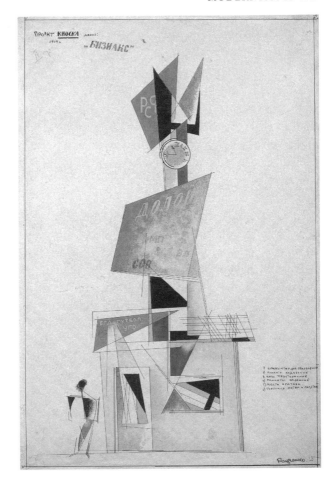

this symbolism, like stalled construction where the money ran out or materials were hard to come by.

Certainly the uncertain conditions gave rise to ambitious plans. The new society for a new kind of man took on architectural form in competitions for new building types like Palaces of Labour or – a junior version – workers' clubs. The most famous of these, the Vesnins' winning entry in a competition of 1922–3, looks like a kit of parts in section with a superstructure of wires and transmitting towers almost as tall again as the building below. The solidest part is like an anthology of different forms of truss. This diagram could be read as an exposition of Marxist theories of superstructure and base or as a new model of culture as propaganda, not conventionally tied to one place but diffusing itself constantly across a vast continent.

In the famous aerial perspective the same project looks like the headquarters of a heavy industry whose elements began as simple cube, cylinder, tube and bridge but had to be armour-coated for their task. In

Vesnin brothers, Palace of Labour, 1922–23, winning entry in a competition, looking massive and like a kit of parts at the same time, with displayed circulation and transmitting apparatus.

this version the scene of leisure seems to be disguised as the grim old territory of labour, perhaps inadvertently exposing contradictions in the idea of a Palace of Labour.

The Vesnins' next notable architectural proposal, for Leningrad Pravda's Moscow offices, is perhaps the purest rendition of the new society as dynamic and transparent. The completed building will resemble flimsy scaffolding and turn over inordinate amounts of space to different means of getting to the top of its spindly form. Appropriately for a newspaper, it bristles with messages, even verges towards becoming simply a frame on which placards are mounted, including changing news flashes displayed via a system like a revolving card index. Here the ephemeral nature of the product infects the process of production to an unheard-of degree.

Konstantin Melnikov is the most interesting early Soviet architect, in part because he could turn the collapsed and primitive building industry to positive advantage. As in Tatlin's reliefs, sophisticated ideas are realized in crude materials and techniques, without a feeling of second best, because the crudity is bound up in what the building wants to say.

His Makhorka pavilion at the Russian Agricultural Exhibition of 1923 was a cheap temporary structure but deserves to stand alongside Mies's more expensive and refined pavilion in Barcelona. Melnikov's building promotes a rock-bottom sort of commodity, *makhorka*, the cheapest tobacco, which almost anyone could afford. Appropriately, then, it looks like a shack and mainly consists of rough-sawn timber, apparently unpainted like an ordinary rural building. But coming closer you notice parts of it jacked up on stilts, its roof slope jagged because masses are offset or turned suddenly at right angles. Sub-bits shelter under the part on stilts, and stairs are separate towers or spirals, roughly and functionally glazed.

The whole is more like the model of a fictional industrial building than an installation in deadly earnest. Then, of course, on top of everything it is unceremoniously treated, boldly written over with simple kinds of advertising and instruction, as if it is perfectly all right for a work of architecture to be a poster as well. Posters, which loom so large in the story of Soviet design in this period, have even infiltrated Melnikov's architecture.

Konstantin Melnikov, Makhorka pavilion at the All-Union agricultural exhibition, 1923, complex fractured geometry executed in crude materials and technique.

His other pavilion of 1924 for the Paris exhibition of decorative art in 1925 is better known, purer and more ambitious, but clearly a descendant of the tobacco pavilion. The geometry is more radical and the timber less rough, but judging from photos the temporary building in Paris also depended on simple materials and skills. Instead of sculpting in concrete like European Modernists, Melnikov created his dramatic shattered forms in timber. The small rectangular plot is riven by diagonals, first of all by a wide stair that splits the building in two and cuts the whole way through it, absence just as powerful as presence. Overhead runs a broken zigzag of awnings like the remnants of a ceiling that the stair's thrust has disrupted. This building tells one that change and growth are productive, a message embedded in the spatial experience, not in external symbols. Except that here structure is symbol. The pavilion signals its presence with a lightweight tower in latticed timber to which the letters CCCP cling, laconic shorthand for the nation.

When Melnikov returned from Paris he found a Russia changing rapidly, even treacherously, in ways he was slow to pick up. In one of the most positive developments for architecture, a new building type, the workers' club, was being defined. For the time being unions could commission buildings from architects and get them built with a minimum of red tape. In a short space between 1927 and 1929 Melnikov built six of these in the Moscow region. The earliest designs are the boldest, like that of the Rusakov factory club for the Municipal Workers' Union, where the plan erupts dramatically into the street as three sloping and diverging masses of auditorium seating. Powerful, even intimidating external forms are matched by unexpected flexibility in internal planning. Six meeting halls can be separated or combined by means of mechanized dividers. Perhaps sensitive to charges of formalism (the worst architectural crime in that era), Melnikov applied a lot of thought to acoustics and heat conservation.

Less monumental in scale but in some way even more flamboyant and eccentric is the house Melnikov built for himself at the same time. Though he introduced ingenious variants on traditional construction and achieved significant economies by accepting the limitations of peasant labour, this wasn't enough to save him from a barrage of criticism, for individual dwellings were beginning to come under collectivist attack, and as if in defiance of the new consensus, Melnikov had signed his work in foot-high letters on the façade.

All jagged angularity, the Paris pavilion might be mistaken for a Functionalist work. Working parts lie stripped bare and open to view, but the attitude to usable space is decidedly cavalier, which passes unnoticed in a place where no one stays long. Melnikov's house is also founded on spatial conflict, or on a geometry of distinct forms caught in the process

Melnikov, house
for himself,
Moscow, 1927,
two cylinders
intersecting,
a surprising
outbreak of
individualism
in its time and
place.

Melnikov's own house, model, showing the project as dynamic interpenetration of form.

of merging. But this time the forms are two large cylinders of equal girth and slightly different height that have collided and become partially joined. The cylinder facing the street has lost a thin slice of the curve so that flat glazing stretching from ground to roof can be inserted, while the cylinder behind is punctured by so many prismatic windows that it looks like an oriental lattice. Internal spaces become most interesting where one curve bites into the other or in sleeping quarters, where Melnikov's odd ideas about dust and dreams have banished internal walls and raised the beds on stone pedestals.

In the same year that this piece of romantic individualism was being built, a precocious architectural student entered a competition with a proposal that makes Melnikov look like a realist. Ivan Leonidov's design for the Lenin Library complex divides the brief into two powerful forms of uncompromisingly modern materials, a spherical glass reading room and a pencil-thin rectangular book shaft, both of them held in place by guy wires and surrounded by empty space of interstellar proportions. In the most familiar image the tower continues out of sight off the top edge. As if in a modern translation of Ledoux and Boullée, the idea of public space sent Leonidov into utopian flight from the scale of everyday life. In plans for ideal communities he went even further. His House of Culture for the Proletarskii District shows zones of activity or accommodation barely anchored in a generous emptiness. Above the sprawling complex is tethered a dirigible, emblem of the drive to escape all confinement.

Perhaps it was inevitable that spatial ideas that went so far beyond the boundaries of reality would fall back on themselves in a kind of implosion, to end as paper fantasies. After 1930 a wide divergence appears between those who would actually get their buildings built and those like Jakob Chernikov, whose utopian renderings of industrial complexes imbibed something of the prevailing Socialist Realism in spite of themselves. This dogmatic new style is realist in reversing the trend towards abstraction in all the arts, a trend towards simplified forms relieved of conventional ornament, whose place was taken by details of construction displayed as almost a form of ornament themselves.

Instead of this the socialist state decreed a return to classically inspired symmetry emphasized to the point of parody, and classically derived detail beefed up and magnified to match the overweening scale of such behemoths as the Palace of the Soviets, subject of an international competition that Le Corbusier, Gropius and Mendelsohn, among others, entered. The winning entry by a shifting team of designers headed by Boris Iofan, a pre-Revolutionary classicist, is a pile of varied forms, starting from a rectangular base enlivened by spurs and wings, modulating to a cylinder of three or four telescoped stages, and crowned by an artwork that grows alarmingly as time passes and construction is delayed. This gigantic figure of Lenin

Jakob Chernikov, *Architectural Fantasy* (1925–33), paper dreams on a huge scale camouflaged as useful building types.

gets bigger and bigger in order to keep the overall height of the building ahead of the latest American skyscraper.

The graphic presentation derives from Piranesi, but the detail of the design is standard Art Deco, shovelled on in a spirit of Baroque excess. Like Nazi and Italian Fascist classicism, Soviet Socialist Realism is always tainted by its political roots, but one still looks for those moments when a talented architect, like a poet submitting to sestina-form, subjects himself to these crushing constraints and brings interesting work out of prison conditions. Or perhaps one waits just as eagerly for a work of architecture that will express, though inadvertently, the full horror of the regime. One of Melnikov's last projects comes nearest to fulfilling this perverse hope.

Boris Iofan and others, *Palace of the Soviets* (1932–41), winning design; Lenin gestures heroically from the top, but this triumph of Socialist Realism is hollow – it could not be built.

If the Palace of the Soviets had ever been built, though physically, technically and economically impossible, it would have made nonsense of its surroundings by the Moscow River. Similarly, Melnikov's Commissariat of Heavy Industry would have reduced Red Square, an imposing public space, to insignificance. Its enormous towers form a double zigzag

Melnikov, *Commissariat of Heavy Industry* (1934), competition entry, his unsuccessful attempt to join the vogue for over-scaled propaganda.

like a giant letter M. Because they are so huge, the entry ramps that collide with the main masses halfway up need to be equipped with high-speed escalators, or the suppliants who enter through gigantic cogwheels will never reach their destinations. A deep pit like an opencast mine yawns in front, necessary to bring light to sixteen storeys of offices buried underground. The pathos of the project breaks through at the point where the structure under the steep ramps turns from a classical aqueduct to a flat-iron building packed with offices, accessible how? It also appears in two gargantuan figures given the impossible task of pushing against the sharp points of the vs that make up the giant M. Except that they are not vs and it is not an M, for the pointed shapes represent the Roman numeral fives of two five-year plans, both exceeded in the brutal drive to industrialize this backward country, and so the straining figures stand for the millions tormented by their ruler's dreams of industrial might.

Because of the chaotic times in which it began and the twists of early Soviet history that brought it to a premature end, Russian Constructivism generated one of the largest archives of unbuilt projects in the whole of twentieth-century architecture. After the lapse of a generation or so, Constructivist ideas began to make a startling reappearance in Western architecture, where, like the African sculpture from which Picasso borrowed, they were bound to carry radically different meanings from those at their first appearance.

Stirling and Gowan's Engineering Faculty at Leicester University, completed in 1963, looks like something straight out of the Vesnin office. It combines bold forms clashed against each other in mixed materials,

James Stirling and James Gowan, Engineering Faculty, University of Leicester, 1959–63, Constructivist ideas of form and materials surface 45 years later in different political circumstances.

themselves combined with deliberate crudity – glass, industrial brick, bare concrete. Large clumsy forms push their way up through others equally strong, the geometry simple but nonetheless impure, full of odd slopes, chopped-off corners and masses dislodged to one side.

Here the old signature of visible circulation in a glazed tube conveys almost the contrary of the optimistic Soviet motif: it feels squeezed from the unwieldy lump of the brick like toothpaste from a tube, and the whole structure seems an intimidating monster set on a fixed, unfriendly course. The mentality behind this is hard to enter now, which presents a place of learning as a whole set of irresolvable stresses and strains. Perhaps it is better understood as a playful kind of theatre. In the bland conformist world it was born into, the idea of dramatic collision, even brutality, among the parts of a building helped wake up the jaded user.

Administering an enlivening shock to a zombie is one way of describing what Frank Gehry had to do to an ordinary suburban bungalow in Santa Monica before he could live in it. The original house has almost disappeared, ensconced in a Constructivist stage set of rough materials haphazardly thrown together or erupting like an uncontrollable nightmare from the complacent old core. Except that the mess is extremely satisfying. All the scrap materials are employed in highly cerebral ways, the shapes portraying dissolution from a consistent vocabulary, and thus the whole decomposed composition is playing with ideas of destruction. It has been said that this house is unthinkable before the Holocaust and its concentration camps, that the chain-link fence, which reminds other critics of the mist of thought or the indefinable physicality of ideas, is after all a hallucinatory reprise of imprisonment like a Wagnerian leitmotif.

At this point in his career Gehry experimented with various ways of defacing or undermining architecture. Other unbuilt dwellings teeter on legs too weak to support them, bump awkwardly into unrecognized parts of themselves, remind us uncannily of Kafka's protagonists whose own

Frank Gehry, house conversion for himself, Santa Monica, California, 1977–8 (revised 1993), where modernist forms erupt from a suburban house like bad dreams it has had.

mental acuity hastens their defeat. Before long, in less than three years, this poignant vulnerability disappeared and the painful centrifugal forces were resolved in comfortable formalist dissociations of parts. The result is a law school or even a private dwelling analysed into a collection of amusing freaks.

Designs that call in question the basic principles of all permanent constructions put themselves at least implicitly in antagonistic relation to existing buildings. Two Austrian designers who took the confusing name Coop Himmelblau (often misheard as Coop Himmelbau), with its contradictory suggestions of earth and sky, began by staging ephemeral performances like *Blazing Wing*, a lightweight construction that sketched an angel's wing in unsuitable materials, suspended it between existing buildings, set it on fire and caused a lot of the surrounding windows to fracture in the flames.

Like Gehry's own house, most of their early buildings were insertions or interventions in existing structures, part of the tired nineteenth-century fabric of Vienna, most moribund of capitals, long a beacon of pomposity that had provoked subversives in many fields to puncture its complacency. Perhaps Coop Himmelblau's most startling project is an eruption on the rooftop of one of those staid old Viennese blocks, a clatter of metal and

Coop Himmelblau, rooftop addition to a 19th-century block, Vienna, 1983–8, an unlikely eruption of congested and unstable fragments into a staid existing setting.

glass like huge bird's wings caught in mid-flutter or a mechanism that has got assembled in the wrong order, something impossibly dynamic but also nonsensical. There it sits, undeniably real, yet defeating any possible notion of intentionality. Intricate yet completely illogical – it lands us with an irresolvable paradox: such objects don't get built without detailed foresight and planning, yet no one could have meant this.

It appears that the process is just as preposterous as the result: initial drawings are done blindfolded or without looking at the page, and the germ obtained this way is refined in a series of models alternating with more precise drawings until presumably an engineer enters the conversation and helps work out thicknesses, materials and articulations of parts.

The result much further down the line remains disquieting – this is its triumph – and serves as lawyers' offices, perhaps an allegory of the unpredictability of legal process, where fresh developments are liable to fall on you out of the sky, altering everything. In the strangest twist of all, this turns out to be practically a non-existent building, because it is almost invisible from the narrow street below, perhaps explaining how it got planning permission in an environment not especially tolerant of oddity.

Other Coop Himmelblau projects from the same period make even less show in the street but wreak havoc with interior spaces, sometimes suggesting that a large writhing creature – always metallic, never organic in texture – has got trapped in rectangular confines too small for it and thrashes helplessly. Two spatial conceptions attempt to inhabit the same space with highly uncomfortable but absolutely un-boring results.

Two conceptions fighting over the same space, or hundreds. I can remember when Daniel Libeskind's series of large drawings called *Micromegas* looked to me like a garbage bin dumped out and its contents recorded where they fell. New kinds of order often look like disorder: I can also remember regarding the Internet as a rubbish heap of appalling extent. The Internet is an order that can't be printed or materialized in one place, and *Micromegas* – its title from an improbable, inappropriate distance, a story by Voltaire – turns to drawing to show an architecture no one could build. Maybe it takes off from exploded technical drawings, those wonderful artefacts that turn a single object into a dozen or a hundred, bringing to individual life and consciousness lots of normally insignificant components.

Libeskind's fragments explode in more than one direction and discard the idea of standard intervals. They shrink and expand, sometimes darting so far back in the space that they make one think of star systems. We could catalogue all the sorts of penetrations of one form by another, the overlays and occlusions, but it would violate the spirit of the drawing to mimic its meticulousness in our looking. We almost wish we hadn't

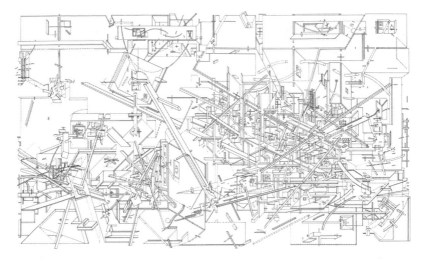

Daniel Libeskind, 'Leakage' from the *Micromegas* series (1979), delighting in architectural impossibility, too many ideas in the same space.

noticed that there's a right way up and something approaching single-point perspective. Here space *recedes*, and obeys Euclidean, not some newer geometry. *Micromegas* work because of this tension: they show believable building components, more like bits of timber than anything else, forming themselves into nebulous clouds.

When Libeskind comes to build actual buildings the polarities are reversed: structures take on some of the properties of drawings – the plan derives from a contorted line and the fenestration resembles marks on a piece of paper, which pay no attention to gravity, while in other ways it never lets itself be mistaken for anything but a building, made up of solid masses.

Early models of the Jewish Museum in Berlin show it leaning like its own shadow. In order to get built it was forced to stand up straight, but allowed to keep its zigzag form in another dimension like an unintelligible scrawl in an unfamiliar language. You can read how this wonderfully arbitrary form was arrived at using the addresses of famous Berliners and the template of a Jewish star. Except that by now the star has disintegrated and become the line of German history crossed by another path, now in fragments, experienced by visitors as dark voids interrupting their progress at intervals.

These manipulations of the user's experience are justified by the building's function as a memorial of its subject, the Holocaust, which is most poignantly present here as emptiness, a strange resting place in a structure that began with such clear if unsettling formal assertions. Every human structure is remembering something and becomes more obviously a memorial the longer it stands. A few buildings have always begun from at or near this endpoint.

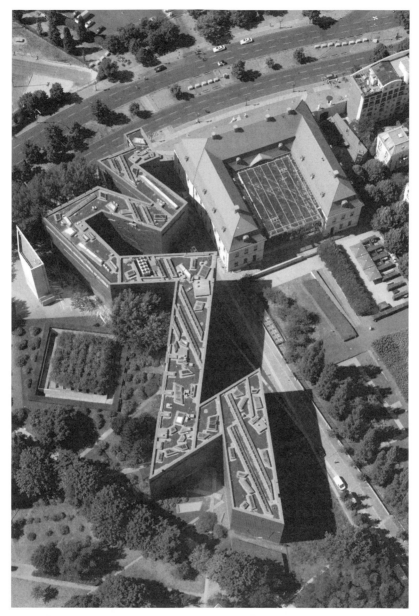

Libeskind, Jewish Museum, Berlin, 1989–2001, zigzag plan and internal voids to embody and memorialize historical catastrophe.

We have not reached a necessary stopping point with the Jewish Museum. Ending the story there might feel to some like a pessimistic conclusion, but others have detected a sort of jauntiness in Libeskind's despairing forms. The old orders no longer inspire belief, we have nothing to replace them with, human culture spins out of control, yet most of those who've thought about all this believe that we will put it right in the end.

Trying to take the pulse of the present, we might very well gravitate to the great globalized architectural practice of the moment, Rem Koolhaas's OMA and its new theoretical arm, AMO. Koolhaas was publishing books before he began building buildings; now the two activities race ahead in tandem, the books looking more like magazines and less like books, and including such titles as the *Harvard Guide to Shopping*.

From the beginning he has sought to turn the world upside down or at least to invert received perception of it: the Berlin Wall was beautiful, the culture of congestion was the best the modern world had to offer, places like Lagos and Atlanta were the world's most interesting cities, because in their different ways centre-less and out of control. In his writing an embrace of the most disorienting features of modern urban life, in his buildings an aggressive undoing of the Modernism he kicks off from, like turning a graffiti artist loose in a museum. So the Villa d'Ava outside Paris of 1984, an early work, looks like a Corb villa carried out in the wrong materials. The latest in the series, CCTV in Beijing, is the most overreaching megalo-idea so far, a square doughnut several hundred metres high with a great hole in the middle.

It performs its necessary subversion by not-being a tower or even two towers (though its vertical elements reach 51 storeys) but a loop that therefore requires the seemingly arbitrary twists in its cross-pieces to maintain its balance. The behemoth is inscribed with thick black lines like the grid of a city falling diagonally across it, not a window pattern as one might at first suppose, but a picture of the uneven disposition of structural members in this erratic monster, which combines impossible bigness and the appearance of instability. A Chinese website claims that it is the first of 200 skyscrapers in the new CBD of Beijing, so perhaps it will not be long before CCTV is outdone in bigness.

Koolhaas the writer sometimes comes across as a strange kind of prophet, on a roller coaster of aphorisms, scattering freely the brand names and capitalized abbreviations of the very latest moment in the history of the world. He has seen it all, and accepted it all, even though he believes less than the critics of Modernism that any good will come of it. In carefully composed pieces like 'Junk Space' one detects a strong undercurrent of despair, springing (can it be?) from a vast foreboding of the futility of human effort, the unhappiness that comes from projecting yourself on a world stage only to find your biggest project submerged in a flood of two hundred more. Perhaps the explosion of a certain number of Western architects onto the whole earth will come to seem, like earlier phases of Western imperialism, a curious interim phase.

Rem Koolhaas and OMA, CCTV headquarters, Beijing, 2002–9, the vogue for buildings that look as if they might fall down continues to grow.

Afterword

Architecture isn't just a matter of individual buildings elevated on pedestals and more or less detached from context. It comes as a shock to the connoisseur of famous landmarks collected from books to find that they often disappear into the actual cities in which they are placed like needles in haystacks. Are we to conclude from this common experience that architecture is a category that isn't really recognized by reality?

One could imagine a history of human building that avoided individual monuments almost completely and concentrated first on the idea of the settlement, picking out individual features only once the sense of the whole had been established. So instead of temples, tombs and palaces it would be a tale of cities and towns, an entirely different starting place from the one chosen here, and a harder story to tell.

Part of the explanation for the unnerving absence of cities from my narrative is that many of the most successful are so splintered and various that they strain the very idea of a single comprehensible thing. And to do justice to the more homogenous kind of settlement, the ones that make the most powerful impression of a large entity with yet a consistent personality like Venice, Bath or Tallinn would lead one decisively away from individual structures to those more indefinable spatial entities hard to put boundaries or names to – streets, squares and the complicated tangles formed from them.

Sometimes one stumbles on essential truths about one's own interests while travelling on circuitous paths. That searcher of seventeenth-century literary byways, Mario Praz, turns out to be a passionate collector, who has hit on the bizarre idea of telling his autobiography by means of an inventory of his prizes as they happen to be laid out in his flat in an obscure Roman palace. This lovingly detailed compendium of the stories his furniture tells seems at times a conscious parody of a topographical narrative, but it has nonetheless helped me understand the pull that guidebooks, especially those to old impacted cities, have exercised on me for almost as long as I can remember. Part of the appeal is their maniacal concentration on a territory that has a clear boundary, a small field into which an intense attention is poured. Such concentration is the plain contrary of the darting sort of attention I find natural.

Nevertheless, I cannot give up the idea of writing someday an exhaustive guidebook to an old, already well-known place. I tell this because it bears on one of the chief peculiarities of the present book, in which there is an undeclared war between a topographical and a chronological arrangement. I think I gravitated to architecture initially because of its anchorage in physical places, and the initial prompting of the book is travel much more than it is reading, so the form of each chapter is a pattern of places more like a map than an ordinary narrative. If a reader remembers this, certain surface oddities will seem less odd, and anomalous elements will fall into place.

This still leaves crucial features unexplained, like the starting place, left until last to be justified, when it is too late. But what and where is the real beginning of this story, the oldest settlement known, or the oldest city, further east than almost anything in this book as it stands, or the oldest art that one might call architectural, cave paintings in places like Lascaux? Any of these could be justified easily enough. Egypt in this book is standing in for much more, the nearest thing to an antecedent of Greece – Greece the absolutely necessary origin – Egypt making the essential point that other forms exist, and that the way Europe has developed is not the only path imaginable, a truth re-found at every step along the way but above all at the setting out.

Too late to apologize for one's omissions, which almost loomed even larger than they have. For years I found Brunelleschi's dome an excrescence on the story, until I took students there and was forced to study it un-flippantly. The work for the book required much more of such study, of course, as one expects when one is telling a story whose outcome is known, which appears to constrain the teller unconscionably. But in the end I understand better why composers of operas, for example, often prefer to work with plots their audiences already know. There are writers (and architects) who are always doing this, like Thomas Mann. The outcome of *Holy Sinner* is known (the material taken from a twelfth-century verse epic), but not by me. So, current students don't necessarily start by knowing who won the Trojan War, any more than everyone who picks up this book knows what happened to Baroque in the end.

It disturbed me growing up to see how quickly New York was taken down and re-erected in larger and, to me, more intimidating, less pleasing form. The history of all the arts, of all human activities, of all change perhaps, is a story of destruction as well as growth, but this is true in a special sense of architecture, which has unusual power to get in the way.

At times the instability or the temporariness of the subjects of this history is brought home with overpowering force. Just look at the last chapters of most histories of architecture or at magazines of twenty or thirty years ago and you will find a record of things forgotten, if not actually torn down.

This may be taken as my excuse for not bringing the story right up to the minute in which I am writing any more conscientiously than I have. I have a strong resistance to dealing in the trademark ideas of the moment, for if fads in architecture tend to be short-lived, styles of interpretation often enough have lives even shorter. At the end of an early chapter in *Rings of Saturn* W. G. Sebald tells of the recorded words of a famous war criminal, who happened also to be head of the United Nations, being fired by a rocket towards distant stars. He neglects to name him and now his name is lost to most readers. So I fear some elements of this story and especially the freshest ones, and some of my attitudes especially the latest ones, might become like those ancient Egyptian nouns that stand for something someone once used, but no one knows exactly what any more.

FURTHER READING

This is neither a full bibliography nor a true bibliographic essay. I have kept it in the form of annotated lists because they are more immediately accessible than continuous paragraphs of prose. Works in languages other than English have been omitted in all but a few cases included for their illustrations. Plenty of the standard works on their subjects appear, along with many books I consider remarkable that cover such tiny parts of the whole field that occasionally it seems almost quirky to include them.

EGYPTIAN

Badawy, A., *History of Egyptian Architecture* (Berkeley, CA, 1954–66), 3 vols
Bard, Kathryn A., ed., *Encyclopedia of the Archaeology of Ancient Egypt* (London, 1999). Fascinating for a concentration on what Egypt has meant to outsiders.
Godley, A. D., *Herodotus I: Books I and II* (London, 1926). The first anthropologist and still one of the liveliest.
Grimal, N., *A History of Ancient Egypt*, trans. Ian Shaw (Oxford, 1992). Unusual concentration on physical remains.
Kemp, Barry J., *Ancient Egypt: Anatomy of a Civilization* (London, 1988/9). Views the study of Egypt as an unfinished work in progress, good illustrations that convey this vividly.
Lichtheim, Miriam, *Ancient Egyptian Literature*, I: *The Old and Middle Kingdoms* (Berkeley, CA, 1973); II: *The New Kingdom* (1976); III: *The Late Period* (1980). A selection of the remarkably wide range of ancient Egyptian writing that survives.
Redford, Donald B., ed., *Oxford Encyclopedia of Ancient Egypt* (New York, 2001), 3 vols
Simpson, W. K., *The Literature of Ancient Egypt* (New Haven, CT, 1973)
www.thebanmappingproject.com/ For tomb-by-tomb treatment of the West Bank at Luxor, including plans and full illustration.
history.memphis.edu/hypostyle/ For the project cataloguing all reliefs and inscriptions on the greatest Egyptian temple at Karnak.

GREEK

Beard, Mary, and J. Henderson, *Classic Art, from Greece to Rome* (Oxford, 2001). Lively, with consistently off-beat examples.
Burkert, Walter, *Greek Religion, Archaic and Classical*, trans. John Raffan (Oxford, 1985). German edition 1977. Very suggestive for the psychological depths of the subject.
Calasso, Roberto, *The Marriage of Cadmus and Harmony*, trans. Tim Parks (New York, 1994). Italian edition 1988. Wilful but sometimes electrifying interpretation of Greek myth.
Camp, John, *The Archaeology of Athens* (New Haven, CT, 2002). Succinct synthesis of current knowledge.
Cooper, Frederick A., ed., *The Temple of Apollo Bassitas*, I: *The Architecture* (Princeton: American School of Classical Studies at Athens, 1996); II: *Sculpture* by Brian C. Madigan (1992);

III: *The Architecture Illustrations*, (1996); IV: *Folio Drawings* (1992), 62pl, 7pp foldout plans. Monumental study of a single badly ruined temple, which it brings back to life.

Coulton, J. J., *Ancient Greek Architects at Work: Problems of Structure and Design* (London, 1977). Constructional perspective was new when it appeared, wonderfully fresh and down to earth.

Crawford, Michael H., and D. Whitehead, *Archaic and Classical Greece: A Selection of Ancient Sources in Translation* (Cambridge, 1983)

Gantz, Timothy, *Early Greek Myth: A Guide to Literary and Artistic Sources* (Baltimore, MD, 1993). The subject in an authentically dismembered state.

Haselberger, L., articles in *Scientific American* (December 1985), pp. 126–32; (June 1995), pp. 84–9 on newly discovered ancient architectural drawings scratched on temple walls at Didyma.

Haskell, Francis, and Nicholas Penny, *Taste and the Antique: The Lure of Classical Sculpture, 1500–1900* (New Haven, CT, 1981). Fascinating accounts of the transmission and interpretation of classical art.

Hurwit, Jeffrey M., *The Athenian Acropolis: History, Mythology and Archaeology from the Neolithic Era to the Present* (Cambridge, 1998). An up-to-date synthesis.

Kazantzakis, Nikos, *Travels in Greece, Journey to Morea*, trans. F. A. Reed (Oxford, 1966) Along with Henry Miller's *Colossus of Maroussi*, a notable contemporary example of a poetic response to classical sites.

Lawrence, Arnold W., *Greek Architecture*, revd R. A. Tomlinson (New Haven, CT, and London, 1996)

Pausanias, *Guide to Greece*, trans. Peter Levi (Harmondsworth, 1971/1979), 2 vols. Like travelling with an ancient connoisseur; Levi's notes are wonderful examples of puzzle-solving.

Pfeiffer, Rudolf, *A History of Classical Scholarship, from the Beginning to the End of the Hellenistic Era* (Oxford, 1968, 1971). Extremely thorough, and thus not to everyone's taste; first of a series of volumes bringing the story up to the 20th century.

Stewart, Andrew, *Greek Sculpture, an Exploration* (New Haven, CT, and London, 1990), 2 vols. Comprehensive and fresh at once; discusses the relation to architecture.

Stillwell, Richard, ed., *The Princeton Encyclopedia of Classical Sites* (Princeton, NJ, 1976). Includes all known sites.

Travlos, J., *A Pictorial Dictionary of Ancient Athens* (London, 1971). Wonderfully detailed description of all remains on the Acropolis from Neolithic times onward.

ROMAN

Adam, Jean-Pierre, *Roman Building: Materials and Techniques*, trans. Anthony Matthews (London, 1994)

Bober, P., and R. Rubinstein, *Renaissance Artists and Antique Sculpture: A Handbook of Sources* (London, 1986). Another fascinating view of the distant past seen through the less distant.

Bowersock, G. W., Peter Brown and Oleg Grabar, eds, *Late Antiquity: A Guide to the Postclassical World* (Cambridge, MA, 1999)

Claridge, Amanda, *Oxford Archaeological Guides: Rome* (Oxford, 1998). Lively, intelligent analysis of the richest of all archaeological sites.

Coarelli, Filippo, *Rome and Environs: An Archaeological Guide* (Berkeley, CA, 2007). This English edition combines *Roma* with relevant chapters from the author's *Italia Centrale* and *Dintorni di Roma* to provide walking tours of the city and its suburbs.

Helbig, Wolfgang, *Führer durch die öffentlich Sammlungen*, ed. Hermine Speier (4th edn, Tubingen, 1963–72), 4 vols. Included as an artefact in its own right: an exhaustive catalogue of classical sculptures in public collections in Rome.

Huelsen, Christian, and Hermann Egger, eds, *Die römischen Skizzenbücher von Martin van Heemskerck* (Berlin, 1913), 2 vols. Reprint facsimile (Soest, The Netherlands: Davaco, 1975) with an English introduction to an interesting Renaissance artist's sketchbook of classical remains.

Kleiner, Diane, *Roman Sculpture* (New Haven, CT, 1992). Consciously planned by the publisher as a parallel to Andrew Stewart's volumes on Greek sculpture, showing the relative poorness of the Roman work.

MacDonald, William L., *The Pantheon: Design, Meaning and Progeny* (Cambridge, MA, and London, 1976). A canonical urban site.

——, and John A. Pinto, *Hadrian's Villa and its Legacy* (New Haven. CT, and London, 1995). The canonical semi-rural site.

Nash, E., *A Pictorial Dictionary of Ancient Rome* (London, 1968), 2 vols

Packer, James E., *The Forum of Trajan in Rome* (Berkeley, CA, 2002). Includes a detailed reconstruction of the most lavish Imperial Forum.

Piranesi, G. B., *Complete Etchings*, ed. J. Wilton Ely (San Francisco, CA, 1994). A powerful 18th-century vision of Antiquity.

Richardson, Lawrence, Jr, *A New Topographical Dictionary of Rome* (Baltimore, MD, 1992). A one-volume catalogue of all existing and lost ancient remains in the city, much handier than E. M. Steinby's *Lexicon Topographicum Urbis Romae* (Rome, 1993–2000), 5 vols and a multitude of languages, now being expanded to include the area suburbana.

Roullet, Anne, *The Egyptian and Egyptianizing Monuments of Imperial Rome* (Leiden, 1972)

Ward-Perkins, J. B., *Roman Imperial Architecture* (Harmondsworth, 1981)

——, *Marble in Antiquity: Collected Papers of J. B. Ward-Perkins*, ed. Hazel Dodge, Archaeological Monographs of the British School at Rome (1992)

Wilson-Jones, Mark, *Principles of Roman Architecture* (New Haven, CT, 2000). Makes one believe in the Corinthian order.

www.karmancenter.unibe.ch/karman-center/the_projects/pantheon   For an elaborate hi-tech study of the Pantheon with good summaries on its history and structure.

formaurbis.stanford.edu/   For the Marble Plan of ancient Rome and the latest word on its decipherment.

BYZANTINE

Brubaker, Leslie, *Byzantium in the Iconoclast Era (ca 680–850): The Sources, an Annotated Survey (with a section on the architecture of iconoclasm, the buildings, by R Ousterhout)* (Aldershot, 2001)

Burns, Ross, *Monuments of Syria: An Historical Guide* (London, 1992). Includes ancestors of Hagia Sophia, now ruins.

Chatzidakis, Manolis, *Mystras, the Medieval City and the Castle: A Complete Guide to the Churches, Palaces and the Castle* (Athens, 1994)

Comnena, Anna, *The Alexiad*, trans. and ed. E.R.A. Sewter (Harmondsworth, 1979). A shrewd account of the reign of the Byzantine emperor Alexius I by his daughter.

Constantine VII Porphyrogenitus, *Le Livre des ceremonies*, trans. into French by A. Vogt (Paris, 1933). An English translation of this work describing the ritual-bound life of the Byzantine court is sorely needed.

Evans, H. C., and W. D. Wixom, eds, *The Glory of Byzantium: Art and Culture of the Middle Byzantine Era, 843–1261*, exh. cat., Metropolitan Museum of Art, New York (1997)

——, *Byzantium: Faith and Power (1261–1557)*, exh. cat., Metropolitan Museum of Art, New York (2004)

Harrison, Martin. *A Temple for Byzantium: Discovery and Excavation of Anicia Juliana's Palace Church* (London, 1989). One of the richest, most interesting Byzantine buildings, its site only recently discovered.

Kazhdan, A. P., ed., *Oxford Dictionary of Byzantium* (Oxford, 1990), 3 vols

Krautheimer, Richard, *Early Christian and Byzantine Architecture* (4th revd edn by S. Curcic; Harmondsworth, 1986)

Mainstone, R., *Hagia Sophia* (London, 1988). Good on its construction.

Mango, Cyril, *Byzantine Architecture* (New York, 1976)

——, ed., *Art of the Byzantine Empire, 312–1453: Sources and Documents* (1st edn 1972; Toronto, 1986). Includes Paulus Silentiarius.

Mathews, Thomas F., *Byzantine Churches of Istanbul: A Photographic Survey* (University Park, PA,

1976). Exhaustive, including many archive views of states and features that no longer exist.

Mueller-Wiener, W., *Bildlexikon zur Topographie Istanbuls* (Tübingen, 1977). Includes the best available maps of districts and plans of buildings.

Nicol, Donald M., *The Despotate of Epiros, 1267–1479* (Cambridge, 1984). An outlying territory whose capital Arta contains many late Byzantine buildings.

Procopius, *The Secret History*, trans. and ed. G. A. Williamson (1st edn 1966; Harmondsworth, 1981)

Psellus, Michael, *Fourteen Byzantine Rulers / The Chronographia*, trans. and ed. E.R.A. Sewter (1st edn 1953; Harmondsworth, 1966). Byzantine history told by intelligent participants.

ROMANESQUE

Cassidy, Brendan, ed., *The Ruthwell Cross* (Princeton, NJ, 1992)

Corpus of Romanesque Sculpture in Britain and Ireland: www.crsbi.ac.uk/
Extremely thorough catalogue treatment of hundreds of sites, primarily churches; exhaustively illustrated.

Cramp, Rosemary, et al., eds, *Medieval Art and Architecture at Durham Cathedral*, British Archaeological Association Conference Transactions (1980)

Focillon, Henri, *The Art of the West in the Middle Ages* (French edn 1963; New York, 1963), vol. I. Pioneering treatment of the Romanesque, imaginative in a way no longer fashionable.

Hohler, E. B., *Norwegian Stave Church Sculpture* (Oslo, 1999), 2 vols. See also http://oslo.arounder.com/city_tour/NO000009415.html for 360 degree views of a stave church interior.

Jenkins, D., and M. Owen, 'Welsh Marginalia in the Lichfield Gospels', *Cambridge Medieval Studies*, 5 (Summer 1983); in Lichfield Cathedral this is known as the 'St Chad Gospels', but it is also called the 'Llandeilo Fawr Gospels', from its 200-year stop (early 9th century to late 11th century) in Llandeilo Fawr, Carmarthenshire. The marginal annotations in this manuscript are among the earliest surviving examples of written Welsh.

Lapidge, M., et al., eds, *The Blackwell Encyclopedia of Anglo-Saxon England* (Oxford, 1999)

Morris, Richard K., and Ron Shoesmith, *Tewkesbury Abbey: History, Art and Architecture* (Logaston, Herefordshire, 2003)

Schapiro, Meyer, 'Romanesque Sculpture of Moissac', in *Romanesque Art: Selected Papers* (New York, 1985)

Webster, L., 'The Iconographic Programme of the Franks Casket', in *Northumbria's Golden Age* (Stroud, 1999)

Zarnecki, George, and Denis Grivot, *Gislebertus, Sculptor of Autun* (London, 1961)

GOTHIC

Bideault, Maryse, and Claudine Lautier, *Ile de France gothique*, 1: *Les églises de la vallée de l'Oise et du Beauvaisis* (Paris, 1987)

Bony, Jean, *The English Decorated Style* (3rd edn, Oxford, 1980)

Branner, Robert, ed., *Chartres Cathedral* (New York, 1969)

British Archaeological Association, *Medieval Art and Architecture at Gloucester and Tewkesbury* (1985)

British Archaeological Association, *Medieval Art and Architecture at Wells and Glastonbury* (1978)

Brown, Sarah. *The Architectural History of York Minster* (Swindon, 2003). The Corpus Vitrearum volume on the Great East window will presumably be replaced when the present lengthy programme of cleaning is complete.

Clark, William W., *Laon Cathedral, Architecture: The Aesthetics of Space, Plan and Structure* (London, 1987)

Cobb, Gerald, *English Cathedrals, the Forgotten Centuries: Restoration and Change from 1530 to the Present Day* (London, 1980). A fascinating story of Gothic despised and disregarded.

Corpus Vitrearum, France, vol. 9, pt 1: *Les Vitraux de la cathédrale Notre Dame de Strasbourg*, by Victor Beyer, Christine Wild-Block and Fridtjof Zschokke (Paris, 1986). Systematic, with diagrams distinguishing authentic medieval glass from replacements for every window.

Focillon, Henri, *The Art of the West*, II: *Gothic*, ed. Jean Bony (London, 1963)

Hamann-Maclean, Richard, *Die Kathedrale von Reims*, I: *Die Architektur*, 3 vols, text, figures, plates. II: *Die Skulpturen*, 5 vols. Volume 5: North portal and nave; 6: West portal; 7: West inner face (Stuttgart, 1993–)

Harvey, John, *English Medieval Architects: A Biographical Dictionary down to 1550* (2nd edn London, 1987). A very expansionist view of the subject, mistrusted by many but fascinating for collating many individuals involved in medieval building.

——, *The Perpendicular Style* (London, 1978)

Leedy, W. C., *Fan Vaulting, a Study of Form, Technology and Meaning* (London, 1980). A very important English development, but this is a prosaic approach to it.

Nussbaum, Norbert, *German Gothic Church Architecture*, trans Scott Kleager (New Haven, CT, and London, 2000). First published in German in 1994. Another school of Late Gothic vaulting to be compared to the English one.

Rodin, Auguste, *Cathedrals of France* (revd edn, Redding Ridge, CT, 1981). Perhaps more illuminating for his own sculpture than for the light it sheds on Gothic.

Ruskin, John, *The Bible of Amiens* (London, 1885). This 'Bible' is the rich collection of quatrefoil scenes on the west facade. Ruskin remains one of the most interesting writers on medieval architecture.

Sandron, Deny, *Picardie gothique: autour de Laon et Soissons* (Paris, 2001)

Simson, Otto von, *The Gothic Cathedral: Origins of Gothic Architecture and the Medieval Concept of Order* (New York, 1964). First published in 1956. A somewhat confused thinker who raises a multitude of interesting questions.

Williamson, Paul, *Gothic Sculpture, 1140–1300* (New Haven, CT, and London, 1995). A wide-ranging survey.

Wilson, Christopher, *The Gothic Cathedral, Architecture of the Great Church, 1130–1530* (London, 1990). The best recent treatment of the subject.

www.cvma.ac.uk/ Corpus Vitrearum survey of medieval stained glass in Britain, with many images and links to other national indexes.

RENAISSANCE

Alberti, Leon Battista, *On the Art of Building*, trans J. Rykwert, Neil Leach and Robert Tavernor (Cambridge, MA, 1988). The first architectural treatise since antiquity.

Benevolo, Leonardo, *The Architecture of the Renaissance* (London, 1970), 2 vols. Much fuller than standard accounts by Peter Murray and others.

Brown, Patricia Fortini, *Venice and Antiquity: The Venetian Sense of the Past* (New Haven, CT, and London, 1996). Interesting illustrations, dull text.

Bruschi, Arnaldo, *Bramante* (1st edn 1973; London, 1977). An exemplary monograph.

Burckhardt, Jacob, *The Civilization of the Renaissance in Italy* (1st edn 1860; London, 1950). Early argument that the Renaissance invented the modern idea of the individual.

——, *Letters of Jacob Burckhardt*, trans Alexander Dru (London, 1955)

Burnett, Charles, and Anna Contadini, eds, *Islam and the Italian Renaissance* (London, 1999)

Fanelli, Giovanni, and Michele Fanelli, *Brunelleschi's Cupola: Past and Present of an Architectural Masterpiece* (Florence, 2004). Comprehensive analysis of Brunelleschi's most famous and perplexing project, extremely well illustrated.

Geanakoplos, Deno John, *Interaction of the Sibling Byzantine and Western Cultures in the Middle Ages and Italian Renaissance (330–1600)* (New Haven, CT, and London, 1976)

Howard, Deborah, *Venice and the East: The Impact of the Islamic world on Venetian Architecture, 1100–1500* (New Haven, CT, and London, 2000)

Manetti, Antonio, *Vita di Brunelleschi*, ed. Howard Saalman, trans. Catherine Enggass (University Park, PA, 1970). Rich in anecdote, a fascinating early instance of the genre.

Millon, Henry, and Vittorio Lampugnani, *The Renaissance from Brunelleschi to Michelangelo: The Representation of Architecture* (London, 1994). Includes fascinating architectural models of the period.

Onians, John, *Bearers of Meaning: The Classical Orders in Antiquity, the Middle Ages and the Renaissance* (Cambridge, 1988). Remarkable for the material it ferrets out, disappointing for what it makes of it.

Palladio, Andrea. *The Four Books on Architecture*, trans. Robert Tavernor and Richard Schofield (Cambridge, MA, 1997). Interesting primarily for the plates.

Portoghesi, Paolo, *Rome of the Renaissance* (London, 1972). Especially good for illustrations of both well-known and obscure palazzi.

Saalman, Howard, *Filippo Brunelleschi: The Buildings* (London, 1993). Full treatment, building by building, including minor works.

Serlio, Sebastiano, *Sebastiano Serlio on Architecture*, trans. Vaughan Hart and Peter Hicks (New Haven, CT, and London, 1996, 2001), 2 vols

Tafuri, Manfredo, *Venice and the Renaissance: Religion, Science, Architecture* (1st edn 1985; Cambridge, MA, 1989). Intricate, knowledgeable treatment of specific buildings, many of which, like San Salvatore, are not usually taken so seriously.

Stegmann, C. von, *Die Architektur der Renaissance in Toscana* (Munich, 1885–1909), 11 vols. Not easy to find, not seen by me, but bound to include unfamiliar material.

MANNERISM

Ackerman, James, *The Architecture of Michelangelo* (revd edn Harmondsworth, 1970). Lively.

Girouard, Mark, *Robert Smythson and the Elizabethan Country House* (New Haven, CT, and London, 1983). For rustic early translations of classical architecture in England.

Hart, Frederick, *Giulio Romano* (New Haven, CT, and London, 1958), 2 vols

Hauser, Arnold, *Mannerism: The Crisis of the Renaissance and the Origin of Modern Art* (London, 1965). Early into a neglected field, its Marxism now seems quaint.

Shearman, John, *Mannerism* (Harmondsworth, 1967). Not a book to agree with, but full of salutary scepticism.

Tafuri, Manfredo, et al., *Giulio Romano* (Cambridge, 1998). Translation of a recent Italian monograph.

Giorgio Vasari, exh. cat., Arezzo, Casa Giorgio Vasari (1981)

BAROQUE

Blunt, Anthony, *Guide to Baroque Rome* (London, 1982). Draws on deep familiarity with buildings and printed sources: gazetteers by building type, much detail compactly presented.

——, *Sicilian Baroque* (London, 1968). Pioneering treatment; there have since been much fuller ones in Italian.

Cache, Bernard, *Earth Moves* (Cambridge, MA, 1995). Deleuzian treatment of slippages in Baroque motifs.

Deleuze, Gilles, *The Fold, Leibniz and the Baroque*, trans. Tom Conley (London, 1993). Has had its influence on contemporary architectural thought; not as clear as it could be, which suits Deleuzians.

Harbison, Robert, *Reflections on Baroque* (London, 2000). Ranges across genres and traces Baroque tendencies in later centuries.

St Ignatius of Loyola, *Personal Writings: Reminiscences, Spiritual Diary, Letters, Spiritual Exercises* (London, 1996). A crucial thinker for the Baroque that came after him; with full annotation.

Kimball, Fiske, *Creation of the Rococo* (Philadelphia, 1943). Sophisticated.

Lyttleton, Margaret, *Baroque Architecture in Classical Antiquity* (London, c. 1974). An important subject prosaically handled.

Mallory, Nina, *Roman Rococo Architecture* (New York, 1977). A dissertation, with disappointing photos; Blunt said there was no such thing as Roman Rococo – here is the counter-evidence.

Norberg-Schulz, Christian, *Baroque Architecture* (London, 1971)

——, *Late Baroque and Rococo Architecture* (London, 1986). Good coverage of Eastern Europe.

Portoghesi, Paolo, *Roma barocca* (1st edn 1966; Bari, 1995). Interesting photos of many obscure works.

Sedlmayr, Hans, and Hermann Bauer, 'Rococo' in *Encyclopedia of World Art* (New York, 1966), XII, pp. 230–70. Captures the essence of the mode imaginatively.

Viale Ferrero, Mercedes, *Filippo Juvarra scenografo e architetto teatrale* (Turin, 1970). 300 drawings for stage scenery well reproduced, giving great insight into his architecture.

Wittkower, Rudolf, *Art and Architecture in Italy, 1600–1750* (Harmondsworth, 1965 and subsequent edns). One of the best volumes in the Pelican History of Art series.

Wölfflin, Heinrich, *Renaissance and Baroque*, trans. Kathrin Simon (London, 1984). 1st pubd Munich, 1888. An influential early treatment of the despised style; Wölfflin treats late Renaissance as Baroque.

Nolli map of Rome, interactive website: http://nolli.uoregon.edu/

The Virtual Architecture Project has interesting computer realizations of Baroque buildings at www.williams.edu/art/architectureVR/

HISTORICISM

Davey, Peter, *Arts and Crafts Architecture* (1st pubd 1980, London, 1995)

Dixon, Roger, and Stefan Muthesius, *Victorian Architecture* (London, 1978)

Eastlake, C. E., *A History of the Gothic Revival in England* (1st pubd 1872; Leicester, 1970). A full contemporary account.

German, G., *Gothic Revival in Europe and Britain* (London, 1972). Wide Continental perspective; good on intellectual underpinnings.

Hersey, George, *High Victorian Gothic, a Study in Associationism* (Baltimore, MD, 1972). Creature and machine metaphors for buildings.

Hitchcock, Henry-Russell, *Architecture: Nineteenth and Twentieth Centuries* (Harmondsworth, 1977)

Howarth, Thomas, *C. R. Mackintosh and the Modern Movement* (1st edn 1952, London, 1977)

Martinell, César, *Antoni Gaudí: His Life, his Theories, his Work* (Cambridge, MA, 1975)

Meeks, Carroll, *The Railroad Station* (New Haven, CT, 1956). From the beginning to the 1950s; the USA is fully covered.

Pevsner, Nikolaus, *Pioneers of Modern Design* (1st edn 1936, Harmondsworth, 1964)

Pugin, A.W.N., *The True Principles of Pointed or Christian Architecture* (London, 1973). First published in 1841, it is still fascinating on abuses, from fringes and wallpapers to building types.

MODERNISM

Banham, Reyner, *Theory and Design in the First Machine Age* (London, 1960). A groundbreaking study by a subtle enthusiast for technological progress.

Le Corbusier, *The City of Tomorrow and its Planning* (London, 1971)

Curtis, William, *Modern Architecture since 1900* (Englewood Cliffs, NJ, 1987)

Frampton, Kenneth, *Modern Architecture, a Critical History* (London, 1992). The best short survey, especially good at connecting contemporary texts to buildings.

Giedion, Siegfried, *Mechanization takes Command* (1st pubd 1948, Cambridge, MA, 1955). His most original work, on some ideological underpinnings of modernism as exemplified in industrial products.

——, *Space, Time and Architecture* (1st pubd 1941, London, 1967). Important early defence of the new architecture of Europe.

Hitchcock, H.-R., and Philip Johnson, *The International Style: Architecture since 1922* (New York, 1932). Polemical accompaniment to an influential exhibition.

Koolhaas, Rem, 'Junkspace', in *Content: Triumph of Realization* (Cologne, 2004)

——, *S, M, L, XL* (New York, 1995). Earlier demonstration of the disquieting combination of cynicism and acquiescence that characterizes his response to contemporary reality.

Kopp, Anatole, *Town and Revolution: Soviet Architecture and City Planning 1917–1935* (New York, 1970). Rich in human detail; reads almost as if written by a participant.

Richards, J. M., *The Functional Tradition in Early Industrial Buildings* (London, 1958). A kind of vernacular pre-history to the functional tradition in early modernism.

Smithson, Alison, and Peter Smithson, *Without Rhetoric – An Architectural Aesthetic* (London, 1973)

Starr, S. Frederick, *Konstantin Melnikov: Solo Architect in a Mass Society* (Princeton, NJ, 1978). Comprehensive, including many drawings not previously seen in the West.

Venturi, Robert, *Complexity and Contradiction in Architecture*, exh. cat., MoMA, New York (1977). Polemic that announced Postmodernism in architecture.

Wigley, Mark, and Philip Johnson, *Deconstructivist Architecture*. exh. cat., MoMA, New York (1988). Polemical accompaniment to an influential exhibition.

www.alvaraalto.fi/ Exemplary website of Alvar Aalto Foundation with particularly good, thoughtful texts attached to each project.

www.coop-himmelblau.at/ Full coverage of all their projects with plentiful images and plenty of text, stylish and easy to navigate.

www.oma.eu/ Rem Koolhaas/ OMA
Appropriately confusing visually with overheated texts (Seattle Central Library especially pretentious) and spectacular panoramas that need Adobe Shockwave.

ACKNOWLEDGEMENTS

The author wishes to thank London Metropolitan University and Robert Mull, Head of the Department of Architecture and Spatial Design, for their strong continued support of this project. Lectures, seminars and student trips have played a large part in shaping the result, so particular thanks to the students who have contributed much to my views.

Colin Davies read an earlier version of the manuscript and made a crucial suggestion about the form of the book, Kelly Zinkowski sent many clues along the way, and Vivian Constantinopoulos has been an ideal editor, alert, responsive and unusually patient.

Finally, thanks to my wife, Esther, who lived through it all and created the setting in which the work was possible.

PHOTO
ACKNOWLEDGEMENTS

The author and publishers wish to express their thanks to the following sources of illustrative material and/or permission to reproduce it (some locations of artworks are also given below):

Photo © Steven Allan / 2009 iStock International Inc.: p. 215; photos by the author: p. 18, 19, 25, 26 (top), 28, 29, 30, 32, 35, 37, 39, 40, 46, 49, 51, 54, 56, 60, 62, 64, 74 (foot), 83, 85, 88, 91, 92, 93, 99, 122, 123, 126, 128, 129, 130, 131, 133, 160, 166, 167, 175, 179 (top), 181, 183, 184, 189 (top, 191, 192, 194 (top), 195, 197, 198, 203, 208, 212, 214, 216, 233, 245; photo courtesy the author: p. 256; photo © AveryPhotography / 2009 iStock International Inc.: p. 240; photo Gibert Bochenek: p. 108; British Museum, London (photo courtesy British Museum Images, © The Trustees of the British Museum): p. 96; photo ©: Andrew Drysdale / Rex Features: p. 219 (foot); © FLC / ADAGP, Paris and DACS, London, 2009: pp. 48, 227, 228, 229, 231, 245; Galleria Nazionale delle Marche, Urbino: p. 149; photo Francesco Gasparetti: p. 147; photo © Steve Geer / 2009 iStock International Inc.: p. 218; photo Arjan Huijzer / BigStockPhoto: p. 226; photo Alain Janssoone: p. 168; photo courtesy Ilpo Koskinen: p. 257; Kunsthistorisches Museum Vienna: p. 75; photo Michael Leaman: pp. 71, 174 (top), 263; photo © LEHTIKUVA OY/ Rex Features: p. 244; photo © Studio Daniel Libeskind: p. 260; photo © Studio Daniel Libeskind / Jüdisches Museum, Berlin: p. 257; photos Library of Congress, Washington, DC (Prints and Photographs Division): pp. 16, 78, 204, 220; photos Joaquin Lorda, Universidad de Navarra: pp. 164, 165; photo Andrew Mawby: p. 115; photo James Mitchell: pp. 124-5; photo courtesy Tina Negus: p. 105; photo © Phooey / 2009 iStock International Inc.: p. 12; photo © Achim Prill / 2009 iStock International Inc.: p. 156; photo © Wolfgang Richter / 2009 iStock International Inc.: p. 153; photo © Roger-Viollet / Rex Features: p. 201; photo © Alastair N. Ross: p. 102; photo courtesy Rachele Rossi: p. 63; photo courtesy the Slater Memorial Museum, Norwich, CT: p. 76; photo © Hannu Vallas / Rex Features: p. 243; photo Velela: p. 208; photo © Niko Vujevic / 2009 iStock International Inc.: pp. 234-35; Woburn Abbey, Woburn, Bedfordshire: p. 170 (top); photo www.grahamcustance.com: p. 169; photo Burçin Yıldırım: p. 224.

INDEX

Page numbers in *italics* denote illustrations